D1264579

Cognitive Systematization

A systems-theoretic approach to a coherentist theory of knowledge

NICHOLAS RESCHER

Cognitive Systematization

A systems-theoretic approach
to a coherentist theory of knowledge

ROWMAN AND LITTLEFIELD
TOTOWA, NEW JERSEY

FIRST PUBLISHED IN THE UNITED STATES 1979

Library of Congress Cataloging in Publication Data

Rescher, Nicholas.
  Cognitive systematization.

  Includes indexes.
  1. Knowledge, Theory of. 2. Cognition. 3. System
theory. I. Title.
BD161.R47 1978   121   78-18317
ISBN 0-8476-6094-X

PRINTED IN GREAT BRITAIN

For W. V. O. Quine

Table of Contents

Preface

The present book has its roots in my earlier one on *The Coherence Theory of Truth* (Oxford: The Clarendon Press, 1973). In reflecting on the role of coherence considerations, it became clear that the concept of system and the ideal of cognitive systematization itself would repay closer scrutiny. Some of these systems-aspects of our scientific knowledge were explored in *Methodological Pragmatism* (Oxford: Basil Blackwell, 1977), and the present work represents a further extension and development of various lines of thought touched upon there. The book thus manages to effect a tightening of the threads that link the coherentist and the pragmatist elements of its author's approach to the theory of knowledge. In particular, the book establishes a closer fusion between the coherentism of *The Coherence Theory of Truth* (which recurs here in Chapters III–V), the evolutionary pragmatism of *Methodological Pragmatism* (which recurs here in Chapters VII–VIII), and the cognitive futuristics of *Scientific Progress* [Oxford: Basil Blackwell, 1978] (which recurs in Chapter VIII–IX). In these previous books the idea of system lies in the background – here it emerges into the foreground of explicit consideration.

Parts of the book were drafted during my tenure of a National Science Foundation Research Grant (GS–37883) awarded during 1973–4 in support of an investigation of "A Coherence Theory of Inductive Inference." The project was carried further during my tenure in the Fall of 1975 of a grant-in-aid from the American Council of Learned Societies in support of work in Oxford on "The Theory of Knowledge of the English Idealists." I am most grateful to these agencies for their support.

The substance of the book was presented in a group of lectures I delivered during the Trinity Term of 1977 in the School of Literae Humaniores of the University of Oxford at the kind invitation of the Sub-faculty of Philosophy. I also very much appreciate the kindness and hospitality of Corpus Christi College in affording me an academic foothold during my stay in Oxford on this as on many previous occasions.

I am grateful to Cynthia Freeland and Jay Garfield for reading the book in draft form and offering some useful suggestions for its improvement. And I wish to thank Mrs. Kathleen Reznik and Mrs. Virginia Chestek for preparing the typescript through many revisions with great patience and competence.

Finally, one terminological point is in order. In this book I have adopted the arbitrary convention of speaking of "justification" specifically in the context of *particular cognitive items* (espoused theses, claims, beliefs, arguments, etc.). At a level of higher generality, where types or large-scale groups of such items are concerned (viz., with *types* of arguments, *systems* of beliefs, doctrines, *principles* of reasoning, or the like), I speak of "validation." Finally, at the still more general methodological level of methods, procedures, standards, etc., I speak of "legitimation." It seemed certainly too monotonous to use a single term throughout, and possibly too confusing to vary them at random. (To be sure, an unawareness of this convention can – as best I can tell – never lead to confusion.)

PITTSBURGH
November 1977

Introduction

This book is a study in systems-epistemology, in fact, a venture in *cognitive metasystematics* – the systematic analysis of knowledge about knowledge. It seeks to examine the systematic aspect of our knowledge and to show why – and how – this represents one of its crucial features.

Philosophers have long recognized the centrality of systematization in the theory of knowledge. In Kant's *Critique of Pure Reason* "the art of constructing systems" is characterized as *architectonic*, and this enterprise plays a prominent role throughout that monumental work, one entire chapter of which (entitled "Transcendental Doctrine of Method") is devoted to its detailed exploration. For Hegel and his school – especially the English Neo-Hegelians – system was not just an important aspect but *the characterizing feature* of our knowledge. The present study of systematization proceeds within the frame of reference set by these large historic claims on its behalf. The aim of the book is to explore the range of issues relating to cognitive systematization posed by the following group of questions: Why is it important that we should develop our knowledge about the world systematically – what is the *point* of systematization in the cognitive domain? How does cognitive systematization aid in the pursuit of truth? What are the major modes and methods of cognitive systematization? What considerations legitimate the principles and procedures of cognitive systematization? Does the systematicity of our knowledge have an ontological basis or is it purely an epistemological issue?

The position to be defended here belongs to the epistemological approach generally characterized as coherentism and associated in particular with the Oxford school of neo-Hegelians inaugurated by T. H. Green in the 1870's. The guiding thought of this doctrine is the idea that systematization is not merely a way of *organizing* our knowledge, but – more fundamentally – a criterial *standard* for determining what it is that we indeed know. An issue of prime concern is that of the rationalization of the systematists' perspective upon the rational validation of our claims to knowledge. It will, moreover, be argued – in an emphatically pragmatic vein – that the splendid success of natural science in its traditional mission of explanation, prediction, and control over nature affords a potent vindication of its systematizing approach to cognitive methodology.

One particularly intriguing issue provides the culminating point towards which the whole discussion moves slowly but surely – the theme posed in the question: Might circumstances so eventuate that our efforts at cognitive systematization will encounter insuperable limits? (I shall not anticipate an answer here, and mention the topic only to give the reader a preview of the overall tendency of the discussion.)

It is clear on the very surface of it that these questions regarding systematization pose important epistemological issues. Yet it appears that no work published in the present century affords any substantial treatment of these matters. And despite the rising popularity of systems-oriented thought in philosophy the theme of systems-epistemology remains very much neglected. The aim of the present book is to take some small steps towards remedying this large deficiency.

I

Historical Stagesetting

SYNOPSIS

(1) A sketch of the origin and development of the concept of a system in classical antiquity. After the Renaissance, the idea came to be applied preeminently to *cognitive* systems. (2) A survey of the historically most prominent components of the idea of system, the traditional "parameters of systematicity." (3) The very conception of a "system" is itself a systemic whole that links distinguishable elements into a unified composite. (4) Consideration of the view – standard in the epistemological tradition of the West – that the totality of "the truth" forms a rational system. (5) Systematicity serves as a regulative ideal of cognitive development and represents the very hallmark of a science. The totality of scientific knowledge is traditionally viewed as constituting one vast synoptic system, a discipline being marked as scientific by its having a place as a subsystem within this overall system. (6) An exposition of the epistemological importance of the systems point of view.

1. THE CONCEPT OF SYSTEMATIZATION

Although use of the term "system" in this connection is of relatively recent date, the underlying *idea* of what we nowadays call a "system" of knowledge was certainly alive in classical antiquity, with the Euclidean systematization of geometry providing a paradigm for this conception. In fact, it has been insisted throughout the history of Western philosophy that men do not genuinely *know* something unless this knowledge is actually *systematic*. Plato's thesis in the *Theaetetus* that a known fact must have a *logos* (rationale), Aristotle's insistence in the

Posterior Analytics that strict (scientific) knowledge of a fact about the world calls for its accounting in causal terms, the Scholastic analysis of *scientia*, Spinoza's celebration of what he designates as the second and third kinds of knowledge (in Book II of the *Ethics* and elsewhere), all instantiate the common, fundamental idea that what is genuinely known is known in terms of its systematic footing within the larger setting of a rationale-providing framework of explanatory order. The root idea of system is that of *structure* or *organization*, of integration into an orderly whole that functions as an "organic" unity.[1]

From antiquity to Hegel and beyond, cognitive theoreticians have embraced the ancient ideal that our knowledge should be developed architectonically and should be organized within an articulated structure that exhibits the linkages binding its component parts into an integrated whole and leaves nothing wholly isolated and disconnected. A cognitive system is to provide a framework for linking the *disjecta membra* of the bits and pieces of our knowledge into a cohesive unity. A cognitive system is to be a *structured* body of information, one that is organized in accordance with taxonomic and explanatory principles that link this information into a rationally coordinated whole.[2] The functional categories governing this organizational venture are those of understanding, explanation, and cognitive rationalization.

The systematicity of knowledge is thus to be construed as a category of *understanding*, akin in this regard to generality, simplicity, or elegance. Its immediate concern is with form rather than matter, and it bears upon the organizational development of our knowledge rather than upon the substantive content of what is known, and deals with cognitive structure rather than subject-matter materials. Just as one selfsame range of things can be characterized simply or complexly, so it can be characterized systematically or unsystematically. Systematicity accordingly relates in the first instance not to *what* we know – the facts at issue in the items of information at our disposal – but rather to *how we proceed in organizing our knowledge of them*. (These two issues are

[1] The systems concept is operative with respect to knowledge at two distinguishable levels: the level of *propositions* (theses, theories, doctrines) and the level of *concepts* (conceptions, ideas). The present discussion will focus upon the former. Conceptual systems are, after all, embedded in thesis-systems: our concepts are defined, specified, determined, and explained in terms of the theses in which they figure. The systematization of our concepts and categories is accordingly supervenient upon that of the propositional systems in which these concepts and categories play their characteristic role.

[2] A cognitive system is never "merely descriptive" – any scientific scheme of classification always proceeds in line with *explanatory* considerations.

– to be sure – not wholly unrelated.) A cognitive system is not just a collection of endorsed (or accepted) *theses*, but embodies also the *rationale* that underwrites in these endorsements. The characterization of a system-included thesis in *normative* terms (as "true," "warrantedly assertible," or the like) is the product of the operations of rationale-establishing *principles* that are no less crucial to the make-up of the system than the theses it accommodates. Christian Wolff's formula applies: *systema est veritatum inter se et cum principiis suis connexarum congeries*; a system embodies the meshing of theses and connecting principles.

But while the concept of cognitive systematization is very old, the term "system" itself was not used in this sense until much later. In ancient Greek, *systēma* (from *syn-histēmi*, "to [make to] stand together") originally meant something joined together – a connected or composite whole. The term figures in Greek antiquity to describe a wide variety of composite objects – flocks of animals, medications, military formations, organized governments, poems, musical configurations, among others.[3] Its technicalization began with the Stoics, who applied it specifically to the physical universe (*systema mundi*) – the composite cosmos encompassing "heaven and earth."[4] But the term continued in use throughout classical texts in its very general ordinary sense (which it shared with terms like *syntagma* and *syntaxis*).

The Renaissance gave the term a renewed currency. At first it functioned here too in its ancient applications in its broad sense of a generic composite. But in due course it came to be adopted by Protestant theologians of the 16th century to stand specifically for the comprehensive exposition of the articles of faith, along the lines of a medieval *summa*: a doctrinal *compendium*.[5]

[3] Much of the presently surveyed information regarding the history of the term is drawn from the monograph by Otto Ritschl, *System und systematische Methode in der Geschichte des wissenschaftlichen Sprachgebrauchs und der philosophischen Methodologie* (Bonn, 1906). Further data are given in the review of Ritschl's work by August Messer in the *Göttinger gelehrte Anzeigen*, vol. 169 (1907), no. 8. See also Aloys von der Stein, "Der Systembegriff in seiner geschichtlichen Entwicklung" in A. Diemer (ed.), *System und Klassifikation in Wissenschaft und Dokumentation* (Meisenheim am Glan, 1968).

[4] See Theodor Zichen, *Lehrbuch der Logik* (Bonn, 1920), p. 821. The foundation of the Stoic's approach lies in Aristotle's *De mundo*. But contrast also Sextus Empiricus, *Outlines of Pyrrhonism*, III, 269, which speaks of the *systēma* of the rules of art, or again *ibid.* II, 173, which speaks of the *systēma* (= collectivity) of the propositions of a syllogism.

[5] Thus Du Cange, *Glossarium mediae et infimae latinatatis* (Paris, 1842): *Systema, proprie compages, collectio. Hinc astronomis pro mundi constitutione et forma usurpatur. Theologis vero pro complexu articulorum fidei*. The term gradually drove its rival *syntagma* from the field in this latter sense.

By the early years of the 17th century, the philosophers had borrowed the term "system" from the theologians, using it to stand for a synoptically comprehensive and connected treatment of a philosophical discipline: logic, rhetoric, metaphysics, ethics, etc.[6] (It was frequently employed in this descriptive sense in the title of expository books.)[7] And thereafter the use of the term was generalized in the early 17th century to apply to such a synoptic treatment of any discipline whatever.[8]

This post-Renaissance redeployment of the term *system* had a far-reaching significance. In the original (classical) sense, a system was a physical thing: a compositely structured complex. In the more recent sense, a system was an organically structured body *of knowledge* – not a mere accumulation of aggregation or compilation of miscellaneous information (like a dictionary or encyclopedia), but a functionally organized and connectedly articulated exposition of a unified discipline. It was just this sense of "system" that was eventually encapsulated in Christian Wolff's formula of a system as "a collection of truths duly arranged in accordance with the principles governing their connections" (*systema est veritatum inter se et cum principiis suis connexarum congeries*).[9] Moreover, a system is not just a constellation of interrelated elements, but one of elements assembled together in an "organic" unity by linking principles within a functionally ordered complex of rational interrelationships. The dual application of systems-terminology to physical and intellectual complexes thus reflects a long-standing and fundamental feature of the conception at issue.

A further development in the use of the term occurred in the second

---

[6] Thus Bartholomaeus Keckerman (d. 1609) wrote in his treatise *Systema logicae tribus libris adornatum* (Hanover, 1600) that what is at issue is the whole organized body of logical precepts. He explained that the term *logic*, like that for every art, stands for two things: the practical skill (*habitus*) on the one hand, and the systematic discipline on the other: *primo pro habitu ipso in mentem per praeceptu et exercitationem introducto: deide pro praeceptorium logicorum comprehensione seu systemate*. . . . (Quoted in O. Ritschl, op. cit., p. 27.) Keckerman's later (1606) handbook of logic appeared under the title *systema minus*. His contemporary Clemens Timpler (d. c. 1625) wrote in his *Metaphysicae systema methodicum* (Hanover, 1606) that in an exposition that is ordered and structured according to proper methodological principles: *systema non confusum et pertubatum, sed bene secundum leges methodi ordinatum et dispositum*.

[7] More than 130 titles of this sort published during the 17th century are listed in Ritschl (*op. cit.*). Some examples: Johann Heinrich Alsted, *Systema mnemonicum duplex* (Frankfurt, 1610); Nicas de Februe, *Systema chymicum* (Paris, 1666 [in French]; London, 1666 [in English]), Richard Elton, *Systema artis militaris* (London, 1669). (For details see O. Ritschl, op. cit.)

[8] There is no entry for *system* in the *Lexicon Philosophicum* of Rudolf Goclenius (Frankfurt, 1623). But in that of Johann Micraelius (Stettin, 1653) the term is explained in its literary sense as a systematic exposition.

[9] *Logic*, sect. 889; cited in Theodor Ziehen, op. cit., p. 821.

half of the 17th century. Now "system" came to be construed as a *particular approach* to a certain subject – a particular theory or doctrine about it as articulated in an organized complex of concordant hypotheses, a *nexus veritatum*. (This new usage is particularly marked in Malebranche's treatise *De la Recherche de la vérité* [*De Inquirenda veritate libri sex* (Geneva, 1685)], where we find a section "*de novorum systematum inventoribus*.") This is the sense borne by the term in such phrases as "the system of occasional causes" or "the Stoic system of morality." Leibniz was a prime promoter of this usage. He often spoke of his own philosophy as "my (new) system" of preestablished harmony, contrasting it with various rival systems.[10] System was now understood as a doctrine or teaching in its comprehensive (i.e. "systematic") development. In the wake of this new redeployment of the term in relation to a baroque proliferation of competing doctrines, philosophy now came to be viewed as a battle-ground of rival systems.

This use of "system" to stand for a comprehensive (if controversial) particular philosophical doctrine opened the conception up to criticism, and brought systems into disrepute in the age of reason. Thus Condillac developed a judicious critique of systems in his celebrated *Treatise on Systems*.[11] He distinguished between systems based on *speculation* ("abstract principles," "gratuitous suppositions," "mere hypotheses") and those based upon *experience*. A system cannot be better than the principles on which it is based, and this – he held – invalidates philosophical systems, since they are based upon hypotheses along the lines disdained in Isaac Newton's famous dictum: *Hypotheses non fingo*. Scientific systems, on the other hand, were viewed in a very different light. For Condillac, systems can thus be either good or bad – the good systems are the *scientific* systems, based on "experience," typified by Newtonian physics, the bad systems are the *philosophical* ones, based on speculative hypotheses, typified by the ideas of the presocratics.

The cognitively oriented conception of an *intellectual* system did not by any means totally displace the thing-oriented idea of an *ontological* (rather than intellectual) system – even among the early modern

[10] Thus Leibniz contrasts his own *système de l'harmonie préétablie* with the *système des causes efficientes et celui des causes finales* as well as the *système des causes occassionelle qui a été fort mis en vogue par les belles réflexions de l'Auteur de la Recherche de la Vérité* (Malebranche). He characterizes his own contribution as the *système nonveau de la nature et de la communication des substances aussi bien que de l'union qu'il y a entre l'âme et le corps*. (O. Ritschl, op. cit., p. 60.)

[11] See his *Traité des systèmes* first published in Paris in 1749.

philosophers. For example, throughout most of modern philosophy the most diversely oriented thinkers (Leibniz, Berkeley, Kant, Mill, etc.) offer an analysis of *substance* – of physical things – that demands an invocation of the systems-idea to furnish the needed integrating principle. (And this line of approach is no less apposite when it is a physical *process* rather than a material object that is at issue; say, a thunderstorm rather than an apple.) The ontological role which is, in effect, accorded to systematicity in much of recent philosophy is no less striking than its key place in the theory of knowledge. The concept has always operated amphibiously, extending over both the physical and the cognitive domains.[12] It is, however, this latter, intellectual side of the issue which will preoccupy us here.

2. THE THEORY OF COGNITIVE SYSTEMS: THE TRADITIONAL PARAMETERS OF SYSTEMATICITY

The post-Renaissance construction of systematicity emphasized its orientation towards specifically *cognitive* or knowledge-organizing systems. The explicit *theory* of such cognitive systems was launched the second half of the 18th century, and the principal theoreticians were two German contemporaries: Johann Heinrich Lambert (1728–1777) and Immanuel Kant (1724–1804).[13] The *practice* of systematization that lay before their eyes was that of the great 17th-century philosopher-scientists: Descartes, Spinoza, Newton, Leibniz, and the subsequent workers of the Leibnizian school – especially Christian Wolff. The main use of the system-concept with all these later writers relates not to its application to material things, but to its specifically *cognitive* applications to the organization of information.

Along these lines, Lambert adduced the following examples of cognitive systems:

(a) the system of truths at large

---

[12] Most writers about systems have recognized and indeed stressed this duality. See, for example, Hugo Dingler, *Das System* (Munich, 1930), pp. 128ff.

[13] The main theoretical works are various essays by Lambert (including the opuscula *Fragment einer Systematologie* [with parts dated 1767 and 1771], *Theorie des Systems* [1782] and *Von den Lücken unserer Erkenntniss* [c. 1785] and, of course, Kant's *Critique of Pure Reason* (1781), esp. Book II, Pt. 3 "The Architectonic of Pure Reason." Lambert's philosophical writings were issued by J. Bernouilli (ed.), *Johann Henrich Lambert: Logische und Philosophische Abhandlungen*, two vols. (Berlin, 1782 and 1787; reprinted Hildesheim, 1967, ed. by H. W. Arndt).

(b) individual systems by way of sciences, or theories, etc.

(c) the thought-systems and belief-systems of particular cultures or individuals

(d) religious systems, creeds, myths and "symbolic" books, etc.

(e) narratives, fables, poems, speeches, etc.

Lambert and Kant stressed that the idea of system applied alike to *material* systems (such as organisms) and *intellectual* systems (such as "organically" integrated bodies of knowledge). The idea is neutral as between its material and its cognitive applications.[14] They also clearly recognized that there are physical as well as cognitive systems, and that, moreover, systems can lie on the practical as well as theoretical side, and that there can be behavioral systems of rules of procedure, or methods of action, or purposive means or instrumentalities, etc.[15]

Traditionally, these two aspects of system – the ontological (material) and the cognitive (intellectual) – were seen as closely connected through the conception of truth as *adaequatio intellectu ad rem*. If the objects we study (nature and its components) are systems, then such a parallelism principle dictates the necessary that the intellectual framework we create in the course of this study should itself also be a system. The pre-Kantian ("dogmatic") tradition thus sees a *metaphysical* basis for the imperative to impart to our thought a systematic order akin to that which we find in its objects. With Kant (as we shall see) this imperative to systematization becomes endowed with a strictly epistemological rationale. But however connected or disconnected, these two facets of system are both ineliminably *there*.

To be sure, some recent writers urge the need for maintaining a careful line of separation between *intellectual* systems, where systems-talk relates to "*formulations* of various kinds that are used for descriptive or conceptual-organizational purposes in science," and *physical* systems as "extra-linguistic entities which, in fact, might be described or referred to by such formulations."[16] But any rigid bifurcation seems ill-advised. It is wrong to think that two different

[14] In view of this fact, it is strange that so little attention has been paid to cognitive ("intellectual," "symbolic") systems within the recent *general systems theory* movement. Thus in Ludwig von Bertalanffy's synoptic survey of *General Systems Theory: Foundations, Development, Applications* (New York, 1968), the distinction is recognized, but without any elaboration or discussion of issues on the cognitive side.

[15] For a fuller account of Lambert's views see Ritschl (op. cit.) and von der Stein (op. cit.).

[16] Richard S. Rudner, *Philosophy of Social Science* (Englewood Cliffs, 1966), p. 89.

systems-concepts are at issue. As our historical considerations show, we are dealing with a deep-rooted parallelism, a pluralized application of one single underlying conception.[17] And actually, the development of *general* systems-theory over the past generation should be seen as an attempt to forge a comprehensive unifying framework within which all of the diverse applications of the systems idea could be accommodated – physical systems (be they natural or artificial), process control systems, and cognitive systems alike.

Lambert contrasted a system with its contraries, all "that one might call a chaos, a mere mixture, an aggregate, an agglomeration, a confusion, an uprooting, etc." ("[*alles*] *was man ein Chaos, ein Gemische, einen Hauffen, einen Klumpen, eine Verwirrung, eine Zerüttung, etc. nennt*").[18] And in synthesizing the discussions of the early theoreticians of the system-concept one sees the following features emerge as the definitive characteristics of systematicity:

1. *wholeness*: unity and integrity as a genuine whole that embraces and integrates its constituent parts
2. *completeness*: comprehensiveness: avoidance of gaps or missing components, inclusiveness with nothing needful left out
3. *self-sufficiency*: independence, self-containment, autonomy
4. *cohesiveness*: connectedness, interrelationship, interlinkage, coherence (in one of its senses), a conjoining of the component parts, rules, laws, linking principles; if some components are changed or modified, then others will react to this alteration
5. *consonance*: consistency and compatibility, coherence (in another of its senses), absence of internal discord or dissonance; harmonious mutual collaboration or coordination of components "having all the pieces fall into place"
6. *architectonic*: a well-integrated structure of arrangement of duly ordered component parts; generally in an hierarchic ordering of sub- and super-ordination
7. *functional unity*: purposive interrelationship; a unifying

---

[17] In an interesting recent article "On the Concept of a System" (*Philosophy of Science*, vol. 42 [1975], pp. 448–468), J. H. Marchal reaches a precisely parallel conclusion on the basis of an examination of systems-discourse emanating from the "general systems theory" movement.

[18] *Fragment einer Systematologie* in *Philosophische Schriften*, ed. H. W. Arndt (op. cit.), vol. 7, p. 386.

rationale or telos that finds its expression in some synthesizing principle of functional purport

8. *functional regularity*: rulishness and lawfulness, orderliness of operation, uniformity, normality (conformity to "the usual course of things")

9. *functional simplicity*: elegance, harmony and balance, structural economy, tidiness in the collaboration or coordination of components

10. *mutual supportiveness*: the components of a system are so combined under the aegis of a common purpose or principle as to conspire together in mutual collaboration for its realization; interrelatedness

11. *functional efficacy*: efficiency, effectiveness, adequacy to the common task

These are the definite *parameters of systemalization*. A *system*, properly speaking, must exhibit all of these characteristics, but it need not do to the same extent – let alone perfectly. These various facets of systematicity reflect matters of degree, and systems can certainly vary in their embodiment.

They are matters of degree, of more or less, which can be realized more or less fully in various applications of the idea. Now systematicity has, *vis-à-vis* its components, the character of a *profile* (rather than an average). Just as the health of a person is determined by a plurality of constituent factors (blood pressure, white cell count, etc.), so the systematicity of a body of knowledge is determined in terms of a wide variety of separable albeit interrelated considerations. And there will be trade-offs as between the various "parameters of systematicity."

Different cases of systematization can offer different circumstances as to the realization of the various parameters. (See the schematic illustration of Figure 1.) And so in looking at *alternative*

Figure 1
A SAMPLE OF SYSTEMATICITY-PARAMETER REALIZATION
PROFILES FOR TWO HYPOTHETICAL
RIVAL SYSTEMATIZATIONS
(NOS. I and II)

Note A, B, C, represent different parameters of systematization.

systematizations, we must face such questions as, for example, whether the extent to which the systematization I outweighs II in point of parameters B and C suffices to compensate for extent to which II outweighs I in point of A. In any concrete application of the idea to the realization of systematic treatment of some body of claims, we might have to trade some of these factors off against others: greater completeness may threaten consistency, consistency may endanger completeness, greater connectedness may require the insertion of disuniform elements, greater uniformity may demand loss of connectedness, etc. Any single parameter of systematization is just one element in the overall cost/benefit calculations. And so, even if we pursue our inquiry into nature under the aegis of certain regulative ideals – such as coherence, etc. – we might nevertheless be driven in the final analysis by systematic considerations for results that some be sacrificed (in part) for the sake of others. Despite our best attempts to produce (say) a simple picture of nature, we might nevertheless find that our systematizing efforts themselves force us willy-nilly into a position that fails to yield this desideratum to any substantial extent.

The basic paradigm of a system is that of an *organism*, an organized whole of interrelated and mutually supportive parts functioning as a cohesive unit. Kant puts the matter suggestively as follows:

In accordance with reason's legislative prescriptions, our diverse modes of knowledge must not be permitted to be a mere rhapsody, but must form a system. Only so can they further the essential ends of reason. By a system I understand the unity of the manifold modes of knowledge under one idea. This idea is the concept . . . [which] determines *a priori* not only the scope of its manifold content, but also the positions which the parts occupy relatively to one another. The scientific concept of reason contains, therefore, the end and the form of that whole which is congruent with this requirement. The unity of the end to which all the parts relate and in the idea of which they all stand in realtion to one another, makes it possible for us to determine from our knowledge of the other parts whether any part be missing, and to prevent any arbitrary addition, or in respect of its completeness [to discover] any indeterminateness that does not conform to the limits which are thus determined *a priori*. The whole is thus an organised unity (*articulatio*), and not an aggregate (*coacervatio*). It may grow from within (*per intussusceptionem*), but not by external addition (*per appositionem*). It is thus like an animal body.... (CPuR, A833 = B861 [Kemp Smith].)[19]

And he goes on to maintain:

[O]nly after we have spent much time in the collection of materials in somewhat random fashion at the suggestion of an idea lying hidden in our minds, and after we have, indeed, over a long period assembled the materials in a merely technical manner, does it first become possible for us to discern the idea in a clearer light, and to devise a whole architectonically in accordance with the ends of reason. Systems seem to be formed in the manner of lowly organisms, through a *generatio aequivoca* from the mere confluence of assembled concepts, at first imperfect, and only gradually attaining to completeness, although they one and all have had their schema, as the original germ, in the sheer self-development of reason. Hence, not only is each system articulated in accordance with an idea, but they are one and all organically united in a system of human knowledge, as members of one whole.... (CPuR, A834 = B862 [Kemp Smith].)

3. THE SYSTEMATIC ASPECT OF THE SYSTEM CONCEPT ITSELF

One and the same system can doubtless be presented differently: it can be developed in an analytic or a synthetic way, or – in the case of an axiomatic system – it can be developed from these rather than those axioms. What counts for a cognitive system is the explanatory connection of ideas and not the particular style or format of their presentation. A system is individuated through general features relating to its content and its rational architectonic, and not through the particular manner of its expository development. As long as we traverse exactly the same cognitive terrain, the way or the order in which we do so is immaterial. Cognitive systematization is thus an epistemological notion and not a literary or rhetorical one – a matter of the organization of information and not its mode of presentation, of *explanation* not *exposition*.

---

[19] Seen in this light, Hermann Lotze's dictum that human thought never does and never can rest until "the whole context of reality is conceived under some principle of organic unity" can be seen in a more prosaic light as indicating man's insistence on achieving scientific knowledge of his environing world.

The idea of systematization is intimately intertwined with that of *planning* in its generic sense of the rational organization of materials.[20] Planning, like organizing, is a mode of intellectual action, and it too exhibits the "amphibious" character of systematization. On the physical side one can have such projects as town planning, architecture, and landscape gardening; on the cognitive side, one can plan the organization for the purpose of explanatory or deductive or dialectical (persuasive) or mnemonic codification. Again, systematization is closely connected with the enterprise of *design*, albeit with a difference in orientation. For design – as generally understood – is oriented towards the realization of *physical* forms,[21] while systematization is no less concerned with *intellectual* ones. But the basic issues are the same on both sides: the articulation of a rational structure on the basis of "best-fit" considerations, with all the parameters of systematization – economy, efficiency, generality, uniformity, etc. – figuring in this role. A cognitive system is, as it were, a "design for knowing," and system building is preeminently a problem of rational design.

A painting or piece of architecture – any good design – must combine a variety of potentially conflicting elements in the conjoining synthesis of a cooperative harmony, and this sort of rational unification is exactly what a *system* is all about. In fact, all the various parameters of systematicity contribute to such an idea of an organic unity in varying ways.

Modern writers generally characterize a system in some such terms as these:

> A *system* is a collection of interrelated entities, the relationships among which are such that information about them affords a basis for inferring conclusions regarding the structure, *modus operandi*, or temporal history of the system as a whole.[22]

Such a formula puts its finger on many key features of a system: wholeness, interrelatedness of parts, functional interrelationships, etc., all of which are present in the traditional explications of the idea. The

[20] For a useful general treatment of planning theory see G. A. Miller, E. Galanter, and K. H. Pribram, *Plans and the Structure of Behavior* (New York, 1960). The parallelism of planning and systematizing was stressed by Hugo Dingler. See his *Das System* (Munich, 1930), pp. 127ff.

[21] See Christopher Alexander, *Notes on the Synthesis of Form* (Cambridge, Mass., 1964).

[22] Compare the definition given by Anatol Rapoport in the article "Systems Analysis: I. General Systems Theory" in the *International Encyclopedia of the Social Sciences*, vol. 15 (New York, 1968), pp. 452–456 (see p. 453b).

concept is a chain that links together many distinguishable elements.

Systematicity, accordingly, emerges an internally complex and multi-criterial conception, which embraces and synthesizes all the various aspects of an organic, functionally effective whole. The paradigmatic system is a whole that has subordinate wholes whose existence and functioning facilitate – and indeed make possible – the existence and functioning of the resulting whole. A true system is subject to a pervasive functional unity of interrelated components, a unity correlative with the notion of completeness.

Interestingly enough, the conception of systematicity is thus itself a system-oriented conception: a whole that represents a congeries of closely interrelated and mutually complementary conceptions. It is a composite idea, a complex Gestalt in whose make-up various, duly connected, structural elements play a crucial role. The conception of organism and organic unity clearly provides a unifying center for this range of ideas. Their focal point is the coordinated collaboration of mutually supportive parts operating in the interest of a unifying aim or principle.[23]

Many such conceptual clusters contain elements that are in theory disparate but in fact held together by the systematic order of the world. Rather than representing a fusion of diverse conceptual elements whose coming together is underwritten by purely *a priori* and semantical relationships, the *concurrence basic to the concept rests on a strictly empirical foundation.* There is no *logical* guarantee that these conceptually distinguishable factors must go together; their by and large coordination is a matter of contingent fact. Concepts of this *fact-coordinative* sort rest on presuppositions whose content is factual, reflecting a view of how things go in the world. Such concepts are developed and deployed against a fundamentally empirical backdrop – a Weltanschauung, or rather, some miniscule sector thereof. The crucial characteristic of such cases is the conjoining of various factors that are *in theory* separable from one another but *in practice* generally found in conjunction. At the base of such a concept, then, lies an empirically underwritten coordination that places the various critical factors into a symbiotic, mutually supportive relationship. Accordingly, the concept is fact-coordinative in envisaging a coming-together of

---

[23] As Lambert puts it, the parts of a system should "*alle mit einander so verbunden sein, dass sie gerade das der vorgesetzten Absicht gemässe Ganze ausmachen.*" (Quoted in O. Ritschl. op. cit., p. 64.)

theoretically distinct factors whose union is itself the product not of conceptual necessity but of the contingently constituted general run of things.[24]

It is clear that systematicity is itself a fact-coordinative concept of just this sort, one which holds together in a symbiotic and systemic union various elements which – from the aspect of purely theoretical considerations – might well wander off on their own separate ways, but which "the ways of the world" – or, rather the conceptualizing mechanisms that afford our instrumentalities for their rationalization — have inseparably joined together.

The parameters of systematicity (simplicity, regularity, uniformity, comprehensiveness, cohesiveness, unity, harmony, economy, etc.), represent certain *intellectual* values or norms within the cognitive enterprise. Three points are of particular importance here:

(1) The issue is one of *cognitive* norms or values that implement the requirements of intelligibility and understandability. The simpler (or more uniform, etc.) an explanation is, the more easily it is formulated, mastered, utilized, etc. The inquiring intellect proceeds standardly with reference to such essentially "aesthetic" principles of order and structure of a very *classical* sort. The theoretical values at issue implement this cognitive approach.

(2) The values at issue are object rather than subject oriented. They relate to the objects or materials of our theorizing inquiry and not to the workers that carry it on. In this respect they differ altogether from such values as perseverance, honesty, probity, cooperativeness, etc., that represent desirable traits of *scientists* rather than of the science they produce.

(3) The values at issue are *tendential*. In adopting simplicity (say) as a cognitive value, we do not say that we will never exchange a simpler theory for a more complex one. Simplicity-preference is not absolute or peremptory in this sense. What we are committing ourselves to is never to pay the price of augmented complexity unless this is made up for by compensating gains elsewhere, through greater gains with respect to other values.

To be sure, the fact that systematicity invokes a coordinated plurality of desiderata does not mean that these may not *conflict* with one another in concrete contexts. The pluralism of desiderata – the fact that

---

[24] For a fuller treatment of such fact-coordinative concepts see Chapter VI of the author's *The Primacy of Practice* (Oxford, 1973).

each must be taken in context of others within the overall picture of systematicity – means that in the pursuit of these factors we must moderate them to one another. Whenever multiple desiderata interact, we cannot appropriately pursue one without reference to the rest.

Consider an analogy. Its "safety" is a prime desideratum in a motor car. But it would not do to devise a "perfectly safe" car which only goes 1·75 m.p.h. Safety, speed, efficiency, operating-economy, breakdown-avoidance, etc., are *all* prime desiderata of a motor car. Each *counts* – but none *predominates* in the sense that the rest should be sacrificed to it. They must all be *combined* in the design of a good car. The situation with respect to our cognitive ideals is altogether parallel. In formulating an effective cognitive system in a particular case, the achievement of completeness may require a sacrifice in simplicity. The need for mutal support and functional unity may countervail against functional elegance and economy, etc. In the cognitive systematization of a certain body of knowledge the various parameters of systematization – simplicity, uniformity, comprehensiveness, and the rest – may represent foci of conflict and tension.

This plurality and interaction of desiderata means that a narrow focus upon a single such cognitive ideal is not very helpful – they must stand in balance. To stress one to neglect of the rest is ultimately self-defeating: in each instance, these parameters are interlocked in a synthesis of coordinative tension. The pursuit of one factor is profitable only within the setting of a concern for the overall "economy" of associated desiderata, providing for the interaction of its component desiderata in the light of mutual interconnections. Each must thus be seen to figure as simply one component within a system which makes it possible to strike a reasonable balance between the different and potentially discordant demands. It is this aspect which – to repeat – renders systematicity itself a systems-oriented conception.

4. THE SYSTEMATICITY OF "THE TRUTH"

The conception that all truths form one comprehensive and cohesive system in which everything has its logically appropriate place is one of the many fundamental ideas contributed to the intellectual heritage of the West by the ancient Greeks. The general structure of the concept can already be discerned in the Presocratics, especially in the seminal thought of Parmenides.[25] The conception that all knowledge – that is all of truth as humans can come to have epistemic control of it – forms a single comprehensive unit that is capable of a deductive systematization on essentially Euclidean lines is the guiding concept of Aristotle's theory of science as expounded in the *Posterior Analytics*.

Inquiry is the pursuit of *truth*. And the overall domain of truth is in itself clearly a system – *das System der Wahrheiten überhaupt* as Lambert calls it. Let us consider the way in which the idea that "truth is a system" is to be understood. Three things are at issue: the set $\mathcal{T}$ of truths must have the features of *comprehensiveness* (or completeness), *consistency*, and *cohesiveness* (unity). The first two of these are familiar and well understood. Let us concentrate on the third.

One way to explicate cohesiveness is in terms of inferential interdependence:

The propositional set $\mathcal{T}$ exhibits the feature of *inferential interlinkage* in that every $\mathcal{T}$-element is inferentially dependent upon at least some others: Whenever $Q \in \mathcal{T}$, then there are elements $P_1, P_2, \ldots, P_n \in \mathcal{T}$ (all suitably distinct from Q) such that:

$$P_1, P_2, \ldots, P_n \vdash Q.$$

This feature is at bottom merely a matter of sufficient redundancy. And it is clear that such redundancy does and must characterize truths. Assume that p and $\sim q$ are both true (and so q false). Then clearly both of the following will also be truths: $p \lor q$, $q \supset (r \& \sim r)$. And so if our initial two propositions were excised from the set that represents the truths, they would both still be derivable from the remainder.

The situation illustrated by such examples is a perfectly general one. Each and every truth P_1 is a member of a family of related truths $P_1, P_2, P_3, \ldots, P_n$ of such a kind that, even when P_1 is dropped from explicit

---

[25] The following passage is particularly apposite here:

The thing that can be thought and that for the sake of which the thought exists is the same; for you cannot find thought without something that is, as to which it is uttered. And there is not, and never shall be, anything besides what is, since fate has chained it so as to be whole and immovable. . . . Since, then, it has a furthest limit, it is complete on every side, like the mass of a rounded sphere, equally poised from the centre in every direction; for it cannot be greater or smaller in one place than in another. For there is nothing that could keep it from reaching out equally, nor can aught that is be more here and less there than what is, since it is all inviolable. For the point from which it is equal in every direction tends equally to the limits. Here shall I close my trustworthy speech and thought about the truth. (Frag. 8, Diels; tr. J. Burnet.)

membership in the list, the remainder will collectively still yield P_1. (The trio $P_1 = p$, $P_2 = p \vee q$, $P_3 = \sim q$ yields an example.) This circumstance reflects what might be called the *systematic constrictiveness* of the truth: the fact that truths constitute a mutually determinative domain such that even if some element is hypothetically deleted, it can nevertheless be restored from the rest.[26]

Thus when we formulate our knowledge-claims systematically, we are endowing them with *verisimilitude* in the root sense of "resemblance to the truth." One arrives at the inference:

> Knowledge must reflect the truth.
> The truth is a system.
> _____
> Knowledge should be a system.

This idea – that if our truth-claims are indeed to approximate to the truth itself, then they too must be capable of systematic development – has historically provided one of the prime grounds for adopting the systematicity of knowledge as a regulative ideal.

5. COGNITIVE SYSTEMATICITY AS A HALLMARK OF THE SCIENTIFIC

Their systematicity authenticates the claims of individual theses as actually belonging to a *science*, as Kant rightly insisted:

> As systematic unity is what first raises ordinary knowledge to the rank of science, that is, makes a system out of a mere aggregate of knowledge, architectonic [the art of constructing systems] is the doctrine of the scientific in our knowledge. . . . (CPuR, A832 = B860.)

Let us explore more extensively the contention – deeply rooted in the epistemological tradition of the West – that the proper, the *scientific* development of our knowledge should proceed systematically.

Scientific systematization has two aspects. The first is *methodological*, and looks to the unity provided by common intellectual tools of inquiry and argumentation. (This aspect of the unity of a shared body of methodological machinery was the focus of the "Unity of

---

[26] See Chapter VII of the author's *The Coherence Theory of Truth* (Oxford, 1973) for a further treatment of relevant issues.

Science" movement in the heyday of logical positivism in the 1920's and 30's.) But, of course, there should be a *substantive* unity as well. Something would be very seriously amiss if we could not bring the various sectors of science into coordination and consonance with one another. And even when there are or appear to be conflicts and discordances, we should be able to explain them and provide a rational account for them within an overarching framework of explanatory principles.

Scientific explanation in general proceeds along *subsumptive* lines, particular occurrences in nature being explained with reference to covering generalizations. But the *adequacy* of such an explanation hinges upon the status of the covering generalization: is it a "mere empirical regularity," or is it a thesis whose standing within our scientific system is firmly secured as a "law of nature?" This latter question leads straightaway to the pivotal issue of how firmly the thesis is embedded within its wider systematic setting in the branch of science at issue. Systematization here affords a criterion of the appositeness of the generalizations deployed in scientific explanation.

An empirical generalization is not to be viewed as fully adequate for explanatory purposes until it can lay claim to the status of a law. And a law is not just a summary statement of observed-regularities-to-date, it claims to deal with a universal regularity purporting to describe how things inevitably are: how the processes at work in the world must invariably work, how things have to happen in nature. Such a claim has to be based upon a stronger foundation than any mere observed-regularity-to-date. The *coherence of laws* in patterns that illuminate the functional "mechanisms" by which natural processes occur is a critical element – perhaps the most pivotal one – in furnishing this stronger foundation, this "something more" than a mere generalization of observations. An "observed regularity" does not qualify for acceptance as a "law of nature" simply by becoming better established through observation in additional cases; what is needed is *integration* into the body of scientific knowledge.[27]

---

[27] The idea that in explicating the idea of a "law of nature" we shall take systematicity as our standard of lawfulness was a standard among the English neo-Hegelians. It recurs in F. B. Ramsey, who in an unpublished note of 1928 proposed to characterize laws as the "consequence of those propositions which we should take as axioms if we knew everything and organized it as simply as possible in a deductive system." (See David Lewis, *Counterfactuals* [Oxford, 1973], p. 73.) Ramsey gives the theory an interesting – but in principle gratuitous – twist in the direction of a specifically *deductive* style of systematization, a specification the Hegelians had made along

Systematicity is thus not only a prominent (if partial) aspect of the structure of our knowledge, but is a normatively *desirable* aspect of it – indeed a *requisite* for genuinely scientific knowledge. It is, accordingly, correlative with the *regulative* ideal presented by the injunction: develop your knowledge so as to endow it with a systematic structure. To understand an issue properly – that is to say, *scientifically* – we must grasp it in its systematic setting. *Sapientis est ordinare* affirms the sage dictum of which St. Thomas Aquinas was fond.[28]

Their methodological role as instruments of scientific reasoning reflects – and makes manifest – the fundamentally regulative nature of the parameters of cognitive systematization (simplicity, uniformity, etc.). They combine to mark the endeavour to instill our knowledge of the world with the hallmarks of system as a definitive feature of scientific inquiry. The parameters of systematicity emerge as prime tools of scientific method.

It is through the heritage of the Leibniz-Wolff tradition in particular that systematization has become for the moderns too an ongoing vehicle for the ancient ideal of a *scientia* – a body of knowledge developed as a comprehensive whole according to rational principles. And indeed, the prospect of organizing a body of claims systematically is crucial to its claims to be a science. Systematization monitors the adequacy of the rational development (articulation) of what we claim to know, authenticating the whole body of claims, collectively, as a science. As Kant put it, "systematic unity is what first raises ordinary knowledge to the rank of science."[29] To know something scientifically is to exhibit it in an appropriate systematic context:

> Every discipline (*Lehre*) if it be a system – that is, a cognitive whole ordered according to principles – is called a science.[30]

Perhaps this puts it a bit too strongly. Systematicity is no doubt a

---

coherentist rather than deductivist lines. The more orthodoxly neo-Hegelian, coherentist version of the theory was refurbished in the author's *Scientific Explanation* (New York, 1970; see especially pp. 110–111). Parts of the present discussion draw upon this work.

[28] St. Thomas also wrote that an "architect" was a man who knew how things should be ordered and arranged, and that the world could be more appropriately applied to a philosopher than to a builder. (Quoted in Paul Frankl, *The Gothic: Literary Sources and Interpretations* [Princeton, 1960], p. 135.)

[29] CPuR A832 = B860 (tr. Kemp Smith).

[30] Immanuel Kant, Preface to the *Metaphysical Foundations of Natural Science* (tr. L. W. Beck).

necessary condition for a science, but scarcely a *sufficient* one, since the rules of an art (sonnet writing, chess playing) can also be systematized. Yet the key point is right: there can be no science without system. Systematicity is the very hallmark of a science: a "science" is – virtually by definition – a branch of knowledge that systematizes our information in some domain of empirical fact. Kant espoused the schema: the science of X = the systematization of all of our attainable knowledge regarding X.[31] In a remarkably Hegelian vein, he wrote:

> Systems seem to be formed . . . in the sheer self-development of reason. Hence, not only is each system articulated in accordance with an idea, but they are one and all organically united in a system of human knowledge, as members of one whole, and so as admitting of an architectonic of all human knowledge, which, at the present time, in view of the great amount of material that has been collected, or which can be obtained from the ruins of ancient systems, is not only possible, but would not indeed be difficult. (CPuR, A834 = B862 [tr. Kemp Smith].)

This idea of the systematically comprehensive self-development of reason is present in much of the subsequent philosophical tradition, and is particularly prominent in the school of Hegel.

To be sure, our main concern here will be with the fact-oriented applications of cognitive systematization – the systematizing of our descriptive knowledge (or *purported* knowledge) of the way in which things work in the world. The *formal* rather than *factual* sphere (i.e. logic, mathematics, theoretical linguistics) and the normative application of system (as regards the aesthetic, moral, or religious sectors of life) lie outside the scope of present concerns.

The systematic idea in the context of science embraces not only the more modest view that the several branches of empirical inquiry exhibit a systematic structure severally and separately, but also the more ambitious doctrine that the *whole* of natural science forms one single vast and all-comprehending system.[32] Prominent in the historical background here is Leibniz's bold vision of a *scientia universalis* – a synoptic treatment of all knowledge – encyclopedic in scope, yet

---

[31] CPuR A834 = B862 (tr. Kemp Smith).

[32] Indeed these boundaries – vast though they are – may seem too restrictive. Parmenides, Aristotle, Spinoza, Leibniz, Hegel, and other great systematizers did not limit their aspirations to the confines of natural science, but extended them over the totality of human knowledge.

ordered not by the customary, conventional, and arbitrary arrangement of letters of the alphabet, but a rational arrangement of topics according to their immanent cognitive principles. The conception of scientific systematization points towards the ideal of a perfect science within which all the available and relevant facts about the world occupy a suitable place with due regard to their cognitive connections. Indeed not only should scientific knowledge approximate – and, ideally, *constitute* – one vast synoptic system, but a discipline is validated as authentically scientific by its inclusion within this over-all system.

6. PERSPECTIVALISM: THE EPISTEMOLOGICAL IMPORTANCE OF THE
SYSTEMS POINT OF VIEW

Consider any item of the world's furniture – that tree, for example. It is quite clear that it can be classified, described, and studied from many different angles of approach – the botanist's, the ecologist's, the zoologist's (as home or source of food for fauna), the meteorologist's (as indicative of the climatic past of its region), the structural engineer's, etc. The same meteorite can concern the chemist, the metallurgist, the cosmologist, the descriptive astronomer, etc. The constituents of nature are always multifaceted – they can always be approached from a diversified plurality of descriptive and explanatory categories.

Is this just a matter of different *explanatory interests*, leading as a consequence to aspectival differences? Surely not. In general, we do not *impose* our purpose-inherent differences *on* nature; rather the aspectival differences operative *in the world* constrain us to diversify our perspectives. (We are naturally lazy and would everywhere prefer a uniform, undifferentiated approach if complications were not forced on us willy-nilly by a complex world.)

It is thus just not a matter of *human* contrivance and convenience in the division of intellectual labor that there are many specialized "dimensions of consideration" or "descriptive and explanatory standpoints." Rather, this circumstance reflects a fact about the world itself – as we have come to know it – namely that its things have different SORTS of properties: that this block of stone has physical and chemical and geological and even (as fossil-container) biological aspects. Our cognitive situation reflects an ontological fact; that what is seen from our different perspectives are very different sorts of things –

very different aspects. (Perspectival pluralism roots in aspectival pluralism.)

The *prismatic* nature of things as inherently embracing different facets is a significant fact of theoretical life. *Description* is – and must be – correlative with *explanation*. Descriptive classifiers are law-correlative. The fact that things hold multiple citizenship in diverse law-frameworks provides the explanatory basis for their falling subject to various different, naturally constituted disciplines.

Perspectivalism is not to be applied *conjunctively*; – we cannot simply add together law-frameworks and say "from this angle *X*" and "for that angle *Y*" *and* "for yon angle *Z*." Rather, we must proceed *compositively*. The different aspects must be seen as so many constituent "moments" (in Hegel's sense) of a unified *whole*. One thing seen from different points of view is still one thing. The prismatic character of things does not destroy their unity. Rather, things must be seen as *systems*, exhibiting plurality of aspects in systemic interrelationship. The concept of a *system* is thus a crucial ingredient in any adequate concept of a *thing*.

Understanding aims not only at the truth but at the whole truth. We do not comprehend *adequately* what we do not comprehend from *all the appropriate perspectives* taken in their proper interrelationship. Adequacy of understanding aims not only at correctness but at comprehensiveness as well. It hinges on how matters stand "with everything taken into account." Consider an analogy. I am going to buy a car, and want to know if it is economical to operate. It might be very economical in part of fuel usage but not (say) in terms of its demand for lubricants or in point of frequency-of-repair considerations. If I want to know if it is "economical on the whole – *with everything taken into account*," then I must combine all these aspects into a single, comprehensive, over-all evaluation.

The achievement of adequacy in understanding is a matter of combining points of view and synthesizing them into a unified whole. It is to be achieved through reproducing the aspectival complexity of the object on the cognitive side through a comprehensive perspectival characterization. *Adequacy lies in wholeness*: it is only achievable through comprehensive synthesis of diverse aspects. In cognitive affairs we do well to hold aloft a methodological banner with Goethe's device: "MANY-SIDEDNESS."

The search for cognitive system brings together man's deepest intellectual and aesthetic aspirations. As Karl Pearson put it some three generations ago:

> There is an insatiable desire in the human breast to resume in some short formula, some brief statement, the facts of human experience. It leads the savage to "account" for all natural phenomena by deifying the wind and the stream and the tree. It leads civilised man, on the other hand, to express his emotional experience in works of art, and his physical and mental experience in the formulae or so-called laws of science.... Science endeavours to provide a mental *résumé* of the universe, and its last great claim to our support is the capacity it has for satisfying our cravings for a brief description of the history of the world. Such a brief description, a formula resuming all things, science has not yet found and may probably never find, but of this we may feel sure, that its method of seeking for one is the sole possible method, and that the truth it has reached is the only form of truth which can permanently satisfy the aesthetic judgment. (*The Grammar of Science* [London, 1892], Chap. 1, sect. 14.)

The drive for system represents a synthesis of the cognitive and aesthetic domains of the human intellect to which no creative scientist is wholly insensitive in his thought. (Recall Rosalind Franklin's remark that the Watson–Crick double-helix model "is just too pretty to be wrong.")

The systematic ideal is a powerfully attractive one. Any rent in the fabric of our scientific knowledge – any failings in point of its unity and orderliness – would clearly deserve to be characterized as flaws, and would be seen as impediments to the adequacy of our understanding and the effectiveness of our intellectual mastery. To be sure, no one claims that such synoptic and comprehensive systematization is a descriptive aspect of scientific knowledge as it stands today (or will stand at some other historical juncture). But it represents an idealization towards which – by general agreement – science can and should progress along an evolutionary route.

This grandiose and heroic vision that all of man's knowledge of his environing universe forms parts of one single all-embracing cognitive system is of ancient and respectable lineage. Adumbrated by Parmenides, this conception was elaborated by Plato, developed in loving detail and with immense labor by Aristotle, and espoused by a whole host of thinkers from the Church Fathers to Leibniz and Hegel and beyond.[33] It is one of the great formative ideas of Western civilization.

[33] Sixteenth-century thinkers inclined to locate "the perfect system" in the mind of God, a stance no longer "available" after Kant's Copernican Revolution. Thus Charles S. Peirce transposed it to be the product of a scientific community projecting its efforts over the idealized long run.

II

The Purpose of Cognitive Systematization: the Quality-control of Knowledge Claims

---

SYNOPSIS

(1) The principal functions of cognitive systematization in the factual domain: the pursuit of intelligibility, the realization of a specifically *scientific* mode of rational development, and the verification of truthfulness. (2) The first aim: providing a vehicle for intelligibility and understandability. The second aim: providing the requisite means for authenticating a body of knowledge claims as scientific. The third aim: providing a testing standard of the acceptability of knowledge-claims. This third function points towards: (3) The "Hegelian Inversion" and the idea of a coherentist criteriology of knowledge. (4) The metaphysical ramifications of the Hegelian Inversion in its relationship to Kant's "Copernican Revolution."

---

1. INTRODUCTION

Systematization provides an ideal for cognitive development throughout the domain of our knowledge – alike in its formal and its factual hemispheres. However, the present discussion will put aside almost entirely the issue of the systematization of *formal* knowledge, and focus upon the *factual* sector. The systematization of formal knowledge – particularly in the spheres of mathematics, logic, and grammar – is, to be sure, a noble and ancient project whose pursuit among the Greeks provided the very foundation of the enterprise of cognitive systematization. But it is the systematization of our factual, empirical knowledge of the contingent arrangements of this world that will primarily occupy us throughout the coming pages.[1]

It is well to begin by facing up to the realities of the situation. There is no rational basis for issuing in advance – prior to any furtherance of the enterprise itself – a categorical assurance that the effort to systematize our knowledge of the world is bound to succeed. The systematicity of our factual knowledge is (as we shall see) not something that can be guaranteed *a priori*, as having to obtain on the basis of the "general principles" of the matter. The parameters of systematicity – coherence, consistency, uniformity, and the rest – represent a family of *regulative ideals* towards whose realization our cognitive endeavours do and should strive. But the drive for systematicity is the operative expression of a governing ideal, and not something whose realization can be taken for granted as already certain and settled from the very outset. There is no valid reason to assume or presume from the very outset that systematicity is ultimately going to emerge at the constitutive level of how inquiry will ultimately picture the descriptive nature of things.

This cognitive drive for orderliness is informed and crucially conditioned by a coordinate cognitive drive for comprehensiveness, variety, novelty, and the like. As students of human biology have shrewdly observed, man's central nervous system demands a novelty of inputs to avoid boredom – exploratory behavior and novelty-tropism are a fundamental aspect of the biological outfitting of higher animals.[2] Clearly systematization has a deep Darwinian rationalization. To make our way in a difficult world, we men, as *rational* animals, need to exploit regularities for our effective functioning. Now rules are easiest to grasp, master, to apply, and to transmit if they themselves are organized in rulish patterns – i.e. are developed systematically. And the concern for system is nothing else than this drive for *metarulishness*, an effort to impart to our principles of behavioral and intellectual procedure a structure that is itself principled.

In explaining the views of the American philosopher Charles Sanders Peirce one commentator has written:

The apparent thirst of the mind for unity and coherence is most

---

[1] It should be stressed that this stance in no way countervails against recognition that formal knowledge is an indispensable part of the rational instrumentalities by which inquiry in the factual domain proceeds. For the writer's views regarding these issues, see his *Methodological Pragmatism* (Oxford, 1976), especially ch. XV.

[2] Compare Robert Ardrey, *The Hunting Hypothesis* (London, 1976).

persistent. The quest for [systematic] unity is of great intensity, and seems to lie at the very root . . . of intellectual activity of any kind. The quest of the mind for comprehensiveness is not, as some have suggested, pernicious, but rather is of the essence of the life of reason. . . . The craving for a unified view of things is as real as any of man's physical cravings, and more powerful than many of them. (William H. David, *Peirce's Epistemology* [The Hague, 1972], pp. 45–56.)

This gets at the heart of the matter. Man as a rational animal exhibits a deep need for understanding, and the facets of rational structure (unity, comprehensiveness, coherence, and the rest) are constitutive components of that systematicity through which alone understanding can be achieved.

But the question remains: what *rational* considerations render systematicity so desirable – what is the legitimative grounding of its status as a regulative ideal in cognition? What, in short, does systematicity do for us? After all, systematization is a pointful action and system is a functional category – systematizing is something that has to have a purpose to it. This teleological aspect of the matter needs closer scrutiny.

Knowledge is organized with various ends in view – in particular, the *heuristic* (to make it easier to learn, retain, and utilize) and the *probative* (to test and thereby render it better supported and more convincing). This latter, epistemological dimension will be our prime focus of concern.

In the present study of cognitive systematization it will, in effect, be the monograph and not the textbook that is the paradigm. We shall put aside the *psychological* aspects of knowledge-acquisition and utilization (learning, remembering, etc.), focusing upon the *rational* aspects of organizing knowledge in its probative and explanatory dimensions. We shall deal with the systematizing of knowledge as a matter of cognitive planning for theoretical and purely cognitive purposes and put heuristic issues aside.

Given a focus on probative and explanatory issues, the systematic development of knowledge – or purported knowledge – may be seen to serve three major interrelated functions:

1. INTELLIGIBILITY. Systematicity is the prime vehicle for understanding, for it is just exactly their systematic inter-

relationships which render factual claims intelligible. As long as they remain discrete and disconnected, they lack any adequate handle for the intellect that seeks to take hold of them in its endeavor to comprehend the issues involved.

2. RATIONAL ORGANIZATION. Systematicity – in its concern for such desiderata as simplicity, uniformity, etc. – affords the means to a probatively rational and scientifically viable articulation and organization of our knowledge. The systematic development of knowledge is thus a key part of the idea of a science.

3. VERIFICATION. Systematicity is a vehicle of cognitive *quality control.* It is plausible to suppose that systematically developed information is more likely to be correct – or at any rate less likely to be defective – thanks to its avoidance of the internal error-indicative conflicts of discrepancy, inconsistency, disuniformity. This indicates the service of systematization as a testing-process for acceptability – an instrument of verification.

Let us consider these three themes more closely.

2. THE FUNCTIONS OF SYSTEMATIZATION

Its orientation towards the provision of a *rationale* makes systematization an indispensable instrument of cognitive rationality. Within a systematic framework, the information to be organized is brought within the control of a network of rule-governed explanatory and justificatory relationships. The facts are thus placed within patterns of order by way of reference to common principles, and their explanatory rationalization is accordingly facilitated.

Systematization is a tool of explanation and we explain things with an end in view – viz., to make them *intelligible.* But what does this "intelligibility" involve? Its definitive themes are reduction to rationally available patterns, rendering matters "only natural and to be expected" through the provision of a suitable rationale. A system-establishing synthesis on the basis of evidential or explanatory cohesion does the job of "accounting for" the theses at issue in both senses of this term – *explaining-the-fact* and also *providing-grounds-for-its-claims-to-*

factuality. In this way, a cognitive system provides illumination: their systematic interconnections render the facts at issue amenable to reason by setting them within a framework of ordering principles that bring their mutual interrelationships to light. Systematicity is the key to understanding – it provides the channels through which explanatory power flows.

A system results when items are linked into an orderly structure of functional unity. In the case of a *cognitive* system, the items are the sundry theses that compare the body of our knowledge or purported knowledge. But what is the nature of the interconnecting linkages?

The two main possibilities here are (1) connections of the probative or *evidential* order, and (2) connections of the justificatory or *explanatory* order. There is an important difference here. In the latter case we are concerned with what the medieval schoolmen called the order of why-it-is-so reasons (*rationes essendi* or ontological reasons), in the latter with what they called why-we-hold-it-to-be-so reasons (*rationes cognoscendi* or epistemological reasons). Consider the height of yonder tree. I say it is roughly 100 feet high. The ontological reason for my claim will lie in the following sort of explanation: that it is a tree of such-and-such a sort, a type which has such-and-such growth characteristics. and that the soil and weather conditions afforded it with such and such requisites for growth. On the other hand the epistemological reason for my claim might simply be that it cast a shadow of approximately 10 feet at a time when a certain 10 foot pole cast a shadow of 1 foot. The one set of reasons deals with the *explanation* of our claims, the other with the *substantiation* we have for making them (with the account *for our holding them to be so*).

It is, or should be, clear that our own present concern with cognitive systems will be oriented almost entirely towards the issue of explanatory linkages and the order of "ontological" reasons.

To be sure, the separation cannot be made with surgical precision and neatness. For the fact is that explanatory considerations will themselves carry evidential and probative weight. The very fact that a certain item fits neatly into an explanatory system provides a powerful indication "that we've got it right" and affords us with a substantial item of evidence for it. (Just this is the basis for the "Hegelian Inversion" to be considered in the next chapter – the policy of taking explanatory systematicity as an index of evidential warrant.)

The urge to understand that affords the impetus to system-construction produces the ebb and flow of a search for new and discordant materials of cognitive disequilibration – succeeded by phases of order-restoration. This ongoing process produces continually recurring discrepancies between the mental plan (the expected) and encountered reality (the experienced).[3] The two key aspects of system – viz., *comprehensiveness* and *order* reflect this fundamental feature of man's cognitive position of a creature emplaced *in medias res* in a world – not of his making, and hostile or at best indifferent – which he must bring under cognitive control.

A second major aim of cognitive systematization is that of providing the requisite means for authenticating a body of knowledge claims as scientific. This is something which we can, at this point, pretty much pass by with a mere "listing for the record," since the issue has already been treated at considerable length in the preceding chapter. There is, however, one further aspect of the matter which deserves closer consideration, namely the utility of systematization as an instrument of inquiry. The endeavour to systematize our in formation greatly facilitates the process of problem-solving. The key issue here is the devising of governing strategies for exposition and rational orientation. A system is akin to a road-map that sets out the network of connections by showing how "places" (i.e., facts) are related by "connecting linkages" (i.e., reasons). Inquiry can only proceed efficiently by means of a system that provides a suitable (intellectual) "map" of the cognitive terrain.[4]

Thirdly, systematic development also provides us with a test of cognitive appropriateness; it serves as a monitor of the adequacy of the articulation of our body of knowledge (or purported knowledge). This is evident from a consideration of the very nature of the various parameters of systematicity: consistency, consonance, coherence – and even completeness (comprehensiveness). The advantages of injecting these factors into the organizing articulation of our knowledge are virtually self-evident. In the pursuit of factual knowledge we strive to secure correct *information* about the world. We accordingly endeavor to reject falsehoods, striving to ensure that to the greatest feasible extent the wrong theses are kept out of our range of cognitive commitments.

---

[3] See the author's discussion of Leibniz' theory of possible-world evaluation in ch. III of his *Essays in Modality* (Oxford, 1974).

[4] On this issue of systematic procedures as a tool of problem solving see Allen Newell and Herbert A. Simon, *Human Problem Solving* (Englewood Cliffs, 1972). See also E. C. Tolman, "Cognitive Maps in Rats and Men," *Psychological Review*, vol. 51 (1945).

And the pursuit of consistency, consonance, coherence, completeness, etc., clearly facilitates the attainment of this ruling objective. Systematization is a prime instrument of error-avoidance – of cognitive quality-control.

There are in fact very different sorts of "errors." There are errors of the first kind – errors of omission arising when we do not accept *P* when *P* is in fact the case. These involve the sanction (disvalue) of *ignorance*. And there are also errors of the second kind – errors of commission arising when we accept *P* when in fact not-*P* is the case. These involve the mark of cognitive dissonance and outright *mistake*. And clearly both sorts of mis-steps are *errors*. The rules of the cognitive game call not only for rejecting falsehoods and keeping the wrong things out but also for accepting truths and assuring that the right things get in. Systematization is a great help in these regards. It is presumptively error-minimizing with respect to the two kinds of cognitive errors. Given its coordinated stress on comprehensiveness and mutual fit, the systematization of our knowledge clearly facilitates the realization of its governing objective: the engrossing of information in the context of an optimal balance of truth over falsehoods. This crucial aspect of truth-determination brings us to the threshhold of an important idea, that of the "Hegelian Inversion."

3. THE HEGELIAN INVERSION: THE TRANSFORMATION FROM A DESIDERATUM OF EXPOSITION TO A TEST OF ACCEPTABILITY

An important development in this range of ideas came into prominence with Hegel and his followers in the 19th century. This is the transformation from the earlier conception of systematicity as the hallmark of science as per the equation

a science = a systematically developed body of knowledge

into its redeployment as *a criterion or standard of cognitive acceptability*, as per the equation:

true (presumptively) = meriting inclusion within a science = capable of being smoothly integrated into the system of scientific knowledge.

We thus arrive at the "Hegelian Inversion" by beginning with the implication-thesis that what belongs to science can be systematized and then transposing it into the converse:

> If an item is systematizable with the whole of our (purported) knowledge, then it should be accepted as a part of it.

Systematicity is now set up as a *testing standard of (presumptive) truth*, and thus becomes a means for enlarging the realm of what we accept as true rather than merely affording a device for organizing preestablished truth.

The earlier discussions stressed the over-all systematicity of "the truth" – the fact that the totality of true theses must constitute a cohesive system – and presented system as a crucial aspect of truth. This pre-Hegelian approach saw systematization as a two-step process: first (1) determine truths, and then (2) systematize them. (Think of the analogy of building: first one assembles the bricks, then one builds the wall.) With the inversion at issue, a single-step process is at issue: the determination of the right components through the very process of their assembling.

This line of development points towards a new and importantly different role for systematicity. Its bearing is now radically transformed. From being *a hallmark of science* (as per the regulative idea that a body of knowledge-claims cannot qualify as a science if it lacks a systematic articulation), systematicity is transmuted into *a standard of truth* – an acceptability criterion for the claims that purport to belong to science. From a *desideratum of the organization* of our "body of factual knowledge," systematicity is metamorphosed into a *qualifying test of membership* in it – a standard of facticity. The effect of the Hegelian inversion is to establish "the claim of system as an arbiter of fact," to use F. H. Bradley's apt expression.

This idea of systematicity as an *arbiter* of knowledge was implicit in Hegel himself, and developed by his followers, particularly those of the English Hegelian school inaugurated by T. H. Green. This Hegelian inversion leads to one of the central themes of the present discussion – the idea of using systematization as a control of substantive knowledge. F. H. Bradley put the matter as follows:

> The test [of truth] which I advocate is the idea of a whole of

knowledge as wide and as consistent as may be. In speaking of system [as the standard of truth] I always mean the union of these two aspects [of coherence and comprehensiveness] . . . [which] are for me inseparably included in the idea of system. . . . Facts for it [i.e. my view] are true . . . just so far as they contribute to the order of experience. If by taking certain judgements . . . as true, I can get some system into my world, then these "facts" are so far true, and if by taking certain "facts" as errors I can order my experience better, than these "facts" are errors.[5]

The plausibility of such an approach is easy to see. Pilate's question is still relevant. How are we men – imperfect mortals dwelling in this imperfect sublunary sphere – to determine where "the real truth" lies? The Recording Angel does not whisper it into our ears. (If he did, I doubt that we would understand him!) The consideration that we have no *direct* access to the truth regarding the *modus operandi* of the world we inhabit is perhaps the most fundamental fact of epistemology. We must recognize that there is no prospect of assessing the truth – or presumptive truth – of claims in this domain independently of our efforts at systematization in scientific inquiry. The Hegelian idea of truth-assessment through systematization represents a hard-headed and inherently attractive effort to adjust and accommodate to this fundamental fact.

To see more vividly some of the philosophical ramifications of this Hegelian approach, let us glance back once more to the epistemological role of systematicity in its historical aspect. The point of departure was the Greek position (in Plato and Aristotle and clearly operative still with rationalists as late as Spinoza) which – secure in a fundamental commitment to the systematicity of the real – took *cognitive* systematicity (i.e., systematicity as present in the framework of "our knowledge") as a measure of the extent to which man's purported understanding of the world can be regarded as adequate via the principle of *adaequatio ad rem*. Here systematicity functions as *a regulative ideal for the organization of knowledge* and (accordingly) as a standard of the *organizational adequacy* of our cognitive claims. But the approach of the Hegelian school (and the Academic Sceptics of classical antiquity who had anticipated them in this regard) moves well beyond this position. Viewing systematicity not merely as a *regulative*

[5] "On Truth and Coherence," *Essays on Truth and Reality* (Oxford, 1914), pp. 202–218; see pp. 202–203 and 210.

ideal for knowledge but as an epistemically *constitutive* principle, it extends what was a mere test of understanding into a test of the *evidential acceptability* of factual truth claims. Explanatory systematicity comes to operate as evidential warrant.

Accordingly, the Hegelian Inversion sees the transformation of systematicity from a framework for *organizing* knowledge into a mechanism for *characterizing* adequate knowledge claims. Fit, attunement, systematic connection become the determinative criteria in terms of which the acceptability of knowledge-claims is assessed. On this approach, our "picture of the real" emerges as an intellectual product achieved under the control of the ideal of system as a regulative principle for our theorizing.

4. METAPHYSICAL RAMIFICATIONS OF THE HEGELIAN INVERSION

Interesting metaphysical implications for the bearing of systematicity on the interrelation between truth and reality emerge from this perspective. Let us approach the issue in its historical dimension. A line of thought pervasively operative since antiquity may be set out by the syllogism:

> Reality is a coherent system
> Knowledge agrees with reality
> ―――――――――――――――――
> Knowledge is a coherent system

With Kant's "Copernican Revolution" this traditional mode of appeal to the classical conception of truth as *adaequatio intellectu ad rem* came to be transformed to:

> Knowledge is a coherent system
> Knowledge agrees with (empirical) reality
> ―――――――――――――――――
> Reality (i.e. *empirical* reality) is a coherent system

While the original syllogism effectively bases a conclusion about knowledge upon premises regarding reality, its Kantian transform infers a conclusion about reality from premises regarding knowledge. In the wake of Kant's Copernican Revolution, the ontological emphasis becomes secondary and derivative, seeing that our only available pathway to reality itself leads via *our* reality: our cognitive endeavors to form picture of the real.

With this aspect of Kant's Copernican Revolution we reach the idea that in espousing the dictum that "truth is a system," what one is actually claiming to be systematic is not the world as such, but rather our *knowledge* of it. Accordingly, it is what is known to be true regarding "the facts" of nature that is systematized, and systematicity thus becomes – in the first instance – a feature rather of knowledge than of its subject-matter. The idea of system can – indeed must – be applied by us to nature, yet not to nature in itself and *an sich*, but rather to "nature insofar as nature conforms to our power of judgement."[6] Correspondingly, system is at bottom not a constitutive conception descriptive of reality *per se*, but a regulative conception descriptive of how our thought regarding reality must proceed.

Kant's successors wanted to "overcome" Kant's residual allegiance to the Cartesian divide between our knowledge and its object. Waving the motto that "The real is rational" aloft on their banners, they sought to restore system to its Greek position as a fundamentally *ontological* – rather than "merely epistemological" – concept. In this setting, however, the concept of the systematization of truth played the part of a controlling ideal more emphatically than ever.

Hegel, in effect, went back to the Greeks and asked: How do we really know that knowledge is a coherent system? He was discontent with Kant's setting up as major premiss what for him (and the Greeks) ought to have been a conclusion, and so insisted once more on the centrality of this question.

But he answered it in a very different way. His starting-point here was the key principle of the Hegelian Inversion:

> If a thesis coheres systematically with the rest of what is known, then – and only then – is it a part of real knowledge (which accordingly characterizes reality itself).

Now it is clear that once we adopt *this* principle as our operative defining standard (criterion, arbiter) of knowledge – so that *only* what is validated in terms of this coherentist principle is admitted into "our knowledge" – then the crucial contention that "knowledge is a coherent system" at once follows, and so returns to the status of a conclusion rather than a premiss. If, as is only sensible the epistemic constituting of our (purported) knowledge takes place in terms of considerations of

[6] Introduction to Kant's *Critique of Judgment* in *Werke*, vol. V; Academy edition (Berlin, 1920), p. 202.

systematic coherence, then it follows – now without any reference to directly ontological considerations – that the body of knowledge so constituted will have to form a coherent system. (But in here taking such an epistemic rather than an ontological route, we Hegelians too reveal ourselves as true children of the era inaugurated by Kant's Copernican Revolution.[7])

The preceding discussion can be summarized in brief compass. We have offered a three-part answer to the question: "What is the point of cognitive systematization?"

(1) Systematization provides a vehicle for making claims *intelligible*.

(2) Systematization authenticates a body of knowledge as developed scientifically: it is a test of the *scientific adequacy* for expositions of knowledge.

(3) In thus providing quality-control at the wholesale level of a body of knowledge, systematicity also provides a means for testing purported knowledge-claims for inclusion in our "body of knowledge." It thus affords a probative instrument – *a test of acceptability* (or correctness) for factual claims.

And to these three fundamental points, the Hegelian Inversion adds yet another:

(4) Systematization provides the definitive constituting *criterion* of knowledge: it is the operative mechanism for authenticating knowledge as such.[8] While (3) comes to a test-standard "if *adequately* systematized, then *presumably* true," (4) comes to "if *fully* systematized, then *certainly true* and conversely."

In these varying but yet related ways, systematization can serve a crucial role in the quality-control of knowledge in the factual domain.

---

[7] However, it will emerge that the "knowledge agrees with reality" principle cannot be construed in such a way that the systematicity of our knowledge of reality guarantees that of reality itself. In this regard our present position parts company with the tradition.

[8] Presumably this is the cash value of the Hegelian view of explanation according to which "nothing can be known rightly, without knowing all else rightly" (Bernard Bosanquet, *Logic* [London, 1888], p. 393). If our system is to control our knowledge, then the system must be constructed before the monitoring can be accomplished.

III

Alternative Modes of Cognitive Systematization: Foundationalism *vs.* Coherentism

SYNOPSIS

(1) What are the major modes of procedure in the systematic development of factual knowledge? (2) The most prominent and historically most influential model of cognitive systematization is the Euclidean model of a *linear*, deductive exfoliation from basic axioms. (3) But the network model of *cyclic* systematization affords a prime alternative to this traditional axiomatic approach. (4) These two different models of cognitive systematization give rise to two rival and substantially divergent epistemic programs for the authentication of knowledge, namely *foundationalism* and *coherentism*. (5) An examination of the structure of foundationalism. (6) The inherent difficulties and limitations of the foundationalist program suggest the advisability of a closer look at the coherentist approach.

1. INTRODUCTION

Cognitive systems can be classified in many ways: by their explanatory methodology, their subject-matter content, the types of data involved, the sources of the data, and so on. The present consideration of the taxonomy of such systems is limited to the first of these, the *methodological* perspective. We shall focus upon the explicative *mechanisms* of cognitive systematization and explore in particular the sorts of explanatory and justificatory linkages that occur in such systems. This issue is particularly pressing because, while there has been widespread acceptance of the systematicity of knowledge as a valid ideal throughout the history of epistemological theorizing, there is a substantial divergence of opinion as to *what sort of system* is to provide the model or paradigm for the enterprise.

The mainstream of the Western tradition in the theory of knowledge has unquestionably cast *mathematics* – and, in particular, *geometry* – in this paradigmatic role. [1] But almost from the very first there has been a succession of rebels sniping from the sidelines and advocating discordant views as to the proper systematic structure for the organization of scientific knowledge regarding how things work in the world. A small but constantly renewed succession of thinkers have steadfastly maintained that the traditional geometric model is not of sufficiently general applicability, and insisted that we must seek elsewhere for our governing paradigm of scientific systematization.

Let us thus begin with a closer look at the two major rivals in this dispute.

2. HIERARCHICAL SYSTEMATIZATION: THE EUCLIDEAN MODEL OF KNOWLEDGE

The model of knowledge canonized by Aristotle in the *Posterior Analytics* sees Euclidean geometry as the most fitting pattern for the organization of anything deserving the name of a science (to put the matter somewhat anachronistically, since Euclid himself postdates Aristotle). This geometric model of cognitive structure holds that the organization of knowledge must proceed in the following manner. Certain theses are to be basic or foundational: like the axioms of geometry, they are to be used to justify other theses without themselves needing or receiving any intrasystematic justification. Apart from these fundamental postulates, however, every other thesis of the system is to receive justification of a rather definite sort. For every nonbasic thesis is to receive its explanation along an essentially linear route of

[1] There is, to be sure, Aristotle's famous disclaimer that one must not expect to obtain in every branch of knowledge the precision of reasoning one meets with in mathematics. But this does not undo the facts that in specifying how scientific knowledge should properly be articulated (in *Posterior Analytics*) Aristotle takes geometry as his model. Aristotle's remark should be understood as pertaining to the exactness or precision of our knowledge and not to its organization.

demonstration (or derivation or inference) from the basic theses that are justification-exempt or self-justifying. There is a step-by-step, recursive process – first of establishing certain theses by immediate derivation from the basic ones, and then of establishing further theses by sequential derivation from already established theses. Systematization proceeds in the manner characteristic of axiomatic systems.

In the setting of this Euclidean model of cognitive systematization, as we shall call it, every (nonbasic) established thesis is ultimately connected to certain basic theses by a linear chain of sequential inferences. These axiomatic theses are the foundation on which rests the apex of the vast inverted pyramid that represents the total body of knowledge.

On this approach to cognitive systematization, one would, with J. H. Lambert, construe such a system on analogy with a building whose stones are laid, tier by successive tier, upon the ultimate support of a secure foundation.[2] Accordingly, the whole body of knowledge obtains with regard to its justificatory structure the layered make-up reminiscent of geological stratification: a bedrock of basic theses surmounted by layer after layer of derived theses, some closer and some further removed from the bedrock, depending on the length of the (smallest) chain of derivation that links this thesis to the basic ones.

A prominent role must inevitably be allocated here to the idea of "relative fundamentality" in the *systematic* order – and hence also in the *explanatory* order of things the systematization reflects.[3] With virtual unanimity, the earlier writers on cognitive systems construed the idea in terms of such a linear development from ultimate premises (or "first principles") that are basic alike in fundamentality and in intelligibility, so that the order of exposition (or understanding) and the order of proof (or presupposition) run parallel.[4] The axiomatic development of our knowledge is seen in terms of both a deepening and a confirming of our knowledge, subject to the principle that clarification parallels rational grounding so that *explanation* replicates *derivation*.[5] (It does not matter

[2] J. H. Lambert, *Fragment einer Systematologie* in J. Bernouilli (ed.), *Johann Heinrich Lambert: Philosophische Schriften* (2 vols; reprinted Hildesheim, 1967).

[3] Think here of Aristotle's extensive concern with "priority" in the order of justification, and his requirement that in adequate explanations the premises must be "better known than and prior to" the conclusion.

[4] Thus Lambert writes: "Grundregel des Systems: Das vorgehende soll das folgende *klar* machen, in Absicht auf den *Verstand, gewiss* in Absicht auf die *Vernunft*. . . . ("Theorie des Systems," in *Philosophische Schriften*, vol. II [op. cit.]. p. 510.)

[5] Compare David Hilbert's view that successful axiomatization affords a "Tieferlegung der

for the fundamental structure of this Euclidean mode of systematization whether the inferential processes of derivation are deducive and necessitarian, or somehow "inducive" and less stringently compelling; in *this* regard the label "*Euclidean Model*" is somewhat misleading. Nothing fundamental is altered by permitting the steps of derivative justification to proceed by means of probabilistic or plausibilistic nondeductive inferences. We are still left with the same fundamental pattern of systematization: a "starter set" of basic theses which provide the ultimate foundation for erecting the whole cognitive structure upon them by the successive accretion of inferential steps.)

Although modern epistemologists generally depart from a traditional Euclideanism in admitting nondeductive (e.g. probabilistic) arguments – thus abandoning the idea that the only available means of linking conclusions inferentially to premises is by means of steps that are specifically *deductive* in character – they still continue for the most part to accept at face value Aristotle's argumentation to the following effect:

> Some hold that, owing to the necessity of knowing the primary premisses, there is no scientific knowledge. Others think that there is, but that all truths are demonstrable. Neither doctrine is either true or . . . necessary. . . . The first school, assuming that there is no way of knowing other than by demonstration, maintain that an infinite regress is involved. . . . The other party agrees with them as regards knowing, holding that it is only possible by demonstration, but they see no difficulty in holding that all truths are demonstrated, on the ground that demonstration may be circular and reciprocal. Our own doctrine is that not all knowledge is demonstrative: on the contrary: knowledge of the immediate premisses is independent of demonstration. (*Posterior Analytics*, I, 3; 72b5–24 (Oxford translation).

The road thus indicated by Aristotle is followed by all those later epistemologists – and their name is by now legion – who feel constrained to have recourse to cognitive ultimates to serve as the basic, axiomatic premises of all knowledge. Accordingly, they commit themselves to a category of basic beliefs which, though themselves unjustified – or perhaps rather *self-justifying* in nature – can serve as a

Fundamente der einzelnen Wissensgebiete" which renders the field at once more intelligible and more secure. "Axiomatisches Denken" (1918), reprinted in David Hilbert, *Hilbertiana* (Darmstadt, 1964).

justifying basis for all the other, nonaxiomatic beliefs: the unmoved (or self-moved) movers of the epistemic realm, as Roderick Chisholm has characterized them.[6] With these epistemologists, axiom-like foundations still play a central role in the criteriology of truth, even when they are no longer used to provide a rigidly *deductive* basis.

It is almost impossible to exaggerate the influence and historical prominence this Euclidean model of cognitive systematization has exerted throughout the intellectual history of the West. From Greek antiquity through the eighteenth century it provided an ideal for the organization of information whose influence was operative in every field of learning. From the time of Pappus and Archimedes and Ptolemy in antiquity to that of Newton's *Principia* and well beyond into modern times the axiomatic process was regarded as the appropriate way of organizing scientific information. And this pattern was followed in philosophy, in science, and even in ethics – as the *more geometrico* approach of Spinoza vividly illustrates. For over two millennia, the Euclidean model has provided the virtually standard ideal for the organization of knowledge. Most early theorists of cognitive systematization viewed the geometric or Euclidean Model as so obviously appropriate that it can virtually be taken for granted. And a rigid insistence on this linear and hierarchial aspect of cognitive systems has continued to characterize the thinking of most recent writers on cognitive systematization. A particularly vivid example is the work of the German philosopher Hugo Dingler,[7] who characterized this linearity as the principle par-excellence of systematically ordered thought ("des geordnetes Systemdenkens") and calls it The System Principle *tout court*. Such a view fails decisively to recognize that this approach characterizes only one particular mode of systematic thought – to be sure a very important one.

3. CYCLIC SYSTEMATIZATION: THE NETWORK MODEL – AN ALTERNATIVE TO THE EUCLIDEAN MODEL

The major alternatives to the Euclidean model that have been supported most prominently have certain general features in common. The present discussion will focus on these shared features to portray

6 R. M. Chisholm, *The Theory of Knowledge* (Englewood Cliffs, 1966).
7 See especially his book, *Das System* (Munich, 1930), pp. 19–20.

what might count as a common-denominator version of these models. This common-denominator theory will be referred to as the *network model*. As we shall see, its approach to cognitive systematization also has an ancient and respectable lineage.

This network model sees a cognitive system as a family of inter-related theses, not necessarily arranged in a *hierarchical* arrangement (as with an axiomatic system), but rather linked among one another by an *interlacing network* of connections. These interconnections are *inferential* in nature, but not necessarily *deductive* (since the providing of "good explanatory accounts" rather than "logically conclusive grounds" is ultimately involved).

Such a network of inferential interrelations will in its over-all aspect have not a hierarchical structure as in Figure 1 but a cyclic structure as Figure 2. The linkages at issue may well be inductive rather than

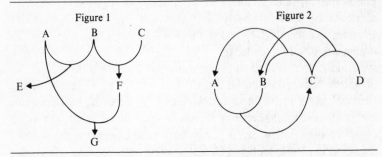

deductive. But even when its linkages operate along wholly deductive lines, this model would still depart drastically from the geometric paradigm. For from the network standpoint, the Euclidean model imposes a drastic limitation in inflating what is at most a *local* feature of derivation from the underived (i.e. *locally* underived) into a *global* feature that endows the whole system with an axiomatic structure. What matters is that the network links theses in a complex pattern of relatedness by means of some (in principle variegated) modes of probative interconnections.

A network system does, however, dispense with one advantageous feature that characterizes Euclidean systems *par excellence*. Since everything in a deductive system hinges upon the axioms, these will be the only elements that require any independent support or verification. Once *they* are secured, all else is supported by them. The upshot is a substantial economy of operation: since everything pivots about the axioms, the bulk of our epistemological attention can be confined to them. A network system, of course, lacks an axiomatic basis, and so lacks this convenient feature of having one delimited set of theses to carry the burden of the whole system upon its shoulders. On the network model, the process of justification need not proceed along a linear path. Its mode of justification is in general nonlinear, and can even proceed by way of (sufficiently large) cycles. To be sure, while a network system gives up Euclideanism at the *global* level of its over-all structure, it may still exhibit a *locally* Euclidean aspect, having local neighbourhoods whose systematic structure is deductive/axiomatic. Some of its theses may rest on others, and even do so in a rigorously deductive sense. For a network system may well contain various deductive compartments based upon locally operative *premisses* rather than globally operative *axioms*.

An important advantage of a network system over an axiomatic one inheres in the former's accommodation of relatively selfcontained subcycles. This absence of a rigidly linear hierarchical structure is a source of strength and security. In an axiomatic system a change anywhere ramifies into a change everywhere – the entire structure is affected when one of its supporting layers is removed. But with a network system that consists of an integrated organization of relatively selfsufficient components, certain of these components can be altered without dire repercussions for the whole.[8] Peirce observed this aspect of network systematization when he wrote:

> Philosophy ought to imitate the successful sciences in its methods, so far as to proceed only from tangible premisses which can be subjected to careful scrutiny, and to trust rather to the multitude and variety of its arguments than to the conclusiveness of any one. Its reasoning should not form a chain which is no stronger than its weakest link, but a cable whose fibres may be ever so slender, provided they are sufficiently numerous and intimately connected. (*Collected Papers*, vol. V, sect. 5.265.)

There is no clear mathematical model to serve the role for network systematization that has been performed for linear systematization by the Euclidean approach. The style of mathematics descriptively best adapted to the network approach lies outside the confines of classical analysis:

[8] Compare Herbert Simon, "The Architecture of Complexity," *General Systems*, vol. 10 (Ann Arbor, 1965), pp. 63–76.

|C|lassical mathematics is not able to handle complex structural features. Organization is best depicted as a network, and the mathematical theory of networks derives largely from certain branches of topology and abstract algebra rather than from analysis, which underlies classical mathematics. Thus the salient feature of a nervous system, of an institution, or of international systems may well reside in the vastly complex network of relations which constitute them: for example, neural pathways, lines of communication and authority, links of alliances or rivalries in international trade . . . [T]he "nature" of the system is indeed embodied in the quality and interrelations of these connections. . . . (Anatol Rapoport, "Systems of Analysis: General Systems Theory," *International Encyclopedia of the Social Sciences*, vol. 15 [New York, 1968], pp. 452–458.)

In the presentation of a network system there is no determinate and inevitable-seeming "logical sequence" and no "natural entry point." Expository convenience is our only resource in transposing the system into a linear order of exposition, rather than any inner "natural ordering." (Think of the "head-to-toe" approach of the ancient medical treatises.)

Three critical points of difference primarily separate the network model of cognitive systematization from its Euclidean counterpart:

(1) The network model dispenses altogether with the need for a category of basic (self-evident or self-validating) foundational or "protocol" theses capable of playing the role of axiomatic supports for the entire structure.

(2) The structure of the arrangement of theses within the framework of the network model need not be geological: no stratification of theses into levels of greater or lesser fundamentality is called for. (Of course, nothing blocks the prospect of differentiation; the point is that this is simply not demanded by the *modus operandi* of the model.)

(3) The network model accordingly abandons the conception of priority or fundamentality in its arrangement of theses. It replaces such *fundamentality* by a conception of *enmeshment* in a unifying web – in terms of the multiplicity of linkages and the patterns of inter-connectedness with other parts of the net.

On the network-model approach to the organization of information, there is no attempt to erect the whole structure on a foundation of basic elements, and no necessity to move along some unidirectional path – from the basic to the derivative, the simple to the complex, or the like. One may think here of the contrast between the essentially linear order of an expository book, especially a textbook, and the inherently network-style ordering of an entire library or an encyclopedia. Again, the contrast between a taxonomic science (like zoology or geology) and a deductive science (like classical celestial mechanics) can also help to bring out the difference between the two styles of cognitive organization.

Two very different conceptions of explanatory procedure are at issue. The Euclidean approach is geared to an underlying conception of fundamentality or logical dependency in the Aristotelian sense of *priority*, in terms of what is sometimes "better understood." Its procedure is one of *reduction by derivation*: reducing derivative, "client" truths to their more fundamental "master" truths. By contrast, the network appeal is unreductive. Its motto is not "Explanation by derivation" but "Explanation by interrelation." It merely seeks to co-ordinate the facts that are at issue. To speak figuratively, it does not view the structure of fact as akin to an organizational manual for a military or beaureaucratic organization than as a novel that traces out a complex web of diversified mutual interrelationships among its cast of characters. In terms of practical advice about scientific procedure, the network model shifts the perspective from undirectional dependency to reciprocal interconnection: "Don't worry about discerning an ordering of fundamentality or dependency; worry about establishing inter-linkages and mutual connections. Just find relationships among your parameters, and forget about which are the dependent and which the independent variables. Bear in mind the dictum from Goethe's 'To Natural Science':

Natur hat weder Kern noch Schale,
Alles ist sie mit einem Male.

Forget about establishing any all-embracing order of fundamentality in your explanatory efforts." The network theorist does not deny that a cognitive system must have a *structure* (how else could it be a system!). But it recognizes that this structure need not be of the form of a rank ordering – that it can provide for the more complex interrelationships that embody a reciprocity of involvement. It is no longer geared to the old hierarchical world picture that envisages a unidirectional flow of causality from fundamental to derivative orders of nature.

One vivid illustration of the network approach to organizing information come from textual interpretation and exegesis. Here there is no rigid, linear pattern to the sequence of consideration. The whole process is iterative and cyclical; one is constantly looking back to old points from new perspectives, using a process of feedback to bring new elucidations to bear retrospectively on preceding analyses. What determines correctness here is the matter of over-all fit, through which every element of the whole interlocks with some others. Nothing need be more fundamental or basic than anything else: there are no absolutely fixed pivot-points about which all else revolves. One has achieved adequacy when – through a process that is continually both forward- and backward-looking – one has reached a juncture where everything stands in due mutual coordination with everything else.

Or again, think of explanation-patterns incorporated in a (single-language) dictionary. Not every word of a language can be defined explicitly in that language. Ultimately this would lead to a circle. For if one starts with any finite list of words, by the time one comes to the last word, all the earlier words in the list will have been "used up," so that a circularity will have to appear in the final definition (if not before). Since standard dictionaries do actually define all the words they use in their definitions, they are guilty of circularity. (Dictionary makers attempt to counteract this problem by confining circularity as much as possible to definitions of words whose generally accepted meaning will be clear and unequivocal to the average reader.) Such circularity ultimately does no harm – most readers have a partial understanding of at least some units of the cycle, and a consideration of the interrelationships serves to clarify the whole series.

But, of course, our present concern is with network-patterned *justifications* rather than with network-patterned *elucidations*. A paradigmatic illustration is afforded by the explanations at issue with the workings of a closed physical or biological system, where every aspect of the *modus operandi* traces back into some of the others. Again, the sort of explanatory justifications at issue with solving a crossword-puzzle or breaking a code or interpreting an ancient document afford other appropriate examples. The key operative idea is that of *explanation through systematization* – i.e. solving the puzzle by "getting all the pieces to fit properly" so that a "comprehensive picture emerges which 'makes sense' by putting everything into place."

Notwithstanding its sharp differences from the axiomatic mode of development, a network approach to cognitive systematization does share some important features in common with the Euclidean organization of a "body of knowledge." The most important of these is that a network system can also exhibit the crucial facet of an axiom system in possessing more content than is overtly explicit. Parts of the network need not be explicity presented, but may be demanded by systematic considerations to round out the systematic structure of otherwise available interrelationships. Like axiom systems, network systems can have both explicit and implicit components.

Moreover, neither approach is smoothly attuned to the linear narrative order of written exposition (whose main implicit connective is "and"). Axiomatic deduction requires constant flashbacks to a plurality of earlier stages; network exposition requires not only this, but also attention to spider-web-like inter-linkages with heretofore unexamined elements. Both procedures invite a recourse to diagrammatic technique that breaks through the confines of verbal sequentialism and suggest the use of mathematical structures rather than merely literary resources.

A heavy charge can be laid against the Euclidean model on grounds of the enormous hold it has established on philosophical and scientific thought in the West. Its exclusion of circles and cycles on grounds of their violating the prohibition of Aristotelian logic against "circular" inferences and reasonings impeded the conceptualization of reciprocal causal models in science for over two thousand years. For we know from Aristotle's own strictures that the core idea of coherentism was astir in his day. He criticizes those who hold of knowledge that

it is only possible by demonstration, but they see no difficulty in holding that all truths are demonstrated, on the ground that demonstration may be circular and reciprocal. (*Posterior Analytics*, Bk. I, ch. 3; 72b5–24.)

Not until the present century have reciprocity-cycles and feedback mechanisms become prominent not only in the domain of causal explanation but in information processing contexts as well. The growing prominence of the Network Model is attributable in no small part to the growing prominence of such examples of its operation in practice.

*   *   *

These then represent the two broad alternative lines of strategy in the systematization of knowledge that have been prominent in the epistemological tradition of the West. To be sure, these strategies both lend themselves to a virtually infinite variety in their detailed implementation. At the level of generality presently at issue, we are dealing with alternative program frameworks rather than concrete procedures. But even in their general aspect the programs envisage very different lines of approach.

4. FOUNDATIONALISM *vs.* COHERENTISM AND THE "HEGELIAN INVERSION"

The prospect of alternative modes of cognitive systematization has far-reaching implications. For only a short and easy step separates a program of cognitive systematization (be it of the Euclidean or of the network type) from a full-fledged criteriology of knowledge, namely that of accepting a thesis as an item of *proper knowledge* if it can be accommodated in smooth systematic fit with the remainder of our *purported (or putative) knowledge*. This step amounts to what we have called "the Hegelian Inversion" – the step from the implication claim KNOWABLE → SYSTEMATIZABLE, or its cognate [PRESUMABLY] KNOWN → [DULY] SYSTEMATIZED, to the reverse implication claim: [DULY] SYSTEMATIZED → [PRESUMABLY] KNOWN. Given this inversion, the criterion for knowledge becomes a matter of being "duly fitted into a systematization of the candidates for cognition." Systematicity becomes the controlling standard of truth and its work shifts from justification to validation.

Now on the basis of a Euclidean model of cognitive systematization, a piece of knowledge must be fitted within the derivational scaffolding: it must either be "immediate knowledge" (form a part of the axiomatic basis), or it must be "derived knowledge" (be justified by derivation from the axioms). Knowledge becomes a complex structure erected on a suitable foundation of basic facts. The theory of cognitive validation based on *combining the Hegelian inversion with a Euclidean model of cognitive systematization*, may accordingly be characterized as *foundationalism*. This foundationalist approach to cognitive justification views certain theses as *self-evident* – or immediately self-evidencing – and then takes these as available to provide a basis for the *derivative* justification of other beliefs (which can then, of course, serve to justify still others in their turn). It is committed to a quest for ultimate bedrock "givens" capable of providing a foundational basis on which the rest of the cognitive structure can be erected.

The foundationalist approach to knowledge has it that every discursive (i.e. reasoned) claim to truth requires *truths* as inputs. If a presumptively true result is to be obtained, the premises on which it rests must themselves be true (or assumed to be so). This foundationalist approach in epistemology is deep-rooted throughout the western tradition from Aristotle through Descartes to C. I. Lewis and R. M. Chisholm. It implements an ancient and enduring idea – based ultimately on the Greek concept of science as a Euclidean system – that *truth is a structure that must have foundations*. There must be a starter set of *primitive* (ungrounded, immediate, "intuitive") truths and, outside this special category, truths can only be established from or grounded upon other truths. We are given an essentially recursive picture of the epistemic process of thesis-justification. There is a special set that is the axiomatic starter-set of truths, and a grounding process for validating certain truth-claims in terms of others. The overall domain of truths is then to be built up by recursion.

Accordingly this foundationalist approach is subject to certain characteristic commitments, as follows:

1. There are two fundamentally distinct sorts of truths, the immediate and the derivative.
2. There is some privileged epistemic process which, like the cataleptic perception of the ancient Stoics or Descartes' clear and distinct intuitions of the mind, is capable of providing immediately evident truths. These initial "givens" are wholly nondiscursive and fixed invariants, which are sacred and nowise subject to reappraisal and revision.
3. All *discursive* – inductive or deductive – epistemic processes require an input of truth if truths are to be an output (which is exactly why an immediate, non-discursive route to justification must be postulated.)

Accordingly:

4. Nothing whatever that happens at the epistemically later stages of the analysis can possibly affect the starting-point of basic truths. They are exempt from any retrospective re-evaluation in the light of new information or insights.

By contrast, *the coherentist program of epistemology implements the Hegelian Inversion by adopting the network model of cognitive systematization*. This coherentist approach thus takes as its index of acceptability *the overall fit of a presumptively acceptable thesis with the rest of what is presumptively acceptable*. On its approach, the standard of the acceptability of theses is not their deductive derivability from some sancrosanct basis, but their systematic connectability with one another. For the coherentist, the network systematizability of best-fit considerations comes to provide the key testing-standard of the acceptability of truth-claims. (After all, scientists have always in fact tended to give weight in considering the acceptability of theories not merely to the status of their evidential support as distinct items considered in their own right, but also to the pattern of their connections with the rest of our knowledge.)

The two approaches to cognitive systematization are thus correlative with two quite distinct programs of confirmatory argumentation or "inductive reasoning." On the Euclidean approach, a thesis derives its evidential support from premises to which it is linked by deductive or probabilistic inference. On the network approach its security of probative standing is largely a matter of the systematic enmeshment of its over-all interlinkage with other elements of the system. Very different theories of supportive reasoning are thus at issue: the one gives exclusive recognition to the weight of supportive evidence, the other goes beyond this in also recognizing – and indeed emphasizing – the probative efficacy of systematic interconnection.

Let us examine these two alternative approaches in closer detail, beginning with foundationalism.

5. MORE ON FOUNDATIONALISM

The idea of *immediate* or *basic* or *"protocol"* truths of fact has a long and distinguished philosophical history that goes back to Aristotle and beyond. Such truths – it is held – are to be apprehended in some direct and fundamental way, typified by the immediate sensory apprehension of phenomenal colors or odors. Within the epistemic structure of our knowledge of truth, such basic truths are to serve as a foundation; other truths are made to rest upon them, but they rest upon no others: like the axioms of a deductive system they provide the ultimate support for the entire structure. Many epistemologists have held that truths – nay even mere probabilities – can be maintained only on a basis of certainty. Thus one very influential recent philosopher writes:

> If anything is to be probable [let alone definitely true], then something must be certain. The data which eventually support a genuine probability [for a warranted truth-claim], must themselves be certainties. We do have such absolute certainties, in the sense data initiating belief. . . . (C. I. Lewis, *An Analysis of Knowledge and Valuation* [La Salle, Ill., 1946], p. 186.)

This essentially *axiomatic* concept of truth finds its formal articulation in the foundationalist (or intuitionist) theory of truth with its invocation of a starter-set of basic truths.

Adhering (at however schematic a level) to the ancient conception of knowledge as true, justified belief,[9] epistemologists have generally arrived straightaway at an essentially foundationalist view of the structure of knowledge. The Euclidean approach of extraction from a secure basis has served as the paradigm model of cognitive systematization throughout the epistemological mainstream of Western philosophy. It underlies Aristotle's thesis that perception provides an ultimate stopping point where the generalizations of inductive reasoning can find a secure axiomatic foothold. It is the mainstay of the Stoic doctrine of "cataleptic" perception which provides failproof certainty. It provides the motive for Descartes' search – basic to the whole Cartesian program of methodological scepticism – for a secure, Archidemean point to serve as fulcrum for the lever of knowledge-acquisition (the "clear and distinct" apprehensions of the mind). And modern epistemologists have continued remarkably faithful in their attachment to the central themes of the Euclidean model of cognitive systematization. It recurs again and again in recent epistemology – in

---

[9] The characterization of knowledge as true, justified belief is first met with in Plato's *Theaetetus* (200 D ff.) where the element added to truth and belief is stipulated to be the existence of a rationale or *account* (*logos*). Since this is bound to be discursive, the thesis is there criticized as conflicting with a foundationalism that admits of basic elements.

Brentano, in C. I. Lewis, in A. J. Ayer, in Roderick Chisholm and in many others.[10] Foundationalism, in sum, represents the predominant and most strikingly prominent approach to Western epistemology, deep-rooted throughout the western tradition from Aristotle through Descartes to the present day.

6. DIFFICULTIES OF FOUNDATIONALISM

Two obvious difficulties confront a foundationalist approach to the criteriology of truth. The first relates to the axiomatic starter-set of basic protocol truths, and the second to the inferential grounding relationship. Let us begin with the first.

The question of the special theses that are to provide the basic foundation by serving in the role of ultimate axioms is clearly bound to be a major source of difficulties for foundationalism. On the one hand, they must be very secure (certain, "self-evident" or self-evidencing) to be qualified themselves to dispense with all need for further substantiation. But on the other hand, they will have to be enormously content-rich, since they must carry on their back the whole structure of knowledge. These two qualifications for the axiomatic role – content and security – obviously stand in mutual conflict with each other. This tension makes for a weak point which critics of the Euclidean model of knowledge have always exploited.

Insofar as any statement provides information about the world (e.g. "I now see a cat there" which entails, *inter alia*, that a cat *is* there), it is not invulnerable to a discovery of error; insofar as it is safeguarded (e.g. by some guarding-locution such as "I take it that . . .", so that we have "It now seems to me that I see a cat there" or "I am under the impression that I see a cat there"), the statement relates to appearance instead of reality and becomes denuded of objective content. Egocentric statements of phenomenological appearances may have the requisite security, but are void of objective information; claims regarding

[10] See F. Brentano, *Wahrheit und Evidenz* (ed. O. Kraus, Leipzig, 1930). The most influential present-day advoctae of an epistemological position along brentanoesque lines is R. M. Chisholm (see his *Theory of Knowledge* [Englewood Cliffs, N. J., 1966]). Compare also R. Firth, "Ultimate Evidence," *The Journal of Philosophy*, vol. 53 (1956), pp. 732–739; reprinted in R. J. Swartz (ed.), *Perceiving, Sensing, and Knowing* (New York, 1965), pp. 486–496. For an informative general survey and critique of present-day foundationalism see Anthony Quinton, "The Foundations of Knowledge" in B. Williams and A. Montefiore (eds.), *British Analytical Philosophy* (London, 1971), pp. 55–86.

impersonal reality are objectively informative, but are in principle vulnerable.[11] The quest for protocol statements as a foundation for empirical knowledge has always foundered on this inherent tension between the two incompatible objectives of indubitable certainty on the one hand and objective factual content on the other.

The second prime difficulty of foundationalism relates to the grounding relationship which governs the derivational process. If this is to have the strength of *deductive* validity, affording a failproof guarantee of the conclusion relative to the premises, then it will be unable to lead us beyond the logical information-content of the premises. If, on the other hand, these inferential processes are in any way inductive or probabilistic – if the inferential derivations at issue are to be able (as they should be) to lead significantly beyond the information-content of the premises themselves – then we are hard put to validate the claims to certainty-preservation that must be established on their behalf.

In the face of such difficulties in the foundationalist program, it deserves emphatic stress that the Euclidean approach to cognitive systematization *does not represent the only way* of implementing the justificatory process inherent in the approach to knowledge as true, justified belief. It is important to recognize that the network model of cognitive systematization affords the prospect of a workable alternative approach – one which leads straightaway to the coherentist program of epistemology. Above all, this variant approach would relieve us of the unhappy burden of a commitment to primary, absolutely sacrosanct propositions on the order of the "first principles" of traditional epistemology. A closer examination of the coherentist program is thus very much in order.[12]

---

[11] Recognition of these and other weaknesses of foundationalism has in contemporary times not been spearheaded by coherentists – the idealistic advocates were ineffectual, the positivist advocates (i.e. Neurath and his sympathizers) were unsuccessful. The only effective opposition has centered about the refutationism of K. R. Popper's *Logik der Forschung* (Vienna, 1935; tr. as *The Logic of Scientific Discovery*, New York and London, 1959; 2nd edn. 1960).

[12] Parts of this chapter draw upon the author's book on *The Coherence Theory of Truth* (Oxford, 1973), and parts upon his paper, "Foundationalism, Coherentism, and the Idea of Cognitive Systematization," *The Journal of Philosophy*, vol. 71 (1974), pp. 695–708.

IV

Advantages of
the Network Approach

SYNOPSIS

(1) Gödel's checkmating of axiomatic systematization in the mathematical domain indicates the potential advantageousness of a non-Euclidean approach. (2) An examination of the idea of the *justificatory completeness* of a cognitive system and a look at some of the ways in which such systems can prove inadequate. The Hegelian Inversion as a means of circumventing possible inadequacies. (3) How the Network Approach to cognitive systematization affords a means of evading some critical limitations of the Euclidean Approach.

1. THE COLLAPSE OF THE EUCLIDEAN APPROACH IN MATHEMATICAL
   SYSTEMATIZATION

From Aristotle's day until the Age of Reason – and well beyond – it was generally thought that all of our knowledge of the observable world could eventually be organized into a single vast deductive system along the lines envisaged by the Euclidean model. The idea of such an overarching synoptic structure underlay Laplace's canonization of the Newtonian world-picture, and continued to be accepted well into the 20th century, both by physicists[1] and by scientifically minded philosophers (including those of the Vienna circle and, more generally, the physicalistic reductivists of the Unity of Science movement that flourished within the logical positivism of the interwar period).

In modern times, this Euclidean picture of scientific cognition was

---

[1] See, for example, Max Planck, *Die Einheit des Physikalischen Weltbildes* (1908; reprinted in *Physikalische Abhandhingen und Vorträge*, vol. III [Braunschweig, 1958].)

first seriously questioned in the wake of the era of Romanticism by those who sought to uphold the existence of distinct scientific methodologies, differing as between the sciences of man and the sciences of (extra-human) nature. The adherents of this view held that within the life sciences, the human sciences, and the social sciences descriptive and explanatory methodologies and approaches are needed that are fundamentally different in nature from those familiar from the physical sciences as currently established. (Think of such examples of Goethe's *Farbenlehre* or the Hegelian phenomenology.) Indeed, this perspective affords one helpful way of viewing the 19th-century attack of the *Geistewissenschaften* movement (the "human sciences") upon the methodological sufficiency of the *Naturwissenschaften* (the natural-science methodology in the human sciences – especially against German participants in this *Methodenstreit* as Wilhelm Dilthey, Wilhelm Windelband, and Heinrich Rickert held in effect that the ahistorical, analytical, and nonevaluative *Naturwissenschaften* are commited to a Euclidean model of systematization, whereas the historical, synthetic and evaluative *Geistewissenschaften* required something along the lines of a network model.[2]

The English neo-Hegelian assault against attempts to propound a natural-science methodology in the human sciences – especially against the associationist psychology of the Mills and the evolutionism of Spencer – ran parallel to this movement in many ways. The work of T. H. Green and his Oxford followers (Bradley, Bosanquet, Joachim) launched an Anglo-American "neo-Hegelian" movement which operated largely from a philosophical base in the tradition of German Idealism from Kant to Hegel. Sharply contesting the claims and credentials of the Euclidean theory of scientific cognition, this school also maintained the appropriateness of a network model in the systematization of knowledge.

Until recently, however, this tendency of thought has been of little effect and influence. Even those few epistemologists in the Western tradition who have doubted the adequacy of a Euclidean approach to cognitive systematization in the *factual* domain, generally inclined to give it unchalleneged passage in the *formal* domain. Throughout those

---

[2] One need not give up unity-of-science ideal in general if one is a network theorist – for one could simply maintain that – while *some* sectors of it are best organized Euclideanly – the network model is indeed correct for our factual knowledge in general. But in the 19th century the prominence of pure and applied mathematics – for which a Euclidean model was generally deemed appropriate – prevented this view from emerging to prominence.

spheres where deductive reasoning is paramount – formal logic and mathematics in particular – the Euclidean approach to systematization has gone virtually uncontested from Greek antiquity to within the memory of living men. To be sure, a substantial shock came with the discovery of effectively alternative systems – first in geometry (with the development of non-Euclidean geometries in the early 19th century) and then in logic (with the development of nonclassical logics in the early 20th century). But still, these systems were different *deductive* systems. The dispute still retained a familiar form, affording a choice between this or that rival *axiomatization*. Revolutionary though these developments were, they were a shock *within* the framework of "Euclidean" systematization rather than a shock *to* this framework itself. In the face of rival systems, it might be difficult to discern how the choice between alternatives might optimally be effected. But once the choice among alternatives is effected, we arrive at last at an essentially axiomatic articulation of "the truth," and thus retain a strictly axiomatic development of our knowledge in this field. The traditional ideal of a Euclidean systematization remained undisturbed.

Difficulties, however, arose from a very unexpected source – the development of modern metamathematics. The shock – nay, the death-blow – to the Euclidean ideal within the domain of formal knowledge came with the work of Kurt Gödel.[3] His discoveries mortally damaged the foundationalist program in the domain of its traditional stronghold – mathematics.

One of the major advantages traditionally credited to the axiomatic systematization is that it greatly facilitates a proof of the *consistency* of a theory, for given an axiomatization one need only worry about the mutual compatibility of the comparatively small group of axiomatic propositions. But Gödel showed that this is an idle hope for *any* formal system as rich as – or richer than – ordinary arithmetic. He devised a cogent demonstration that the consistency of such a formal system can never be proved. And so the consistency of interesting formal systems (those that are at least sufficiently capacious to encompass arithmetic) is inherently unprovable, *even when these systems themselves have a "merely deductive" or axiomatic systematization.*

And worse was yet to come. For Gödel also managed to demonstrate the inherent *incompleteness* of the deductive axiomatization of formal

---

[3] See the helpful and (relatively) informal exposition in E. Nagel and J. R. Newman, *Gödel's Proof* (New York, 1958).

systems that are "interesting" in the aforementioned sense. To the surprise and chagrin of everyone committed to the foundationalist systematization of mathematics, Gödel demonstrated that no formal system as rich (or richer than) ordinary arithmetic can ever be deductively complete. No matter how we twist and turn in our endeavors to axiomatize such a system finitely, there will always be some "true" statements in its domain that cannot be derived from the chosen axioms. In the wake of these results, it was no longer a tenable step to equate mathematical truth with deducibility from a suitable list of specified axioms. This collapse of the prospect of a deductive axiomatization of arithmetical truths brought the whole foundationalist program to checkmate within its traditional stronghold – the mathematical domain.

This failure of the foundationalist approach even in mathematics provides yet another incentive for closer and more sympathetic concern with the coherentist approach, its historic rival.

2. JUSTIFICATORY COMPLETENESS

The previous section has focused upon the completeness of systematizations of one particular – and very limited – branch of knowledge, namely arithmetic. Let us now examine the issue from a more general point of view.

It will be useful to adopt some notational machinery:

(1) Let $\mathscr{T}$ represent a given range of presystematic truth: the set of the theses to be systematized. And let these $\mathscr{T}$-included theses be represented by p, q, r, etc.

(2) Let $\mathscr{S}_{\mathscr{T}}$ (or sometimes simply $\mathscr{S}$) represent the system of justificatory arguments ("rationales") that support the $\mathscr{T}$-theses at issue. And let the $\mathscr{S}$-included arguments in support of $\mathscr{T}$-theses be represented by α, β, γ, etc.

One further bit of notation is helpful, viz., "!" for "justifies" or "validates," which provides for the abbreviative specification:

$\alpha ! p$ for "the argument α validates the thesis p"

And this in turn gives rise to the relationship:

$\mathscr{S}!p$ for "the system $\mathscr{S}$ validates the thesis p":

$\mathscr{S}!p$ iff $(\exists\alpha)\,(\alpha\in\mathscr{S}\,\&\,\alpha!p)$.

We can thus introduce the further definition:

$\mathscr{S}$ is justificatorily *complete* with respect to $\mathscr{T}$:

$(\forall p)\,(p\in\mathscr{T}\supset\mathscr{S}!p)$.

For adequacy we would, of course, regard it as so desirable as to be necessary that our system $\mathscr{S}\mathscr{T}$ did not systematize any theses that failed to belong to its correlative range $\mathscr{T}$ of presystematically given truths:

$\mathscr{S}$ is justificatorily *adequate* with respect to $\mathscr{T}$:

$(\forall p)\,(\mathscr{S}!p\supset p\in\mathscr{T})$

Errors of the first kind arise when:

$p\in\mathscr{T}\,\&\,\sim\mathscr{S}!p$

These are clearly failures in justificatory *completeness*, in that $\mathscr{S}$ fails to provide for all the $\mathscr{T}$-truths. Errors of the second kind arise when:

$p\notin\mathscr{T}\,\&\,\mathscr{S}!p$

These are clearly failures in justificatory *adequacy* in that $\mathscr{S}$ validates something not countenanced within the range of presystemative $\mathscr{T}$-truths. An ideally satisfactory system, would avoid errors of both kinds. Like the perfect witness, it would tell the truth, the whole truth, and nothing but the truth.

The idea of incompleteness as it has figured in this discussion revolves about an imbalance between $\mathscr{S}$ and $\mathscr{T}$ — to wit, the prospect of $\mathscr{T}$-theses that cannot be rationalized through $\mathscr{S}$-arguments: $(\exists p)\,[p\in\mathscr{T}\,\&\,(\forall\alpha)\,(\alpha\in\mathscr{S}\supset\sim\alpha!p)]$. To be sure, such an imbalance between on the one hand the theses established (or establishable) through $\mathscr{S}$-arguments and the $\mathcal{T}$-truths on the other, is predicated on the existence of an independent standard of $\mathcal{T}$-membership – "independent," that is of any considerations relating to $\mathcal{S}$-supportability. The prospect of imbalance thus roots in the potential irrelevance of $\mathcal{S}$-supportability to $\mathcal{T}$-truth, an irrelevance which allows possible discrepancies to arise.

All prospect of such a discrepancy is, however, abolished *by fiat* through the Hegelian Inversion which, after all, *specifies* theses as $\mathcal{T}$-*truths on the basis of their $\mathcal{S}$*-validation. Here we adopt its stance that $\mathcal{S}$-validation is *the* route – and the *only* route – to $\mathcal{T}$-membership. That is, we propose to determine $\mathcal{T}$-membership *on the basis of $\mathcal{S}$-systematization:

$$p \in \mathcal{T} \text{ iff } \mathcal{S} \ !p, \text{ for all } p$$

It is now clear that any threat of *incompleteness* must at once vanish. For the condition of the $\mathcal{T}$-*completeness* of $\mathcal{S}$†, viz.,

$$(\forall p)(p \in \mathcal{T} \supset \mathcal{S} \ !p)$$

now drops out as an immediate consequence of the defining condition of $\mathcal{T}$-membership. And the same situation applies with respect to *adequacy* as well. (To be sure, if we adopt merely the weaker *criteriological* condition that duly systematized theses are to count as true,

$$\text{If } \mathcal{S}!p, \text{ then } p \in \mathcal{T}$$

then the completeness thesis represented by its converse does not necessarily obtain. Now we can still use systematization to *identify* specific members within the family of truths but not to *constitute* this family.) With the Hegelian Inversion we abandon the view that our systematizing comes to grips with a *preestablished* domain of truth, in that this domain itself comes to be determined as a *product* of the systematization in view.

This line of thought indicates that the availability and plausibility of the Hegelian Inversion will turn crucially on our assuring ourselves – on the basis of the "general principles" of the matter – that there is no discrepancy between the $\mathcal{S}$ and the $\mathcal{T}$ at issue – that the systemic range of justificatory arguments we are considering is actually sovereign over the intended domain of truth we seek to encompass. This assurance can come either from weakness or from strength. It comes from strength when there is some independent, pre-systematic realm of truth whose correlativity with our systematization we can in fact demonstrate. (This is the case, for example, with the various well known axiomatizations of truth-functional propositional logic.)[4] And it comes from weakness when we recognize that we simply have no *presystematic* or *system-independent* means of truth-assessment at all, one that does not hinge on our attempts at systematization themselves and plays the role in the factual sphere which "intuition" can play in the spheres of logic and mathematics. (And it can be plausibly argued that just this is the situation in the sphere of empirical inquiry into the domain of contingent facts.)

3. THE NETWORK APPROACH TO SYSTEMATIZATION AS A MEANS OF AVOIDING LIMITS OF THE EUCLIDEAN APPROACH

Problems of justificatory completeness will clearly arise when $\mathcal{T}$ is numerically "outsize" in relation to $\mathcal{S}$, and in particular when:

Case 1: $\mathcal{S}$ is finite, while $\mathcal{T}$ is infinite.
Case 2: $\mathcal{S}$ is denumerably infinite, while $\mathcal{T}$ is nondenumerably infinite.

For when such a circumstance is realized, the systemization at issue will of necessity be inherently inadequate to the group of facts it is supposed to accommodate. Thus consider some mathematical examples. Let $\mathcal{S}$ be a recursive axiomatization, while $\mathcal{T}$ is the whole of real-number theory. Or again, let $\mathcal{S}$ be based on an organon of recursive – and thus inherently finitistic – mensuration, while $\mathcal{T}$ envisages a domain of continuous parameters. In all such cases, the systematization at issue cannot but prove inadequate to the family facts whose rationalization lies within its purposive purview.

This line of thought points to a very fundamental consideration. As long as we proceed within the framework of a Euclidean (i.e. finitely axiomatic) approach to cognitive systematization, it is clear that *the set of (finitely) systematizable/axiomatizable theses can never be larger than denumerably infinite.* And this reflects a drastic limitation *vis-à-vis*

---

[4] However, such correlativity fails – as Gödel has shown – with all attempts to axiomatize our "intuitively" guided grasp of arithmetical truth.

any system of truths whose range is nondenumerably infinite. Hence whenever we know on the basis of the "general principles" of the matter that the relevant set of facts is transdenumerably infinite – as we presumably do with truths in general, or factual truths, or even physical laws – we thereby know (*a priori*, so to speak), that a Euclidean systematization cannot possibly encompass this range. Trans-denumerability is a sufficient condition for Euclidean nonsystematiz-ability – though (as Gödel showed for arithmetic) it is not a necessary condition.

The Euclidean, axiomatic approach is thus of an emphatically limited capacity. As we have just seen, it can validate only a denumerable number of theses. And from this fact it emerges that – quite generally – a comparable denumerability-limit must attach to any approach to systematization based on justificatory relationships built into classificatory hierarchies. For it is easy to see that all hierarchial classifications are enumerable. Consider, for example, the following hierarchical ordering:

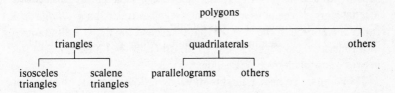

We first represent this pattern by a numerical code that presents its abstract structure:

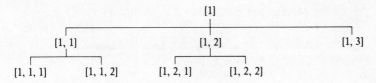

This pattern is straightforwardly transformed into a rank-order listing:

$$[1]\ [1, 1]\ [1, 2]\ [1, 3]\ [1, 1, 1]\ [1, 1, 2]\ [1, 2, 1]\ [1, 2, 2]$$

And it is clear that all such lists can be similarly enumerated. The set of explanatory distinctions that can be incorporated within hierarchical classifications is accordingly denumerable. Thus any approach to validation based solely on hierarchical relationships will also be inadequate to capture a family of justificatory processes of greater than denumerable size.

A significant advantage of the network approach can be discerned against this background. Any hierarchical approach to cognitive validation (preeminently including the Euclidean/axiomatic) is inherently finitistic — each thesis is ultimately supported by a *finite* number of premisses: a terminating list of supportive considerations. A network approach — on the other hand — will not be subject to such finitistic constraints. Each thesis is linked to some others in patterns of order which need not themselves be of finite diversity. Ever more elaborate cycles can open up — at least in principle, if not in actual practice — the prospect of justifying a family of theses larger than denumerable in scope. There are as many connective patterns among the elements of a set as there are ways of partitioning it into subsets. Hence even a denumerably infinite set of elements can give rise to a superdenumerable set of linking connections. This feature of network mechanisms is crucial to making the Hegelian Inversion *available* as a rational resource in those cases that transcend the finitistic limitations of an hierarchical scheme, and so affords a crucial advantage to the network approach over its Euclidean rival.

To be sure, someone might argue as follows against this line of thought:

> Even if the network approach could in principle systematize a transdenumerable set of facts, this is immaterial. The finitary character of language means that the totality of actually statable theses is denumerable. Therefore a systematizing mechanism like the Euclidean approach which can handle denumerably many theses is bound to prove sufficient.

That is well as far as it goes. But we are left with the question: Sufficient for what? Sufficient to systematize those truths we can actually formulate, all truly stated theses? There are two different ideas at work here, one narrower, one wider:

> truth = something *truly stated* in some language
> fact = something *truly statable* in some (possible) language

There are bound to be more facts than we are able to capture in our particular linguistic net. The principle of the Hegelian Inversion – the thesis that *truth* is coordinative with systematizability – is geared to the wider issue of facticity in general. It envisages not just a "rule of thumb" for practical procedures in relation to actually entertained theses, but a general criterion that is (arguably) adequate on theoretical grounds. And this inversion accordingly opens up the at least *theoretical* prospect of a systematically ordered range of potential theses answering to a transdenumerable domain of facts.

V

Coherentism and the Role of Systematicity as a Standard of Presumption

---

SYNOPSIS

(1) The general strategy of the coherentist approach to inquiry: truth without true foundations. (2) An examination of the mechanism of the coherence analysis. (3) A detailed overview of the contrast between foundationalism and coherentism. (4) Coherentism and the view of knowledge as "true, justified belief." (5) How coherentism utilizes the parameters of systematicity as regulative principles of presumption.

---

1. THE COHERENTIST APPROACH TO INQUIRY

At the basis of coherentism lies what we have called the Hegelian Inversion – the transition from system as organizer of what is accepted to that of system as arbiter of what is acceptable. The coherentist approach to epistemic justification results when this inversion is joined with the network theory of cyclic systematization. Coherentism thus views the network-interrelatedness of factual theses as the criterial standard of their acceptability. But just how does such a theory work?

To begin with, the coherentist approach to truth-determination must be seen in an essentially *regulative* role with regard to validating factual propositions as true, rather than as claiming to present the *constitutive* essence of truth as such; it affords a *standard* of truth, not a *definition* or meaning-explicative analysis of it. The stance of the theory is to be articulated in terms somewhat as follows:

Acceptance-as-true is in general not the starting-point of inquiry but is terminus. To begin with, all that we generally have is a body of *prima facie* truths, i.e., propositions that qualify as potential – perhaps even as promising – *candidates* for acceptance. The epistemic realities being as they are, these candidate-truths will, in general, form a mutually inconsistent set, and so exclude one another so as to destroy the prospects of their being accorded *in toto* recognition as truths pure and simple. The best that can be done in such circumstances is to endorse those as truths that best "cohere" with the others so as to "make the most" of the data as a whole in the epistemic circumstances at issue. Coherence thus affords the criterial validation of the qualifications of truth-candidates for being classed as genuine truths.

A coherentist epistemology thus views the extraction of knowledge from the data in terms of an analysis of best-fit considerations. Its approach is fundamentally holistic in judging the acceptability of every purported item of information by its capacity to contribute towards a well-ordered whole.

Such a coherentist theory of knowledge stands in sharp contrast with the foundationalist approach of the mainstream tradition of western epistemology. Unlike foundationalism, coherentism dispenses with any appeal to basic, foundational truths of fact, diametrically opposing the view that knowledge of the actual, and even of the probable, requires a foundation of certainty. The coherence approach maintains that truth is accessible in the extralogical realm on the basis of best-fit considerations, without any foundation of certainty. (The qualifier "factual" occurs here because the instrumental need for the resources of logic is, of course, conceded, seeing that they are needed as a mechanism for best-fit judgments, since logic must be used in determining what does and does not "fit.") This entire procedure goes wholly counter to the classical epistemologists' axiomatic quest for basic or foundational truths.

Foundationalism might be caricatured as an essentially "aristocratic" view of truth: truths as such are not equal; there are certain "master" truths on which the other "client" truths are totally dependent. Negating the need for any axiomatic truths, the coherence theory sets out to implement a rather more "democratic" concept of treating all the truth-candidates not necessarily as equal but at any rate as all more or less plausible. The possibilities rendered available by the data at our disposal are treated with a complete "equality of opportunity"; truthfulness is determined from them only through a process of interaction – that is, by considerations of a best fit in terms of *mutual* accord and attunement (rather than their falling into the implicative captivity of certain basic prior truths).

The coherentist's approach effectively *inverts* that of the foundationalist. The foundationalist begins his epistemological labors with a very small initial collection of absolutely certain truths from which he proceeds to work *outwards* by suitably *additive* procedures of supplementation to arrive at a wider domain of truth. By contrast, the coherentist begins with a very large initial collection of insecure pretenders to truth from which he proceeds to work *inwards* by suitably *reductive* procedures of elimination to arrive at a narrower domain of truth. The expansive approach of the foundationalist is the very opposite of the contractive approach of the coherentist. The foundationalist is forced to a starting-point of few but highly secure items, and immediately faces the dilemma of security *vs.* content. The coherentist bypasses this difficulty altogether. He begins with too many items – far too many since "the data" generally stand in a conflict of logical incompatibility – but he proceeds to undo the damage of this embarrassment of riches by suitably reductive maneuvers. This approach avoids altogether the characteristic perplexity of foundationalist epistemology in finding appropriate candidates to supply the requisitely secure foundation.

For the coherentist, knowledge is not a Baconian brick wall, with block supporting block upon a solid foundation; rather, an item of knowledge is like a node of a spider's web which is linked to others by thin strands of connection, each alone weak, but all together adequate for its support.

2. THE MECHANISM OF COHERENCE ANALYSIS

In general terms, the coherence criterion of truth operates as follows. One begins with a datum-set $S = \{P_1, P_2, P_3, \ldots\}$ of suitably "given" propositions. They are not given as secure truths, in a foundationalist's manner of theses established once and for all, but merely as *presumptive* or *potential* truths, i.e. as *truth-candidates* – and in general as *competing* ones that are mutually inconsistent. The task to which a coherentist epistemology addresses itself is that of bringing order into **S** by separating the sheep from the goats, distinguishing what merits acceptance as true from what does not. The governing injunction is: Maintain as best you can the overall fit of mutual attunement by proceeding – when necessary – to make the least plausible competitors give way to the more plausible. On this approach, a truth candidate comes to make good its claims to recognition as a truth through its consistency with as much as possible from among the rest of such data. The situation arising here resembles the solving of a jigsaw puzzle with superfluous pieces that cannot possibly be fitted into any maximally orderly picture representing the "correct solution."

The procedure at issue such a coherence analysis calls for the following epistemic resources:

I. INPUTS

(i) *"Data"*: theses that can serve as *acceptance-candidates* in the context of the inquiry, contentions which, at best, are merely *presumptively* true (like the "data of sense"). These are not certified truths (or even probable truths) but theses that are in a position to make some claims upon us for acceptance: They are *prima facie* truths in the sense that we would incline to grant them acceptance-as-true *if* (and this is a very big IF) there were no countervailing considerations upon the scene. (The classical example of "data" in this sense are those of perception and memory.)

(ii) *Plausibility ratings*: comparative evaluations of our initial assessment (in the context of issue) of the relative acceptability of the "data." This is a matter of their relative acceptability "at first glance" (so to speak) and *in the first analysis*, prior to their systematic evaluation. The plausibility-standing of truth-candidates is thus to be accorded without any prejudgements as to how these theses will fare *in the final analysis*.

It is important to stress that the need for inputs is inevitable in the realm of factual knowledge; but this unavoidable recourse is not a concession to foundationalism. The coherentist's inputs are raw materials and not themselves finished products.

Given inputs of this sort – plausibilistic data – the coherence analysis sets out to sift through these truth-candidates with a view to minimizing the conflicts that may arise. Its basic mechanism is that of best-fit considerations.

II. MACHINERY OF "BEST FIT" ANALYSIS

That family embracing the truth candidates which are maximally attuned to one another is to count – on this criterion of over-all mutual accommodation – as best qualified for acceptance as presumably true, implementing the idea of compatibility screening on the basis of "best-fit" considerations. Mutual coherence becomes the arbiter of acceptability which make the less plausible alternatives give way to those of greater plausibility. The acceptability-determining mechanism at issue proceeds on the principle of optimizing our admission of the claims implicit in the data, striving to maximize our retention of the data subject to the plausibilities of the situation.[1]

Against this background, the general strategy of the coherence theory lies in a three-step procedure:

(1) To gather in all of the "data" (in the present technical sense of this term).

(2) To lay out all the available conflict-resolving options that represent the alternative possibilities that are cognitively at hand.

(3) To choose among these alternatives by using the guidance of plausibility considerations, invoking (in our present context) the various parameters of systematicity as indices of plausibility.

The coherence theory thus implements F. H. Bradley's dictum that *system* (i.e. systematicity) provides a test-criterion most appropriately fitted to serve as arbiter of truth.

The process of deriving significant and consistent results from an inconsistent body of information is a key feature of the coherence theory of truth, which faces (rather than, with standard logic, evades) the question of the inferences appropriately to be drawn from an inconsistent set of premises. The initial mass of inconsistent

---

[1] The formal mechanism of best-fit analysis is described more fully in the author's books *The Coherence Theory of Truth* (Oxford, 1973) and *Plausible Reasoning* (Assen, 1976).

information are the data for applying the mechanism of coherence as a criterion of truth, and its product is a consistent system of acceptable truths. On this approach, the coherence theory of truth views the problem of truth-determination as a matter of bringing order into a chaos comprised of initial "data" that mingle the secure and the infirm. It sees the problem in transformational terms: incoherence into coherence, disorder into system, candidate-truths into qualified truths.

The interaction of observation and theory provides an illustration. Take grammar. Here one moves inferentially from the phenomena of actual usage to the framework of laws by the way of a best-fit principle (an "inference to the best systematization" as it were), and one checks that the cycle closes by moving back again to the phenomena by way of subsumption. Something may well get lost en route in this process of mutual attunement – e.g. some of the observed phenomena may simply be dismissed (say as "slips of the tongue"). Again, the fitting of curves to observation points in science also illustrates this sort of feedback process of discriminating the true and the false on best-fit considerations. The crucial point for present purposes is simply that a systematization can effectively control and correct data – even (to a substantial extent) the very data on which it itself is based.

The coherentist approach is thus quite prepared to dispense with any requirement for self-evident protocols to serve as the foundations of the cognitive system. the justification of a system-included thesis will not proceed by derivations from the *axioms*, but comes to obtain through the pattern of its interrelationships with the rest. On a coherence approach, the truth is not seen as a tree-like structure supported by a firm-rooted trunk, as it is on the foundationalist theory. Rather, it appears like a multitude of tied objects thrown into water: some of them rise to the surface themselves or are dragged there by others, some of them sink to the bottom under their own weight or through the pull of others.

The coherentist criterion accordingly assumes an entirely *inward* orientation: it does not seek to compare the truth candidates directly with "the facts" obtaining outside the epistemic context; rather, having gathered in as much information (and this will include also *misinformation*) about the facts as possible, it seeks to sift the true from the false *within* this body. On this approach, the validation of an item of knowledge – the rationalization of its inclusion alongside others within "the body of our knowledge" – proceeds by way of exhibiting its interrelationships with the rest: they must all be linked together in a connected, mutually supportive way (rather than having the form of an inferential structure built up upon a footing of rock-bottom axioms). On the coherentist's theory, justification is not a matter of derivation but one of systematization. We operate, in effect, with the question: "justified" = "systematized." The coherence approach can be thought of as representing, in effect, the systems-analysis approach to the criteriology of truth.

One critic of coherentist epistemology has objected:

> According to . . . [one] version of the coherence theory a certain given statement, of which we do not know whether it is true or not, is to be accepted as true if (and only if) it coheres with the statements we have previously accepted. This version has the effect of making our knowledge utterly conservative: 'entrenched' knowledge can hardly be overthrown. (K. R. Popper, *Objective Knowledge* [London, 1973], p. 309.)

But this objection misses its mark if directed against the present version of the theory. For "entrenchment" (acceptance, actual credence) is, as we shall see, not the only path to plausibility, and certainly not the strongest one. Even a well-entrenched item can be dislodged in the face of more plausible data: little is better entrenched than "what one sees with one's own eyes" – yet even here one can be brought to recognize that one has fallen victim to an illusion. Entrenched data may have a "benefit of doubt," but that is not to say that their lease on life is absolute.

3. THE CONTRAST BETWEEN FOUNDATIONALISM AND COHERENTISM

The essential difference between the coherence theory and any foundationalist approach to acceptance-as-true lies in the fact that on the latter line of approach every discursive (i.e. reasoned) claim to truth requires *truths* as inputs. If a (presumptively) true result is to be obtained, the premises on which it rests must themselves be true (or assumed to be so). The only strictly originative provider of *de novo* truths is the process that yields the "immediate" truths of the starter-set. The decisive difference of the coherence theory is its capacity to extract (presumptive) truths discursively from a basis that includes no conceded truths whatsoever – i.e. from data that are merely truth-candidates and not truths. The foundationalist requirement for basic truths is something that the coherence theory – proceeding as it does from a basis of data that need be neither compatible nor true – has been designed to overcome. The analysis seeks to provide a procedure for arriving at output truths without requiring any input truths as an indispensable starting basis. The motto "Truth without true foundations" may properly be inscribed on the banner of the coherence theory of truth.

The contrast between a foundationalist *Aufbau* of the domain of truth and the approach of the coherence analysis is set out graphically in Figure 1.

Figure 1

FOUNDATIONALISM *vs.* COHERENTISM IN FACTUAL INQUIRY

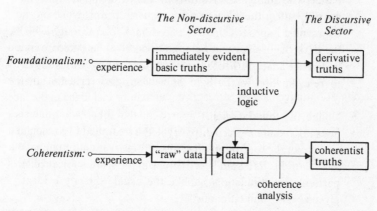

This diagram makes plain the basic similarities between the two approaches, but also brings out their significant differences, which are as follows:

1. On the foundationalist approach there are two distinct sorts of knowledge, the immediate and the derivative, while for the coherentist all knowledge is essentially of a piece.
2. On the foundationlist approach experience is called upon to provide basic knowledge (in the form of certain immediately evident truths), while for the coherentist it only provides the "raw" data for knowledge.

3. On the foundationalist approach all discursive – inductive or deductive – processes require an input of known truths if truths are to be an output (which is exactly why an immediate, nondiscursive route to truth must be postulated). The coherence analysis differs fundamentally in this regard.

4. On the foundationalist approach the initial "givens" are wholly nondiscursive and fixed invariants, while on the coherence approach the "data" represent a *mixture* of experiential and discursive elements. (The "raw" data are, to be sure, nondiscursive, but for the coherentist they are only one part of the total data and are by no means fixed and sacred but subject to a cyclic process of reappraisal and revision.) In consequence:

5. On the foundationalist approach nothing whatever that happens at the epistemically later stages of the analysis can possibly affect the starting-point of basic truths, while on the coherentist approach there is a feed-back loop through which the data themselves can be conditioned by the outcome of a coherence analysis (in other contexts) and their status is subject to re-evaluation in the light of new insights regarding their plausibility.

6. Unlike the foundationalist approach, the coherence analysis does not require a sharp disparity in the treatment of particular and general propositions (between "observation statements" and "laws"). Its "data" for factual inquiry are subject to no particularity stipulations, unlike the usual "directly evident" givens of the foundationalists.[2]

7. On the foundationalist approach the body of "evidence" from which the reasoning proceeds must be self-consistent. The coherence analysis has no need for this unrealistic supposition.

The diagram also brings to the fore one further facet of coherentist method that merits special emphasis. Foundationalist inductivism adopts the basically *linear* systematization of reasoning typical of mathematics: here once a result is obtained one simply passes on to other matters – there is no need ever to return to the reappraisal or resubstantiation of something that has already been "established." But with coherentist inductivism the case is quite otherwise, as the feedback

---

[2] Compare R. M. Chisholm, *The Theory of Knowledge*, 2nd ed. (Englewood Cliffs, 1977).

loop of the diagram illustrates graphically. Here there is a definite place for a dialectical process of cyclical structure, where one returns repeatedly to an item already "established." For the process of confirmation is now more complex, and a thesis might first appear on the status of a mere datum of low plausibility, later as one of higher plausibility, and ultimately even as a validated truth.

Rather than proceeding linearly, by fresh deductions from novel premisses, one may be in a position to cycle round and round the same given family of prospects and possibilities, sorting out, refitting, refining until a more sophisticatedly developed and more deeply elaborated resolution is ultimately arrived at. The information-extracting process developed along these lines is one not of advance into new informative territory, but one of a cyclic reappraisal and revision of the old, tightening the net around our ultimate conclusion as we move round and round again, gaining a surer confidence in the wake of more refined reappraisals. This cyclic process of reappraisal is such that one can even – in suitable circumstances – dispense with the need for "new" data-inputs in an endeavor to squeeze more information out of the old. It is readily observed that this repeated reappraisal of claims is in fact closer to the processes of thought one generally employs in scientific reasoning.

4. COHERENTISM AND THE VIEW OF KNOWLEDGE AS TRUE, JUSTIFIED BELIEF

The coherentist unhesitatingly espouses the historic thesis that knowledge is "true, justified belief," construing this as tantamount to claiming that the known is that whose acceptance-as-true is adequately warranted *through an appropriate sort of systematization*. However, since the systematization at issue is viewed as being of the network type, the impact of the thesis is drastically altered. For we now envisage a variant view of justification, one which radically reorients the thesis from the direction of the foundationalists' quest for an ultimate basis for knowledge as a quasi-axiomatic structure. Now "justified" comes to mean not "derived from basic (or axiomatic) knowledge," but rather "appropriately interconnected with the rest of what is known."

This thesis that knowledge is tantamount to true, justified belief is currently much controverted. The controversy has in large measure revolved about Edmund Gettier's well-known counterexamples, which show that certain claims that one would not wish to countenance as knowledge at all can yet represent both true and justified beliefs when the elements of truth and justification reach them by sufficiently different routes. (For example, the man who believes P-or-Q, when all his justification relates solely to Q, which is false, whereas the truth of the disjunction inheres in that of P alone, for whose belief no justification is at hand.)

Interestingly enough, one way of reading the literature of this dispute is as showing that knowledge *can only be extracted* INFERENTIALLY *from knowledge*, and not from something that is epistemically less than knowledge (such as justified belief). And this is wholly congruent with the stance of coherentism. The coherentist continues to recognize the force of the Aristotelian argument that when one knows the conclusion of a demonstration *on the basis of* this demonstration, then one must also know the premises, and that there is no *demonstrative* route to the extraction of knowledge from something that is less than knowledge. From the standpoint of the network theory of cognitive sytematiza-tion, there is no harm in drawing the conclusion that *ex nihilo nihil* operates as an epistemic principle with respect to knowledge. Such a result is unpalatable only for those who propose to use the formula at issue (viz., that knowledge is true, justified belief) as a *reductive analysis* in seeking to define "knowledge" in other terms, rather than merely as a *descriptive remark* about the systematic interrelatedness among the various items that comprise our "body of knowledge."

The view that there is some rational justification for every item of knowledge, combined with the view that only the known can serve in the rational justification of knowledge appears to lead to the conclusion that nothing can be known because a vitiating regress is involved. But this appearance is misleading – indeed mistaken. We are not saying that the grounds must "first" be known "before" the conclusion can be known. No such temporal ordering is at issue. On the network approach, the relevant items may all lie on the same plane rather than in some linear hierarchy of before and after. (Here the distinction between networks and sequences becomes crucial.) The aspect of vicious regress arises for a mistaken *causal* view of the relation between what is known and its grounding – it confuses the order of *reasons* with that of *causes*. One should not attempt to assimilate the epistemic order of grounding or justification to the causal order of precedence or priority. There is no need to take the stance that grounds must be more "basic" than what is grounded, reflecting the linear, axiomatic order of justifying the less basic in terms of the more basic.

The network concept of grounding offers a perfectly viable alternative here. Our concern with the rational structure of knowledge is, after all, not primarily a matter of learning-theory (the dynamics of extracting real out of proto-knowledge), but of probative systematics. It is not – or need not be – an issue of extracting "real knowledge" from "mere beliefs" by use of a philosopher's stone of epistemic justification. This entire reductive or extractive impetus is absent from a preoccupation with the *rational structure* of knowledge, which represents a concern with the *rational cognitive systematics* of what is known rather than with its *heuristic origin*. And here a coherentist's network approach is not only a possible, but an emphatically attractive alternative to the foundationalist's axiomatic methodology.

5. COHERENTISM'S RELIANCE ON REGULATIVE PRINCIPLES OF PLAUSIBILITY AND PRESUMPTION

Philosophers of science have frequently been exercised by the prominent but yet problematic role in science of such theoretical parameters of inductive reasoning as *continuity, uniformity, regularity, conservation,* and *simplicity*. They are generally approached from one of two directions. Sometimes they are regarded as objective tendencies of nature – constitutive facts regarding a world whose mode of functioning exhibits not the *horror vacui* of the medievals but an analogous principle like *amor simplicitatis*, etc. On the other hand, they are sometimes cast in the role of principles whose weight bears wholly on the *subjects* who do scientific theorizing rather than in the *object* of their theories, and to reflect the subjective intellectual predilection of the working scientist rather than any objective features of the natural universe itself. But in fact neither side of this subjective/objective dichotomy is wholly appropriate. For all these various parameters of systematicity are most advantageously seen as principles of an essentially epistemological, or rather *methodological* character. They represent *regulative* principles for the construction of *adequate* explanatory accounts: *procedural principles of plausibility* that afford evaluative standards governing the provision of such accounts.

Accordingly, it would be an ill-advised and wholly unnecessary complication to regard such principles as representing fundamentally *ontological* factors, as indicating a straightforward fact about the world – an inclination on the part of nature itself towards certain principles of operation (to put it somewhat anthropomorphically). The probative methodology of scientific inquiry requires principles of this sort as part of the evaluative machinery of its own *modus operandi*. One should thus avoid treating such factors as the *results* of an inquiry for which they must in fact serve as *inputs*. It is best to view these parameters of systematicity as a (duly warranted) regulative or procedural or methodological facet of explanatory accounts, rather than a constitutive or descriptive (world-oriented) facet of nature. They represent not so much substantive findings about nature as procedural and regulative ground-rules for the conduct of scientific inquiry.[3] (Just this view of, specifically, the *uniformity* of nature has been advanced by several recent writers.)[4]

We have seen that the coherence analysis sets out from a starting-point of data together with certain characteristic initial assessments of presumption and plausibility. Just what is the basis for these assessments? The answer to this crucial question is simply that *these standards of plausibility and presumption are, for the coherentist, provided by the very conception of systematicity itself*.

Once one adopts the Hegelian Inversion of the implication relationship

acceptable as true → systematizable

into its converse

systematizable → acceptable as true

---

[3] Compare T. S. Kuhn's statement that: "nature is vastly too complex to be explored even approximately at random. Something must tell the scientist where to look and what to look for." ("The Function of Dogma in Scientific Research," in B. A. Brody [ed.], *Readings in the paradigms* provide, for him, the main source of such presumptions.) Most writers on the subject simply invoke *analogy*. See, for example, the interesting cases treated in G. Polya, *Induction and Analogy in Mathematics* (Princeton, 1954). The point at issue goes back at least to C. S. Peirce. See the author's book on *Peirce's Philosophy of Science* (Notre Dame, 1978).

[4] Cf. Stephen Toulmin, *The Philosophy of Science* (London, 1953), see especially sect. 5.2 "Physicists Work on Presumptions, Not Assumptions," pp. 144–148; and J. P. Day, "The Uniformity of Nature," *American Philosophical Quarterly*, vol. 12 (1975). Compare also the author's essay "On the Self-Consistency of Nature," in *The Primacy of Practice* (Oxford, 1973), pp. 88–106.

it becomes reasonable – and, if not actually inevitable, then at any rate only natural – to construe the parameters of systematicity as themselves affording acceptability-indicators. If systematicity is to be our standard of acceptability, then the sundry facets of system will themselves count as acceptability-indicative.

A positive presumption of acceptability is therefore to operate in favor of all the traditional parameters of systematization: consistency, uniformity, regularity (causality, rulishness and lawfulness in all forms), simplicity, connectedness/coherence, unity/completeness, etc. These are now to function as regulative presumptions – as principles of epistemic preferability. This is readily exemplified in cases of circumstances of attuning theory and data in curve fitting:

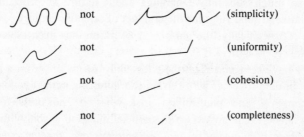

The various parameters of systematicity now recur as principles of presumption, dictating where our epistemic preferences ought to lie (other things being equal). For the coherentist, systematicity thus come to do double duty as a general criterion of acceptability-as-true and as a regulative principle of plausibility and presumption.

On the coherentist approach, the choice between alternative "rival" systematizations in the same cognitive domain is not absolute – not a matter of yes-or-no, right-*vs.*-wrong. It is a matter not of *forced* choices but of *preferential* choices in the light of plausibilistic constraints. The basic process is one of cost-benefit analysis. The benefits are the information afforded by the acceptance of the candidate-theses (the "data"); the costs are the incurring of implausibilities – violations of simplicity, regularity, etc. And these determinative plausibilities are themselves of an economic character: simplicity, regularity, etc. The regulative resort to smoothness of fit is itself a matter of the rational economy of thought.

Coherentism is, in effect, the very quintessence of a systematist's approach. Taking systematicity as the standard of truth, it casts the parameter of systematization as *prima facie* determinants of the epistemic preferability of alternatives. The principles of systematicity now represent *presumptive principles regulatively governing the conduct of inquiry.* The regulative standing of such parameters as principles of epistemic preferability is reflected in the schema:

> Other things being (anything like) equal, give precedence in acceptance-deliberations to those alternatives that in the context of other actual or putative commitments are relatively more uniform (or coherent or simple or complete, etc.) than their alternatives.

The coherentist thus transforms the adequacy principles of system *structure* into selection principles for system *inclusion.* Their crucial features from this perspective are:

1. They are *regulative,* that is, they guide our cognitive actions by telling us how to proceed in system design. ("Of alternative accounts, *adopt* the most simple, uniform, etc.")
2. They are *preferential,* that is, they guide the issue of cognitive precedence and priority. ("Of alternative accounts, give precedence [priority, preference] to the most simple, uniform, etc.")
3. They are *essentially negative,* that is, like the Old Testament rules implicit in the injunctions of the *Pentateuch,* they are to be construed negatively in terms of *avoid*!, *shun*!, *minimize*! with respect to such factors as complexity, disuniformity, etc.

C. I. Lewis has spoken of the "imperative force" of *deductive* logic in relation to the normative bearing of consistency subject to the governing injunction "Keep your assertions mutually consistent with each other!"[5] The present approach contemplates an analogous "imperative force" for *inductive* reasoning (or its coherentist functional equivalent) in relation to the parameters of systematicity as instruments of inquiry in the factual domain. The underlying unifying injunction is simply: "Construct the best (most adequate) cognitive systems that you can!" The regulative status of the parameters of systematicity is a consequence of this prime imperative, via the reasoning:

---

[5] C. I. Lewis, *Values and Imperatives* (ed. by John Lange; Stanford, 1969), p. 192.

Render your knowledge systematic!
The systematic is what conforms to the
 parameters of systematicity.
———————————————————————
Conform your knowledge to the parameters
 of systematicity!

The conception of a synoptic cognitive system embracing all of our knowledge of the world represents an *ideal* in the Kantian sense – a regulative principle of reason.

Seen in this light, the regulative presumptions which provide coherentism with its mechanisms of plausibility assessment are closely akin go the "regulative ideas" (maxims) of Kant's *Critique of Practical Reason* – such as those of uniformity (or "resemblance"), affinity, symmetry, purposive orderliness, etc. Such factors are not absolutes or even *givens* whose presence in our corpus of knowledge is a matter of established *fait accompli* – they represent cognitive *desiderata* which we try to inject into the framework of our knowledge insofar as this is conveniently and unproblematically possible.

VI

Coherentism, Induction, and Scientific Systematization

SYNOPSIS

(1) How coherentism accommodates the standard methodology of scientific inference and inductive reasoning by using the parameters of systematicity as principles of plausibility-assessment. (2) How coherentism provides a natural framework for the rationalization of our inductive practices. It is a point of probative strength of the coherentist approach that what it bases on systematic considerations is not an imputation of *truth*, but merely an imputation of *plausibility*.

1. COHERENTISM AS A FRAMEWORK FOR SCIENTIFIC REASONING

The opening chapters have expounded the thesis that cognitive systematization is the instrument for a specifically *scientific* development of our knowledge. On such a view, far-reaching implications for the theory of scientific method must clearly result from the transition from a Euclidean to a network model of cognitive systematization. It is thus worthwhile to consider more closely how coherentism can furnish the mechanism of cognitive systematization in the context of the inductive sciences, and indeed – more generally – how the coherentist can provide a means for the rationalization of inductive reasoning.

Throughout the history of philosophy in the West, the major theorists of scientific rationality have always stressed such factors as causal regularity (Aristotle), simplicity (Occam), order (Bacon), continuity, conservation, and minimization (Leibniz), uniformity (Hume, Mill), systematicity (Kant), and consilience (Whewell). The ongoing stress upon all such facets of systematic order rightly suggests the suitability of coherentism as a framework for scientific and "inductive" reasoning. And it is clear that considerations of systematic fit must play a crucial role here. One rejects theories because they do not fit the data in hand. And one sometimes (and not infrequently) proceeds conversely as well, rejecting data because they do not fit our accepted theories.[1]

As we saw in the preceding chapter, the strategy of coherentist analysis involves three essential steps:

1. to lay out the available alternative options relative to the possibilities cognitively at hand.
2. to choose between these alternatives on the basis of plausibility considerations.
3. to use systematicity itself as the guide to plausibility, using the various parameters of systematicity as indices of plausibility.

This procedure makes for an intimate linkage between coherentism and the standard processes of inductive reasoning. For it is clear that *the parameters of systematicity – simplicity, uniformity, cohesiveness, and the rest – are one and the same as the guiding standards of inductive reasoning.* Seen from this angle, the inductive process of scientific reasoning embodies a straightforward commitment to maximize the systematicity of our knowledge.

Induction, that characteristic instrument of scientific reasoning, is a search for order – in short, for system. In view of this, the capacity of coherentism to provide a framework for scientific reasoning is scarcely surprising. Let us consider, at least in rough outline, how some standard processes of inductive inference can be accommodated by coherentist means.[2]

Induction by simple enumeration – that paradigm inductive argument – proceeds by noting first that all the objects (of a certain type) that have been observed to date – say, $a_1, a_2, \ldots, a_n$ – have a certain (genuinely qualitative) property F, and then maintaining on this

---

[1] Not only in common life – as per the ancient sceptic's favorite example of the straight stick that looks bent under water – but in science as well. Cf. Henry Margenau, *The Nature of Physical Reality*, 1st edn. (New York, 1950), p. 463.

[2] The following discussion draws on Chapter IX of the author's *The Coherence Theory of Truth* (Oxford, 1973), where this range of issues is treated more extensively.

ground that the next object a_{n+1} will also have F.[3] The argument thus in effect moves from the premises of the form $F(a_1), F(a_2), \ldots, F(a_n)$ to the (inductive) conclusion $F(a_{n+1})$.

The problem of justification here is that of exhibiting the rational warrant for this inferential procedure and its cognates. We must thus grapple with a variant of Hume's puzzle: what could possibly assure that a *future* instance (a_{n+1}) will be like the *past* ones $(a_1, a_2, \ldots, a_n)$? Given that $F(a_1), F(a_2), \ldots, F(a_n)$, what authorizes us to claim the conclusion $F(a_{n+1})$ rather than its contradictory $\sim F(a_{n+1})$?

In the context of our present concerns, it is tempting to think of answering such a question in terms of a coherence analysis. And this can indeed be done. For let it be that the evidential base $F(a_1), F(a_2), \ldots, F(a_n)$ is given and that we are to judge in this context between the rival truth-candidates $F(a_{n+1}), \sim F(a_{n+1})$. From the coherentist's angle of approach we are thus to begin with the following overall set of "data" (in the here-operative sense of truth-candidates):

$$S = \{ F(a_1), F(a_2), \ldots, F(a_n), F(a_{n+1}), \sim F(a_{n+1}) \}.$$

This datum-set has exactly two maximal consistent subsets:

$$S_1 = \{ F(a_1), F(a_2), \ldots, F(a_n), F(a_{n+1}) \}$$
$$S_2 = \{ F(a_1), F(a_2), \ldots, F(a_n), \sim F(a_{n+1}) \}.$$

The issue of justifying the outcome of $F(a_{n+1})$ from these data – rather than $\sim F(a_{n+1})$ – comes down to showing that S_1 is to be preferred over S_2 on the basis of a suitable criterion of epistemic preference. Given the general strategy of coherentism, this comes down to the rather less problematic issue of showing that $F(a_{n+1})$ is more *plausible* than $\sim F(a_{n+1})$. Let us consider how this can be accomplished within the coherentist framework.

The given evidence $F(a_1), F(a_2), \ldots, F(a_n)$ clearly establishes a certain particular pattern: all its items answer to one and the same logical structure, that of the generic form $F(x)$. From this standpoint $F(a_{n+1})$ plainly appears as pattern-concordant while $\sim F(a_{n+1})$ is pattern-discordant. But now consider the following plausibility-delimiting rule:

---

[3] The qualification "genuinely qualitative" is introduced to block such constructs as the "property" of "*having been observed to date.*"

When the initial evidence exhibits a marked logical pattern, then pattern-concordant statements are – *ceteris paribus* – to be evaluated as more plausible than pattern-discordant ones.

This rule of uniformity-precedence is clearly part and parcel of the coherentist's commitment to the parameters of systematicity as principles of plausibilistic precedence. And given such a rule of plausibility-determination, the "inferential" step from the given premises to the pattern-conforming result $F(a_{n+1})$ is at once made available through the general mechanism of a coherence analysis.

A further example of the operation of this plausibility rule may be helpful. Consider yet another paradigm of inductive reasoning, the "argument by analogy":

We have observed that the properties F and G have been conjoined in the case of objects $a_1, a_2, \ldots, a_n$. We now observe further than a_{n+1} has F. Hence we infer "by analogy" that a_{n+1} will also have G. Thus we move from the premises $F(a_1)$ & $G(a_1)$, $F(a_2)$ & $G(a_2)$, $\ldots, F(a_n)$ & $G(a_n)$, $F(a_{n+1})$ to the conclusion: $G(a_{n+1})$.

Again, contemplating the contrary result $\sim G(a_{n+1})$ as a truth-candidate, we arrive at the following set **S** of data:

$$\mathbf{S} = \{ F(a_1) \ \& \ G(a_1), F(a_2) \ \& \ G(a_2), \ldots, F(a_n) \ \& \ G(a_n),$$
$$F(a_{n+1}) \ \& \ G(a_{n+1}), F(a_{n+1}) \ \& \sim G(a_{n+1}) \}.$$

Once more, just two maximal consistent subsets are available, namely those conjoining the initial premises with the two propositions $F(a_{n+1})$ & $G(a_{n+1})$ and $F(a_{n+1})$ & $\sim G(a_{n+1})$, respectively. The preference of one of these over the other is justifiable in terms of a differential judgment of the plausibility of these two propositions. Again, given that the initial evidence exhibits the generic pattern $F(x)$ & $G(x)$, it is clear that one of these propositions is pattern-concordant and the other pattern-discordant. Resort to our plausibilistic uniformity-precedence rule once more suffices to underwrite drawing the "inductively proper" conclusion as emerging from a coherence analysis.

These illustrations show how a coherentist approach proposes to handle the problem of justifying the usual sorts of inductive inference. It proceeds by way of a process that involves two steps:

1. to rely on pattern-conformity considerations to support a differential assessment of the *plausibilities* of the truth-càndidates involved, and then

2. to use the general procedure of the coherence analysis of best-fit considerations to vindicate "the inductively right conclusion" in the move from plausibility to acceptance as a presumptive truth.

Of course there will be situations that do not fit the textbook patterns of inductive inference, but reflect more closely the complex realities of actual scientific practice. The workings of plausibility-considerations would have to be deployed in somewhat more sophisticated ways to accommodate such complexity. (For example, when judging between hypotheses some of which explain a great deal more of the observed evidence than others, one would – other things being equal – definitely incline to consider the former as significantly more plausible than the latter.) But the general principles at issue remain the same.

The coherentist approach to inductive reasoning thus deploys pattern-conformity as a guide to plausibility in strict accord with the doctrinal spirit epitomized in Bradley's dictum: "If by taking certain judgments of perception [for us, 'data'] as true, I can get more system into my world, then these 'facts' are so far true. . . ."[4] The reliance upon pattern-conformity – an obvious facet of orderliness and system – as a guiding criterion to plausibility, and hence to alethic preferability, is clearly one way to "get more system into my world." And in so far as system is – as the coherence theory insists – a guide to truth, the regulative reliance on the inductive parameters of simplicity, regularity, pattern-conformity (etc.) as indices of plausibility simply implements the basic systematic commitments of the whole approach.

All this points to a central and crucial feature of the coherence approach: the plausibilistic reliance on the parameters of systematicity that is part and parcel of its striving towards systematization. If, as the coherence theory insists, truth is appropriately to be sought in maximal systematization, then the stress on inductive procedures based upon pattern-conformity can simply be viewed be seen as a special facet of the general approach. The very rationale of the theory is such that not only does coherence *qua* consistency contribute to the potential for

[4] F. H. Bradley, "On Truth and Coherence," *Essays on Truth and Reality* (Oxford, 1914), pp. 202–218; see pp. 210–211.

truth, but so does coherence *qua* orderliness – that is to say, *systematicity*. The controlling role which the coherentist approach assigns to the standard inductivist parameters (uniformity, regularity, simplicity, etc.) as regulative principles of presumption in plausible reasoning simply mirrors their role as parameters of cognitive systematization as such.[5]

Little wonder, then, that coherentism provides a natural framework for inductive reasoning. Inductive reasoning is based upon the procedure Charles Sanders Peirce called "*hypothesis*" – the practice of adopting the best (=the most smoothly systematizable) among the available explanations.[6] The very nature of inductive reasoning invites an explication of its workings in system-relative terms.

2. HOW THE COHERENTIST APPROACH CAN VALIDATE INDUCTIVE INFERENCES

But can such an inductive procedure – with its collaborative division of labor between system-grounded plausibility and systematic coherence – actually succeed in its intended mission of *validating* the standard gamut of inductive inferences? One must first get clear about just what "validation" can effectively mean in this context. It could in principle mean one of two things:

1. to establish that the "inductively proper" conclusion is *rationally warranted* in the epistemic circumstances, and
2. to establish that the "inductively proper" conclusion is *correct*, in that matters will (always or generally) in fact so eventuate as the inductive argument maintains.

Clearly the coherence analysis does not provide a "validation" in the second sense. But we may take Hume to have shown with all the lucidity that philosophical arguments admit of that there simply can be no "justification of induction" in sense (2). And it is senseless to make demands or impose conditions which cannot in the very nature of things

---

[5] The logic of plausibility and presumption is discussed more fully in the author's *Plausible Reasoning* (Assen, 1976).

[6] "Hypothesis is where we find some very curious circumstance, which would be explained by the supposition that it was a case of a certain general rule, and thereupon adopt that supposition." (*Collected Papers*, vol. II, sect. 2.624.)

be satisfied. But if one is willing to rest satisfied with a "validation" in the former sense – as we indeed *must* be – then the coherence approach can indeed yield the sort of justification we seek. It can provide an instrument for making manifest the *rational warrant* that supports the "inductively proper" conclusion. For the coherentist legitimation of induction is achieved through an assimilation of induction to the general paradigm of rational procedure manifested in the coherence approach to truth.

The tactics characteristic of inductive reasoning all emerge simply as facets of the same fundamental strategy – a drive towards systematicity. For example, the invocation of *uniformity* (of the examined with the unexamined or of the known with the unknown), and *simplicity* (in the choice among alternatives), etc., are simply so many applications of the parameters of systematicity in their regulative, methodological guise as means for imparting structure to our knowledge.

In any ampliative mode of argumentation, induction preeminently included, one infers a conclusion on an evidential basis that is deductively insufficient, so that a divergent imputation always remains *logically* possible. How are we to justify this specific resolution, given that alternative possibilities exist? The coherentist answer is that we do so by selecting that resolution which best fits the given evidential basis, so that the rational basis for the inductivist imputation of truth is provided in terms of the general rationalizing procedure of coherentist systematization. From this standpoint, induction is seen as ultimately a tool for achieving systematic best fit on the basis of experience.

But what sort of legitimative warrant is to be at issue with such a validation of induction, seeing that it cannot be the warrant of guaranteed truth (which one must join Hume in admitting as in principle unavailable)?

The answer here lies in retracing the line of reasoning at issue in such validations of the various modes of inductive reasoning as have just been considered. We have certainly *not* attempted to argue directly that the future will be like the past – i.e. that statements about the future will prove true if they are past-conforming. The crucial fact is that conformity to established patterns is not used on the coherence approach as a criterion of truth *per se*, but only as a guide to *plausibility*. Our coherentism requires merely that statements about the future be viewed as relatively *more plausible* when they conform to the past. The inductive application of the coherence analysis thus brings about a crucial division of labor. On the standard view, the "justification of induction" would require us to make the somewhat drastic move from pattern-conformity to *truth*; but all that is asked by a coherentism along the presently envisaged lines is the more modest move from pattern-conformity to *plausibility*. For on this basis, *the coherence analysis itself can then function – in its characteristic way – to provide the vehicle of rational warrant for the move from plausibility to acceptability.*

The analysis of inductive reasoning in the coherence framework accordingly effects an essential reduction of the problem of "justifying induction." Seemingly, the task of justifying induction is the impossible one of arguing *directly* for the truth of certain propositions about the future on the basis of (clearly insufficient) evidence relating to the past. What the coherence approach does is to shift the requisite argument from an argument for truth to an argument for plausibility. It invokes pattern-conformity merely as a *basis of plausibility*, not as a *basis for truth*. The burden of the rationalizing move from plausibility to presumptive truth is then borne by the generic mechanisms of the coherence analysis.

Induction thus represents a process of reasoning which can be made to conform to the general canons of rationality through its assimilation to the coherence approach. For if the inductive rationality of science is construed (as it should be) in terms of the introduction of systematic order into our understanding of things, and if coherentism is simply a natural program for the realization of systematicity (as is indeed the case), then the rational warranting of inductive reasoning becomes relatively straightforward.

This defense of induction in terms of systematization thus in effect shifts the difficulty, displacing it to another spot. But such a tactic is not without problems of its own. For our favored procedures of cognitive systematization themselves stand in need of a reasoned defense – a rational legitimation. This large and important issue merits a separate chapter.

VII

Legitimating the Coherentist Approach to Cognitive Systematization

SYNOPSIS

(1) How the coherentist policy of using systematization as a criterion of acceptability can be legitimated by a methodology-oriented approach. (2) A system-centered coherentism can be shown to provide for the two main controls of theoretical adequacy upon methods of cognitive quality-control: selfcorrectiveness and selfsubstantiation. (3) This essentially circular process of *self*-reliance does actually manage to avoid viciousness. (4) Still, such a purely theoretical legitimation remains ultimately insufficient: the need for theory-external controls remains unsatisfied. Here the element of successful praxis and effective application must play a key role. (5) This aspect of applicative efficacy provides a theory-external reality principle that leads outside the problematic cycle of selfsubstantiation. (6) The coherentist methodology does indeed satisfy this further requirement of pragmatic efficacy. For a closer scrutiny of the historical dimension of validation yields a fundamentally *evolutionary* view of the pragmatic aspect of cognitive quality-control – a "struggle for survival" in which "the scientific method" (and thus the coherentism inherent in its approach to systematization) has been transparently successful. (7) The procedural principles of cognitive systematization which, seemingly, are strictly the *inputs* of inquiry emerge as its *outputs* as well. The legitimation of systematicity as a cognitive resource is thus ultimately contingent, not necessitarian. (8) Recourse to a network theory of explanatory justification averts the objection that it is circular to validate induction

as a mode of coherentist systematization, and then use induction to justify our procedures for systematization.

---

1. HOW CAN THE ADEQUACY OF A COGNITIVE SYSTEM BE ASSESSED? THE *DIALLELUS* PROBLEM AND THE METHODOLOGICAL TURN

In organizing our information about the world − as in organizing anything else − one cannot begin wholly empty-handed, without bringing the needed tools to the task: in this case, the methods and principles of cognitive organization. A family of structural organizing principles is required from the very outset in the systematization of knowledge, principles which can guide, regulate, and control the organizing processes at issue. The *coherentist* approach envisaged here casts the parameters of systematicity themselves in this pivotal role of regulative principles of cognitive validation. With the Hegelian Inversion, systematicity comes to serve as the arbiter, the controlling standard of our knowledge. But *quis custodiet . . . ?* When systematization is the quality-control standard of our claims to our knowledge, how are our systematizing methods themselves to be monitored? How, in short, can one establish the propriety and legitimacy of the coherentist's penchant for systematicity and the coherentist strategy of cognitive systematization?

This general line of questioning has been familiar from the days of the sceptics of antiquity, who presented it as a particular sort of *circulus in probandi*, under the title of the "diallelus" or Wheel Argument. Montaigne formulated this argument as follows:

> To adjudicate [between the true and the false] among the appearances of things we need to have a decision method (*un instrument judicatoire*); to validate this method we need to have a justifying argument; but to validate this justifying argument we need the very method at issue. And there we are, going round on the wheel.[1]

[1] "Pour juger des apparances que nous recevons des subjects, il nous faudrait un instrument judicatoire; pour vérifier cet instrument, il nous fault de la démonstration; pour vérifier la démonstration, un instrument: nous voilà au rouet." *Essaies*, Bk. II, ch. 12 ("An Apologie of Raymond Sebond"); p. 544 of the Modern Library edition of *The Essays of Montaigne* (New

The significance of this extremely simple line of reasoning is difficult to exaggerate. It shows, in as decisive a manner as philosophical argumentation admits of, that our operative standard of factual truth cannot be validated by somehow exhibiting directly that it does indeed accomplish properly its intended work of truth-determination.[2]

The usual tactic of assessing process in terms of product is thus seemingly not practicable in the case of a cognitive procedure: it is in principle impossible to make a direct check of *this* sort on the functioning of our truth-determining methods. Specifically, if systematicity is to be our arbiter of truth – of correctness – then we cannot argue in support of this standard that system-endorsed theses are acceptable because they are correct. This line of legitimation would be vitiatingly circular if system-endorsement is indeed to serve as our standard of correctness.

Since we cannot show the acceptability of our thesis-validating methods through the correctness of their results, a different approach becomes necessary. We must instead maintain that the system endorsed theses are actually acceptable *just because* they belong to a properly constructed system. And "properly constructed" does not mean "made up of correct theses" (here circularity looms up again), but must be construed to mean "made up by appropriate methods." The crucial result of this *Methodological Turn* is that a system of accepted theses is validated not by the "correctness" of its contents, but by the suitability of the construction-methods used in constituting it. The quality of the product is not assessed directly, but only mediately, through the adequacy of the productive process that leads to it.

It warrants note in this connection that if our thesis-validation method is specifically that of systematization, then "yielded by method"

York, 1933). Francis Bacon, with the characteristic shrewdness of a lawyer, even manged to turn the *diallelus* into a dialectical weapon against his methodological opponents: "no judgement can be rightly formed either of my method, or of the discoveries to which it leads, by means of . . . the reasoning which is now in use, since one cannot postulate due jurisdiction for a tribunal which is itself on trial." (*Novum Organon*, Bk. I, sect. 33.) The argument plays a major role in the *Outlines of Pyrrhonism* of Sextus Empiricus.

[2] Notwithstanding its intrinsic significance, this line of reasoning has lain dormant in modern philosophy until J. D. Mercier's monumental *Critériologie générale ou theorie générale de la certitude* (Louvain, 1884; 8th edn. 1924). This book gave the argument a currency in Catholic circles – see, for example, P. Coffey, *Epistemology or the Theory of Knowledge* (2 vols., London, 1917). It figures centrally in two recent coincident publications, my own book on *The Primacy of Practice* (Oxford, 1973), and Roderick Chisholm's interesting lecture on *The Problem of the Criterion* (Milwaukee, 1973).

="is duly systematized." And the characterization "is true on the ground of being yielded by the method" because tantamount to "is true on the ground of being duly systematized." We have come the full circle and returned to the principle of the Hegelian Inversion, which establishes systematicity as the arbiter of truth.

The motivation for this approach to cognitive justification lies in a recognition that the things one rationally accepts are not of a piece. Specifically, careful heed must be given to the distinction between *theses* on the one hand and *methods* on the other. It is indeed ultimately problematic to persist in justifying theses in terms of further theses in terms of further theses, and thus onwards. But there are alternatives to such an approach to the methodology of truth-determination. For one can also justify the acceptance of specific theses on the grounds that they are validated by an appropriately warranted inquiry procedure (in effect the scientific method, on our view). Accordingly, it becomes possible to break the regress of justifying theses by theses: a thesis can be justified by application of a method, and the adoption of this method is justified by reference to certain *practical* criteria (preeminently, success in prediction and efficacy in control). This two-stage division of labor represents the characteristic idea of a specifically *methodological* pragmatism.

2. THEORETICAL CONTROLS: SELFCORRECTIVENESS AND SELFSUBSTANTIATION

What sort of legitimating considerations support our cognitive methods of thesis-substantiation? It will be maintained that two types of controls are primarily operative here:

1. *theoretical* controls: the cognitive methods at issue must be selfcorrective and selfsubstantiating, as well as unrestricted in scope in point of place, time, user, etc.
2. *applicative* controls: the system that results from the application of these methods must be validated by the applicative adequacy of its results. (When its findings are implemented, matters work out well.)

Let us consider more closely these two aspects of the quality-control of a method of cognitive systematization.[3]

On the "theoretical side" of this issue of their legitimation, our procedures for cognitive systematization are subject to crucial methodological requirements of adequacy: selfcorrectiveness and selfsubstantiation. But the "selfcorrectiveness" of any synoptic cognitive method (such as the coherence analysis purports to be) must – if circularity is to be avoided – be understood in a rather special way. There will, to be sure, have to be iterative or repeated applications of the method that eventually *improve* upon earlier ones, but we cannot understand the later ones to "correct" the earlier ones by furnishing identifiable truths where the earlier have yielded identifiable falsehoods, since this would require an external "third party" arbiter of truth for the ascertainment of the truth-status at issue. (This is the lesson of the Wheel Argument.) Rather, the later applications will "correct" the earlies ones by showing that they are *deficient* (rather than *wrong*); later results improve on the earlier ones by removing certain defects (limitations, insufficiencies) with respect to their basis or the procedure by which they were obtained. (For example, a statistic obtained through inferior vs. superior sampling.) On this perspective, a method is self-corrective if it can monitor itself, that is if it functions in such a way that *its later applications themselves will so operate as to reveal eventually certain deficiencies and limitations in the earlier ones.*

The "selfsubstantiation" of a systematizing method will also have to be understood in a rather special way. Any attempt to argue the appropriateness of a systems-constructing approach in the cognitive domain will rest on certain premises which initially, in the first instance, have the status of regulative principles (procedural presumptions). And the crucial issue in point of selfsubstantiation is that the system that ultimately emerges from the applications of these methods must be such as to provide a retrospective revalidation ("retrovalidation") for these initial presumptions. (Thus if, for example, our cognitive methodology of inquiry is *inductive*, then the results of its applications – the particular inductions it validates – must be such as to indicate an essentially induction-amenable world.)

---

[3] There are, to be sure, other controlling considerations than those mentioned here. The further theoretical factor of *unboundedness* is one example. It would be a serious defect in a cognitive method to have blind spots. That is, if certain facts were actually the case (certain circumstances obtained) then the method would preclude (be inherently impotent to discover) that these facts obtained. Such a method involves in effect a *prejudgment* that certain things just are not there to be discovered, and thus produces *a priori* exclusions from the system.

Let us examine in closer detail how this sort of selfcorrectiveness and selfsubstantiation characterize the specifically coherentist approach to cognitive systematization.

A. *Selfcorrectiveness with Respect to Data*

Two sorts of "selfcorrection" are especially germane to our deliberations regarding the coherentist standard of acceptability: the one relating to the initial "data" (in our technical sense) that it makes use of, and the other to its mechanisms of plausibility-evaluation. Let us begin with the former, and consider the important idea of a retrospective reappraisal of data-sources.

For present purposes, the crucial structural feature of the coherence analysis is that it (1) begins with "raw" data, (2) refines these into revised and "cooked" (or duly processed) data, and then (3) deploys plausibility considerations in applying the coherence analysis to these processed data in the endeavor to extract from them those theses which, relative to these data, are qualified for acceptance-as-true.

Now it is clear that as this process works its way along one can discover that the basic resource of our initial policies in the setting-up of data was defective, in that certain sorts of "initially recognized truthcandidates" (= data) turn out in retrospect – in a systematic and regular way – to be found wanting. For example, if our "data" consist in the reports of various witnesses, we may well discover that the reports given by certain of these are wrong so uniformly and regularly, that we can simply eliminate these "witnesses" as a source of usable data. On the other hand, the analysis may – indeed, if all goes well, ought – to provide for the retrospective resubstantiation of our initial acceptance of data sources.

The relevant aspect of the structure of the coherence analysis may be portrayed from this standpoint as in Figure 1. This circular process clearly embodies an element of "SELFcorrection" in applications of the coherence analysis, in making room for a revised and reformed view of the initial data that afford the very materials of the analysis, arriving at this result in the light of the workings of the analysis itself. There is a cyclic movement, a closing of the cycle that requires a suitable meshing – a meshing process that should eventually *retrovalidate* (retrospectively revalidate) the initial criteria of datahood with reference to the results to which they lead.

Figure 1

THE RETROSPECTIVE REAPPRAISAL OF DATAHOOD ON A
COHERENTIST EPISTEMOLOGY

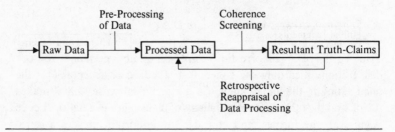

B. *Selfsubstantiation with Respect to Plausibility Judgments*

As such a process of retrospective reassessment works its way along, one can also discover that something is seriously amiss with the principles of our initial evaluation of plausibilities. For it can, of course, happen that certain types of data which we initially regarded as highly plausible turn out to be generally or systematically rejected as unacceptable by the workings of the coherence mechanism. Or, in an essentially converse way, some category of data that we initially tended to consider as low in plausibility-rating may turn out to prevail generally as truths, once we let the wheels of the coherence machinery grind away. A reappraisal of plausibility judgments is thus also possible.

The relevant aspect of the structure of the coherence analysis may be portrayed from this standpoint as in Figure 2, which brings to view another facet of selfmonitoring in the coherence analysis. For the workings of this analysis provide for a revised and reformed view of the principles determining initial plausibilities of the data that provide the input materials of its own operation.

For example, this sort of reappraisal is clearly possible with respect to such principles of plausibility as the principle of the "uniformity of nature," encapsulated in the formula: "Of alternative and in other respects comparable accounts of the world, the most plausible is that which to the greatest feasible extent subsumes similar cases under common principles." It is clear on the very surface of it that this is a procedural principle of plausibility-determination governing the

Figure 2

THE RETROSPECTIVE REAPPRAISAL OF PLAUSIBILITY
EVALUATIONS ON A COHERENTIST EPISTEMOLOGY

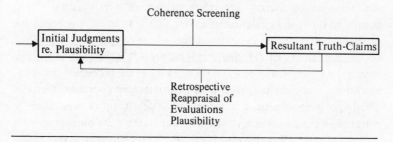

acceptability of explanations. Much the same holds for the principle of the "simplicity of nature" ("of alternative and in other respects comparable accounts of the world, accept the simplest"), the principle of the "consistency of nature" ("mutually inconsistent accounts of the world cannot be accepted"), and the various other analogous principles. It is retrospectively clear that these principles have served us well in our efforts at cognitive systematization. And this is crucial. To be rationally justified, our regulative presumptions of plausibility, such as those reflected in the parameters of systematicity, must (in the final analysis) be retrospectively revalidated through the adequacy of the accounts that are generated by their means.

The parameters of systematicity – considered in this, their fundamental cognitive role – function as guides to the plausibility of the accounts regarding the *modus operandi* of nature that lie at the basis of our descriptions or explanations. If we are to be justified in setting up the parameters of systematicity as such procedural presumptions regulative for inquiry, then the world-picture that results from that inquiry must retrovalidate these presumptions by depicting a world that is adequately systematic. Procedural presumptions that govern inquiry regulatively are not justified if they do not eventually emerge as being in due conformity with the results of inquiry. (No doubt, this matter of "due conformity" is very complicated, since what is at issue is conformity "on balance" and not conformity "in every point and detail.") Systematicity – in its various dimensions – emerges as a regulative *presupposition* of inquiry – a presupposition that inquiry itself must ultimately reauthorize.

3. IS A VICIOUS CIRCULARITY AT ISSUE IN "SELFCORRECTIVENESS" AND "SELFSUBSTANTIATION"?

An autonomous inquiry procedure cannot rely on external "fixed points" to provide the fulcrum of an Archimedean lever. Any probative procedure of cognitive systematization whose operation is dependent on the availability of *certified truths* as prior "givens" will inevitably have to be *incomplete*. For when the working of the procedure demands a *prior* basis of certifiedly true materials for its own operation, then it is clearly not autonomous. It is, rather, other-dependent in its reliance for extraneous inputs upon an external mechanism quite *outside* its own scope. Thus the self-monitoring correctiveness of procedures that aspire to completeness is pretty well inevitable. Any appropriate cognitive method must be selfcorrective if it is sufficiently comprehensive to be autonomous in precluding the prospect of correction by *another* method, "external" to it, as it were.

To be sure, a complete or autonomous probative procedure in the factual domain will also require "inputs" or "givens," but it must be in a position itself to assess and to criticize, to question and to reject them; in sum they must fall *within* its scope rather than lying outside it. Any such procedure for cognitive systematization must make room for *self*-criticism, since we must be able to turn its testing-processes upon the starting-points of its own applications.

Such a circular-seeming process of validation conforms to the performance-monitoring *modus operandi* of a self-evaluating servomechanism, since it provides for a quality-control feedback loop that leads from the *products* ("factual theses") back to the *process* ("the methodology of cognitive systematization") which generated them. Just this retrospective character ultimately assures the adequate functioning of the whole machinery. The mechanism is equipped with a warning buzzer, as it were, that sounds when something is badly amiss with its workings. There is thus no reason to concede that the circle at issue is vicious or otherwise vitiating, for what is actually involved is simply a feedback process of a type nowadays familiar from the study of self-regulatory systems. The sort of "self-criticism" at issue does not represent a vicious circularity, but in effect amounts simply to a *feedback* process that uses later, more refined stages of the analysis to effect revisionary sophistications in the materials from which earlier stages proceeded.

The key point emerges that circularity in a cognitive method or procedure would be bad only if this procedure commits the fallacy of question-begging (*petitio principii*) so as to preempt the prospect of error-discovery and correction. Circularity is harmless when it is compatible with defeasibility – the potential discovery of mistakes. What is critical is corrigibility – and *self*-correctiveness will (if genuine) serve perfectly well.

However, the circular nature of such a self-monitoring process still invites the following line of objection:

> This entire methodological approach fails to accomplish its intended objective because of its circularity. For it legitimates cognitive methods in terms of their producing acceptable (because applicatively successful) theses, and theses are then warranted as acceptable because they are produced by duly legitimated methods. This process is surely viciously circular.

The proper response to this objection is to concede the circularity while denying its harmfulness. For what is basically at issue is not a harmful circle, but a recognition of the fundamentally symbiotic relationship of two interdependent elements. The warranting of theses and methods is *not* successive and sequential. If this *were* the case – if the course of justificatory argumentation were strictly linear – then the circle would indeed be vicious, but this is emphatically *not* so. It is not simply a matter of first settling this and then that, advancing ever further in a fixed direction. The essentially linear order of premiss and conclusion is surely not operative with the feedback loop cycle of argumentation at issue here. Rather, the argumentation is *comprehensively systematic*, placing its several elements into a coordinative framework which unites them within one overall nexus of mutual substantiation.

Our principles of systematization consequently have the feature that they are themselves monitored by conditions of systematic order. This aspect of fit, of conformation, of a closing of the cycle of retrovalidation is itself an aspect of systematicity. The adequacy of our cognitive systematizing is thus itself controlled by systematic considerations. We have envisaged a validation of systematicity on systematic principles. This self-supportingness is a key facet of the enterprise of rational legitimation. It is a crucial aspect of cognitive adequacy – even on uncoherentist approaches – that standards should emerge as proper and appropriate on their own telling, and a failure in this regard would be a grave anomaly. This is not something vitiating, but a necessity.

4. APPLICATIVE CONTROLS: PRAGMATIC VALIDATION

Yet even when all this is said and done, room for queasiness remains. To be sure, the self-support of a cognitive method is crucial. But it is not enough: the process of SELF-monitoring is at bottom inadequate in allowing a cognitive procedure to sit as judge in its own case. The issue of the legitimation of such a method points beyond itself to "the real world." We thus come to the second category of rational controls upon cognitive methodology, the applicative monitoring of pragmatic efficacy.

The adequacy of our methodological tools of cognitive systematization hinges on that of the whole framework of inquiry – the entire methodological *modus operandi* of which the tools at issue are themselves a key part. But by what theory-external reality-principle can the entire "framework of inquiry" that embraces our principles of cognitive systematization possibly be legimated as *more* than selfsubstantiating? Clearly only by its applicative *results* – by that dialectical feedback process which validates the workings of the method in terms of its actual products. Apart from how it fares from its own *internal* standpoint, there remains the more "objective," duly externalized issue of the rational qualifications of the inquiry procedure. Room must be made for the operation of the *theory-external* controls of a factor that is essentially disjoint from the purely cognitive realm – to wit, pragmatic efficacy.

The principles of systematicity (simplicity, regularity, uniformity, etc.) represent *regulative precepts* of inquiry – i.e. methodological injunctions of the sort "Avoid . . ." Maximize. . . ." They are not constitutive theses (descriptive clauses) of the form "The world is of such-and-such a sort." Their normative status does not lie in the range of the correct/incorrect (true/false) spectrum, but rather in the appropriate/inappropriate and functional/disfunctional range. Their validation is ultimately methodological and turns on their capacity to further a realization of the aims of scientific inquiry: the explanation, prediction and control of the phenomena of nature. The legitimation of a coherentist approach which deploys the parameters of systematicity as principles of plausibility and presumption is accordingly ultimately *pragmatic*.

The most promising course in dealing with the issue of cognitive legitimacy is thus *to approach the issue from a methodology-oriented point of departure.* Given the regulative, procedural, in short, *methodological* character of our systematizing principles, the question can be handled in the standard way by which *any* method is ultimately justified, namely by the *pragmatic* route of the questions "Does it work?" – "Is it successful in conducing to the realization of its correlative objectives?" The pragmatic standard is patently the right approach to the legitimation of tools, instrumentalities and all other sorts of methodological devices, and there is no reason to exempt our specifically *cognitive* tools from this general approach.

Just how does this pragmatic legitimation proceed? The rational structure of a pragmatic justification of a methodology of inquiry would have the cyclic format outlined in Figure 3.

Figure 3

THE PRAGMATIC JUSTIFICATION OF AN
INQUIRY-METHODOLOGY

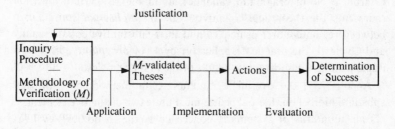

Our methodology of inquiry validates certain truth-claims. We proceed to utilize these by acting upon them, and the resultant success (or lack thereof) provides a basis for the retrospective reappraisal of the adequacy of the inquiry methodology with which the process began.

Everyone is familiar with the occasional surfacing even today of some occult or pseudo-scientific methodology leading to views of the world which substantiate fact-purporting theses of the strangest sort. It is always striking here how beautifully everything meshes at the theoretical level – one bit of strangeness being supported by others. The crunch comes only with the tough question: Does this approach to the warranting of claims actually enable its proponents to navigate more successfully and effectively amidst the rocks and shoals of this world? This issue is vital to the justificatory capacities of the whole process, because it blocks the prospect of a futile spinning around in reality-detached cycles of purely theoretical gyrations. Someplace along the line of justification there must be provision for a corrective contact with the bedrock of an uncooperative and largely unmanipulable reality – a brute force independent of the whims of our theorizing. This crucial reality-principle is provided for in the framework of the present approach by the factor of the reactive success consequent upon implementing action. Its capacity to underwrite successful praxis emerges as the ultimate arbiter of cognitive adequacy.

5. VALIDATION THROUGH A CLOSING OF THE CYCLES

The overall line of validation we envisage for a probative methodology of cognition produces a double circle, by supplementing the theory-internal cycle of theoretical selfsubstantiation of Figure 1 with a theory-external cycle of pragmatic validation as in Figure 4. Here Cycle I represents the theoretical/cognitive cycle of *intellectual consistency* between regulative first principles and their substantive counterparts, and Cycle II, the practical/applicative cycle of *pragmatic efficacy* in implementing the substantive results of the first principles.

Accordingly, the overall legitimation of a methodology for the substantiation of our factual beliefs must unite two distinctive elements: (1) an apparatus of systematic coherence at the theoretical level (a coherence in which factual presumptions and metaphysical presuppositions both will play a crucial part), and (2) a controlling monitor of considerations of pragmatic efficacy at the practical level. Neither can appropriately be dispensed with for the sake of an exclusive reliance on the other. The proof of the theoretical pudding must, in the final analysis, lie in the applicative eating, by monitoring the adequacy of our procedures of cognitive systematization through an assessment of their applicative success in prediction and control over nature.[4]

The legitimative process at issue thus relies on an appropriate fusion

---

[4] The question "Why should pragmatic success of the applications of the products of a cognitive method count as an index of its *cognitive* adequacy?", though seemingly straightforward, in fact plumbs hidden metaphysical depths. The complex issues that arise here are examined at considerable length in the author's *Methodological Pragmatism* (Oxford, 1976), where other considerations relevant to the present discussion are also set out at greater length.

Figure 4

THE TWOFOLD CYCLE OF THE LEGITIMATION OF SYSTEMATIZING METHODOLOGY

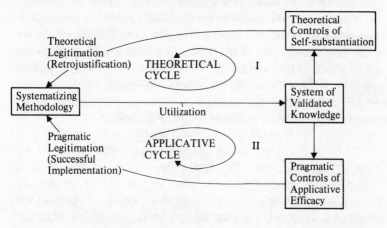

of considerations of theory and praxis. It is a complex of two distinct but interlocked cycles – the *theoretical* cycle of cognitive coherence and the *pragmatic* cycle of applicative effectiveness. Only if both of these cycles dovetail properly – in both the theoretical and the applicative sectors – can the overall process be construed as providing a suitable rational legitimation for the cognitive principles at issue. The symbiotic and mutually supportive nature of the enterprise is fundamental: its structure must afford a systematic union in which *both* methods and theses are appropriately interlinked. Legitimation once more inheres in an appropriate sort of systematization in which both cognitive and ontological factors play a role.

On this approach, the strictly *intellectual* aspect of explanation and understanding is coordinate in important in the teleology of science with its *pragmatic* aspect of "control over nature." Indeed control – throughout the range from prediction as minimal control (the adequate alignment of our own expectations) to the more elaborately modificatory change in the course of nature through effective interaction – comes to be seen in the pivotal role of the final arbiter of adequacy. This aspect of the cognitive centrality of control over nature leads us to an *interventionist* theory of knowledge, one which sees the issue of *monitoring the adequacy* of our theorizing to reside ultimately on the side of efficacy in application.[5]

This line of thought leads inexorably towards a Kant-reminiscent "Copernican Inversion." Later findings do not rest on a superior methodological basis because they are "truer"; rather they must count as truer because they rest on a superior basis. In effect this Copernican Inversion proposes that we not judge a method of inquiry by the truth of its results, but rather judge the claims to truth of the results in terms of the merit of the method that produces them (assessing this merit by both internal [coherentist] and external [pragmatist] standards). We are not to evaluate an inquiry procedure by the truth of its results, but conversely, to assess the truthfulness of the results in terms of rational merits of the procedure (which merits are (1) internal, systematic, and coherentist, and (2) external, applicative, and pragmatist). With an *autonomous* inquiry procedure – where an *independent* "quality control" (check on output) is impossible – one has to rest content with checks on systematic functioning, including controls of pragmatic efficacy at the methodological level. The inversion at issue thus proceeds by *replacing* the direction of reasoning "demonstrably truer" → "worthier of acceptance" by a line of reasoning of an essentially *inverted* order: "better (i.e., more adequately) grounded" → "rationally more acceptance-worthy" → "presumptively truer." The direction of the reasoning thus does not proceed from "greater truth" to "more adequate warrant," but the very reverse. Precisely because the later stages of the application of our inquiry procedure are more fully developed and more fully warranted, we take the stance that it is *rational to view them as better qualified for endowment with the presumption of truth*.

On the standard, pre-Copernican, and seemingly most straightforward view, an inquiry procedure is taken to acquire rational warrant on the basis of the truthfulness of its results. The reasoning is seen to proceed from "greater truthfulness" to "greater rational warrant," with truth as the independent variable and rational warrant for acceptance as the dependent variable in the linking equation between truth and

[5] It is worth stressing an important aspect of the pivotal role of pragmatic efficacy in the quality-control of cognitive systematization. Most of the theoretical parameters of systematizing adequacy (unity, uniformity, cohesiveness, etc.) exert an impetus in the direction of simplicity (economy austerity). Their operation would never in itself induce us to move from a system-in-hand that is relatively simple to one that is more complex. But the pursuit of applicative adequacy can reinforce the operation of completeness and comprehensiveness in counteracting the simplicity-oriented tendency of those parameters.

warrant. But once we turn to our very mechanisms for determining where the truth may be taken to lie (which, in the factual area, is scientific inquiry), the matter can no longer be seen in this light. For one cannot avoid a vitiating circularity in seeking to validate the procedure in view through its capacity to lead to the truth, given that what is to count as true is to be determined by this very procedure itself. To be sure, the linking equation between truth and warrant need not be abandoned, but it must now be viewed in a very different light. For, at this stage, warrant must be seen as the independent variable and truthfulness as the dependent variable; and so, in consequence, it emerges that our inquiry procedures are not seen as warranted because truth-producing, but are presumed to be truth-producing because of their greater rational warrant. On this approach, it appears that to validate the propriety of an inquiry procedure in terms of its truthfulness is simply to pick up the wrong end of the stick: truthfulness should be seen as the output of warrant rather than its input – one does not approach warrant by way of truthfulness, but truthfulness by way of warrant.

Accordingly, there is no question here of denying the crucial fact that superior methodology is *correlative* with greater truthfulness. But the question is: which factor is the dog that wags and which the tail wagged? The inevitable implication of the Wheel Argument (*diallelus*) is that the proper view is that one does not possess a superior methodology thanks to the greater truthfulness of its results, *but rather* that their greater (presumptive) truthfulness derives from possession of a superior methodology (through the operation of a rational presumption connecting superior methodology with the rational warrant for truth-claims).

This line of approach calls for a shift of the center of gravity in regard to the issue of "self-correctiveness" away from *correction* as such to the enhanced methodological adequacy of our probative procedures. To characterize science as *self-corrective* in this sense is thus emphatically *not* to commit oneself to saying that science possessed methods that provide automatically effective cook-book procedures for finding alternative theories once the evidence in hand leads to a loss of trust in the existing ones. (And so the manner in which science is selfcorrective does not help the scientist in his work – it does not afford him with any *devices* for replacing defective theories with more adequate ones.)

Our perspective postulates an effective reversal of the "natural" interpretation of the Hegelian dictum that the real is rational. This is now not so much a remark about the nature of the real, as one about the nature of cognitive rationality. The thesis is that we are warranted in our claims to truth (accuracy, correctness) in matters regarding reality insofar as these claims proceed from adequate methods of inquiry. The "real truth" is thus rational precisely in that it is determined through the output of a rationally warranted methodology.

6. THE EVOLUTIONARY DIMENSION OF SYSTEM-DEVELOPMENT

But how can it be shown that the specifically coherentist approach to cognitive systematization meets the demands of a pragmatic-efficacy standard of quality control? The argument here has two stages: (1) recalling our earlier thesis that the coherentist approach to cognitive systematization can assimilate the standard mechanisms of scientific method, and then (2) noting the dramatic efficacy of science *vis-à-vis* any even remotely available alternative candidate as a mechanism of prediction and control over nature. One can thus invoke on coherentism's behalf the pragmatic efficacy of science, holding that coherentist accommodation of scientific method gains to the credit of a coherentist approach the dramatic success of science in realizing its conjoint purposes of explanation, prediction, and control over nature. On this perspective, the pragmatic warrant of coherentism is seen to reside in its capacity to serve as organon of scientific reasoning. But how can this capacity be made manifest?

The Figure 4 picture of the interlocked circles of the theoretical and applicative validation of cognitive systems portrays the process of system-validation in the essentially timeless terms customary in epistemological discussions. This *static* view of system-validation needs to be supplemented – indeed corrected – by considering the issue in its *temporal and developmental* aspect. The atemporal relationships of probative justification must be augmented by examining the justificatory bearing of the historical dynamics of the matter – the evolutionary process of system development. After all, the articulation of cognitive systems is a matter of historical development, of repeated efforts at improvements in systematizing in the light of trial and error. We are faced with a fundamentally *repetitive* process of the successive revision and sophistication of our ventures at cognitive systematization, a process which produces by way of iterative elaboration an increasingly satisfactory system, one that is more and more adequate in its internal articulation or effective in its external applicability. There are iterative cycles of tentative systematizations followed by resystematizations in the light of the feedback provided by its utilization for theoretical application and practical implementation.

This process is depicted in the diagram given in Figure 5, which presents the cycle at issue in an *historical* perspective, regarding it as a dynamically iterative feedback process. What is at stake is not just *retrospective reappraisal* in the theoretical order of justification, but an actual *revision or improvement* in the temporal order of development.

Figure 5
FEEDBACK CYCLE OF LEGITIMATION

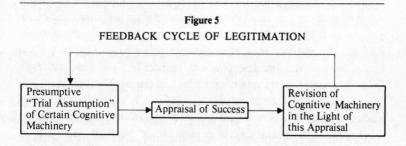

This sequential and developmental process of historical mutation and optimal selection assures a growing conformation between our systematizing endeavors and "the real world." In the final analysis our systematized cognition fits the world for the same reasons that our eating habits do: both are the product of an evolutionary course of selective development. It is this evolutionary process that assures the *adaequatio ad rem* of our system-based claims to knowledge. The legitimating process at issue here is not only a matter of a static cycle of relationships in the probative order of rational legitimation, it also reflects a temporal and developmental process of successive cyclic iterations where all the component elements become more and more attuned to one another and pressed into smoother mutual conformation.

This evolutionary development of intellectual methodologies proceeds by *rational* selection. As changes come to be entertained (within the society) it transpires that one "works out for the better" relative to another in terms of its fitness to survive because it answers better to the socially determined purposes of the group. Just what does "better" mean here? This carries us back to the Darwinian perspective.

Such a legitimation needs a standard of survivalistic "fitness." And this normative standard is provided by considerations of *theoretical adequacy and applicative practice*, and is inherent in the use to which conceptual instrumentalities are put in the rational conduct of our cognitive and practical affairs. Our legitimation of the standard probative mechanisms of inquiry regarding factual matters began with the factor of pragmatic success and subsequently transmuted this into an issue of Darwinian survival. As the discussion has already foreshadowed at many points, it is clearly the *method of scientific inquiry* that has carried the day here. The mechanisms of scientific reasoning clearly represent the most developed and sophisticated of our probative methods. No elaborate argumentation is necessary to establish the all-too-evident fact that science has come out on top in the competition of rational selection with respect to alternative processes for substantiating and explaining our factual claims. The prominent role of the standard parameters of systematization in the framework of scientific thought thus reflects a crucial aspect of their legitimation.

The methodological directives that revolve about the ideal of systematicity in its regulative role ("Of otherwise co-eligible alternatives, choose the simplest!", "Whenever possible invoke a uniform principle of explanation or prediction!", etc.) form an essential part of the methodological framework (the procedural organon) of a science. Experience has shown these methodological principles to be rooted in the functional objectives of the enterprise, being such as to conduce efficiently to its realization of its purposes. We have every reason to think that an abandonment of these regulative principles, while not necessarily spelling an abandonment of science as such, would make hopelessly more difficult and problematic the realization of its traditional goals of affording intellectual and physical control over nature. Considerations of functional efficiency – of economy of thought and praxis – militate decisively on behalf of the traditional principles of scientific systematization.

The key considerations are *effectiveness* and *efficiency*, purposive adequacy and functional economy, acceptability of product and workability of procedure. (And systematicity is, of course, an ideal vehicle here in its stress on simplicity, regularity, uniformity, etc., all of which have to do with the minimizing of unnecessary complications and the pursuit of intellectual parsimony.) A quasi-economic dialectic of *costs* and *benefits* is operative here. And the question of system-choice can ultimately be seen as a matter of "survival of the fittest," with *fitness* ultimately assessed in terms of the theoretical and practical objectives of the rational enterprise. Legitimation is thus evidenced by the fact of survival through historical vicissitudes.

To be sure, there are a *variety* of approaches to the problem of systematizing "how things work in the world." The examples of such occult cognitive frameworks as those of numerology (with its benign ratios), astrology (with its astral influences), and black magic (with its mystic forces) indicate that alternative explanatory frameworks exist, and that these can have very diverse degrees of merit. Thus the orthodox scientific approach to cognitive systematization is simply one alternative among others, and it does not have an irrevocably absolute foothold on the very constitution of the human intellect, nor indeed any sort of abstract justification by purely "general principles." Its legitimation is not *a priori* and absolute, but *a posteriori* and experientially determined.

William James wrote:

Were we lobsters, or bees, it might be that our organization would have led to our using quite different modes from these [actual ones] of apprehending our experiences. It *might* be too (we cannot dogmatically deny this) that such categories, unimaginable by us to-day, would have proved on the whole as serviceable for handling our experiences neutrally as those we actually use. (*Pragmatism* [New York, 1907], p. 114.)

Unlike most philosophers since Kant, James was prepared to consider the prospect of radically different conceptual schemes which dispense with the familiar concepts of space, time, causality, the self, etc. Now the premiss of the first sentence is true enough. But the implication present in the "our" of the second sentence goes badly awry. The prospect that beings constituted as *we* are should function more effectively with the experiential modes of creatures constituted on *different* lines can be dismissed as simply untenable on Darwinian grounds. The serviceable handling of *our* experiences by our cognitive instruments is guaranteed – not by a preestablished harmony but by the processes of evolution.

It is not difficult to give examples of the operation of Darwinian processes in the domain of the instrumentalities of cognitive systematization. The intellectual landscape of human history is littered with the skeletal remains of the extinct dinosaurs of this sphere. Examples of such defunct methods for the acquisition and explanatory utilization of information include: astrology, numerology, oracles, dream-interpretation, the reading of tea leaves or the entrails of birds, animism, the teleological physics of the Presocratics, and so on. There is nothing intrinsically absurd or contemptible about such unorthodox cognitive programs; even the most occult of them have a long and not wholly unsuccessful history. (Think, for example, of the long history of numerological explanation from Pythagoreanism, through Platonism, to the medieval Arabs, down to Kepler in the Renaissance.) But there can be no question at this historical juncture that science has won the evolutionary struggle among various modes of methods of cognitive procedure, and this more than anything else makes it manifest that the inherent coherentism of the orthodox scientific approach to cognitive systematization satisfies the requirement of pragmatic efficacy.

It makes perfectly good sense to ask: "Why should our scientific deliberations proceed in the usual way – with reference to the pursuit of systematicity, etc.?" And it is possible to answer this question along two seemingly divergent routes:

(i) the pragmatic route: it is efficient, effective, successful, "it works," etc.

(ii) the intellectual route: it is rationally cogent, cognitively satisfying, aesthetically pleasing,[6] conceptually "economical," etc.

But the divergence here is only seeming, for Darwinian considerations assure that the two will stay in a convergent conformity.

The merit of entrenched cognitive tools lies in their (presumably) having established themselves in open competition with their rivals. It has come to be shown before the tribunal of bitter experience – through the historical vagaries of a Darwinian process of selection – that the accepted methods work out most effectively in actual practice *vis-à-vis* other tried alternatives.

[6] On this item compare Michael Polanyi, *Personal Knowledge* (New York, 1964).

The conformity between the regulative presumptions and other methodological instrumentalities of inquiry and its *results* is not guaranteed by a preestablished harmony. Nor is it just a matter of contingent good luck. It is the product of an evolutionary pressure that assures the conformation of our systematizing efforts and the real world under trial and error subject to controlling constraint of applicative success (pragmatic efficacy). The evolutionary process assures the due coordination of our cognitive systematizing with the "objective" workings of a nature that is inherently indifferent to our purposes and beliefs.

7. THE CONTINGENCY OF THE GOVERNING PRINCIPLES OF SYSTEMATIZATION

The resulting theory of validation thus takes the stance that the legitimation of a coherentist approach to cognitive systematization turns on the implicational thesis:

(T) IF objective knowledge of nature can be obtained, THEN the coherentist methodology will afford a way to secure it.

And this thesis is itself argued for through a combination of two premises:

1. objective knowledge = a body of appropriately systematized information (i.e. one systematized in line with the general strategy of coherentism)
2. IF systematized information can be obtained at all, THEN the coherentist methodology will afford a way to secure it.

Now (2) here is an *a priori*, necessitarian thesis, obtainable by conceptual analysis alone. Coherentist methodology – with its epistemic canonization of the parameters of systematicity – is in its very nature the most direct route to cognitive systematization. To be sure, we cannot say *a priori* whether our information (our purported knowledge) about the world can be effectively systematized. But we can make do with whatever comfort is afforded by the truism that only by running in the race do we stand a chance of winning it. It is *this* kind of *a priori* assurance that is at issue in the purely theoretical "this or nothing" argument that validates thesis (2).

But thesis (1) has a very different footing. Its contention that properly systematized information is thereby such as to be *true* of the world is simply the "Hegelian Inversion" (as we have called it) all over again. And this thesis is certainly not a matter of *a priori* necessity.

It is perfectly possible for the world – or, rather, for *a* world – to be such that our way of systematizing information about it (via a pivotal reliance on the usual parameters of systematicity such as simplicity, uniformity, and the rest) would not yield an appropriate cognitive *modus operandi*. It is just here – with the validation of (1) – that the complex dual cycle of theoretical and pragmatic retrovalidation comes into play. It is this crucial "closing of the cycles" which – on our theory – is needed to substantiate the status of our systematized information as objective knowledge. Validation roots in Darwinian conformation.

It is clear that if the legitimation of the regulative principles of cognitive systematization is construed as proceeding along such pragmatic/evolutionary lines, then these principles come to stand on an ultimately factual footing – one that is *a posteriori* and contingent. The "first principles" by whose means we constitute our factual knowledge of nature (uniformity, simplicity, and the other parameters of systematization that make up our guide-lines to plausibility) are themselves ultimately of an *a posteriori* and factual standing in point of their controlling force. Seemingly serving merely in the role of *inputs* to inquiry, they emerge in the final analysis as its *products* as well, and accordingly have a contingent rather than necessary status. For then the legitimation of our methodological guidelines to cognitive system- atization in the factual domain is ultimately not a matter of abstract theoretical principle, but one of *experience*.

Our "first principles" of cognitive systematization have no claims to "necessity" – initially and in the first instance, at any rate.[7] Conceivably things *might* have eventuated differently – even as concerns the seemingly *a priori* "first principles of our knowledge." (Why didn't they so eventuate? The question "Why these principles rather than something else?" is *not* illegitimate – it is indeed answerable in terms of the over-all double-circle of methodological legitimation.)

Are such first principles *a priori* and analytic (a part of the

---

[7] The qualification "in the first instance" is made advisedly. For there is no harm in ultimately accommodating our inclination to view these are necessary – once they have become sufficiently firmly entrenched.

"conceptual schema" of our science) or are they *a posteriori* and synthetic (a product of scientific inquiry)? This question now looks naïve – for they are both. The idea of a feedback cycle of evolutionary legitimation indicates that we are ill advised to put the question in terms of a logically tidy yes-or-no. Such first principles are thus "first" only in the first analysis. Their theory-internal absoluteness is deceptive – it represents but a single phase within the historical dialectic of evolutionary legitimation. They do not mark the dead-end of a *ne plus ultra*.

To be sure, all this is to say no more than that circumstances *could* arise in which even those very fundamental first principles that define for us the very idea of the intelligibility of nature might have to be given up. In other "possible worlds" reliance on simplicity, uniformity, etc. could conceivably prove misleading and cognitively counterproductive. But to concede the *possibility* is not, of course, to grant the likelihood – let alone the reality – of the matter as regards our actual world. The first principles at issue are so integral a component of *our* rationality that we cannot even conceive of *any* rationality that dispenses with them: we can conceive *that* they might have to be abandoned, but not *how*.[8]

The very circumstance that these principles are *in theory* vulnerable is a source of their strength *in fact*. They have been tried in the history of science – tried long, hard, and often – and yet not found wanting. They are founded on a solid basis of trial in the harsh court of historical reality. Forming, as they do, an integral component of the cognitive methods that have evolved over the course of time it can be said that for them – as for all our other strictly methodological resources – "*die Weltgeschichte ist das Weltgericht*." A quasi-Lamarckian process of *rational* selection is the key to quality control in the cognitive domain.

8. A RESIDUAL DIFFICULTY

One seeming difficulty remains. Chapter VI offered a validation of induction in terms of its being part and parcel of a properly conducted enterprise of cognitive systematization. And the present chapter proposes to legitimate our mechanisms of cognitive systematization on the basis of considerations which can only be established inductively, viz., applicative success and pragmatic efficacy. Is there not a vicious circle in validating our patterns of inductive argumentation with

[8] On this fact-ladenness of the fundamental ideas by which our very conception of nature is itself framed see Chapter VI, "A Critique of Pure Analysis" of the author's *The Primacy of Practice* (Oxford, 1973).

reference to systematization and then legitimating our systematizing practices by inductive means?

This aspect of self-supportingness can be set out somewhat more strictly by the following question-and-answer dialogue regarding our broadly inductive legitimation of the methodological recourse to systematicity: Q. What legitimates systematization? A. Its relative success *vis-à-vis* the alternatives. Q. How is this success established? A. By the record – i.e. inductively. Q. But how is induction itself to be legitimated? A. With reference to systematicity – i.e. as constituting an efficient route to the systematization of our information. The circle is clear here: systematization validates induction, induction substantiates systematization; inductive methods validate the systematizing rationale of inductive reasonings while inductive reasonings support the recourse to inductive methods.

There is in fact nothing vicious here. One would not (i.e., *should* not) want it any other way. One cannot validate deductive inferences without the use of deductive methods, and one cannot legitimate deductive methods without using deductive inferences. All that one can ask – all that is needed – is that the legitimative arguments should hang together in the proper way. And the use of induction is wholly parallel. The circularity at issue is not vicious or vitiating – it is simply a part of that self-supportingness that is a requisite of any adequate cognitive instrumentality.

It suffices to reconsider the fundamental difference between the network and the axiomatic processes of supportive argumentation to see that nothing is amiss here. As we have seen, the network theorist rejects the whole program of the rigorously linear order of substantiation as a throwback to the Aristotelian theory of unidirectional validation. Abandoning the idea of a linear order of fundamentality, the network theory of validation asks only that everything hang together in a smooth and comprehensive dovetailing. Provided that the cycles are of the sort as to yield inclusiveness and smoothness of mesh, the network theorist views them rather as factors of substantiation than as being in any way vitiating or vicious. And this general position applies with full force in the present case. The mutual support of induction and systematization is rather a mark of adequacy than a defect.[9]

[9] Some of the lines of thought of the present chapter are developed at greater length in the author's *Methodological Pragmatism* (Oxford, 1976).

VIII

The Status of Systematicity

SYNOPSIS

(1) Is systematicity basically *an epistemic desideratum for our knowledge regarding nature* or *an ontologically descriptive feature of nature itself?* (2) The former is maintained, it being held that systematicity is a cognitive ideal whose espousal involves no irreducible ontological prejudgments or presuppositions. And it remains an ultimately *contingent* question whether adequately systematic knowledge of the world can indeed be obtained. (3) In its cognitive bearing, systematicity is a regulative/methodological issue which does not prejudge ontological issues. (4) To be sure, one proviso must be added: the world must clearly be systematic enough – ontologically speaking – to make feasible the attainment of knowledge about it by inquiring beings evolved and operating within it. However, this degree of ontological systematicity is rather a *causal prerequisite* of inquiry than a *rational presupposition* thereof. A validation of the systematizer's venture in the face of the widely current contention that the discovery of answers to our question about the lawful *modus operandi* of nature is inexplicable, vastly improbable, and indeed *miraculous.* (5) Although ontological systematicity is not a *precondition* for cognitive systematicity – save in the minimalistic manner of point (4) – nevertheless cognitive systematicity of a suitable type can serve as an *indicator* of ontological systematicity. (6) The crucial point is that systematicity is a regulative ideal of inquiry – a *methodological* commitment which certainly does not prejudge, let alone preempt, any substantial part of the question of the systematicity of nature on the ontological side. Its legitimation as a *valid* ideal is accordingly teleological – it lies in the methodological efficacy of the pursuit of system in facilitating the efficient realization of the goals of inquiry.

1. COGNITIVE VS. ONTOLOGICAL SYSTEMATICITY

As the opening chapter observed, the conception of a system has historically been applied both to *things* in the world and to *bodies of knowledge*. It is thus important to distinguish between the *ontological* systematicity (simplicity, coherence, regularity, uniformity, etc.) of the *objects* of our knowledge – that is, between systematicity as a feature pertaining to existing things – and the *cognitive* systematicity of our (putative) knowledge or *information* regarding such things. In fact, three significantly distinguishable roles must be assigned to systematicity:

I. COGNITIVE SYSTEMATICITY

1. *Codificational systematicity* – systematicity as a regulative ideal or methodological desideratum for the organization of our knowledge.
2. *Criterial systematicity* – systematicity as a regulative standard for the acceptability of theses – in the wake of the "Hegelian Inversion."

II. NONCOGNITIVE (ONTOLOGICAL) SYSTEMATICITY

3. *Ontological systematicity* – systematicity as a descriptive characteristic of objects – in principle including the whole of the natural universe.

Given these distinctions, there at once arises the question of the relative fundamentality of these several modes of systematicity. Preeminently we must ask: is systematicity at bottom an *epistemic desideratum for our knowledge regarding nature* or an *ontologically descriptive feature of nature itself*?

2. THE RELATIONSHIP OF COGNITIVE AND ONTOLOGICAL SYSTEMATICITY

From the standpoint of coherentism, the parameters of systematicity – simplicity, coherence, regularity, etc. – serve to regulate and control the claims to rational acceptability of our explanatory-descriptive accounts of the world. They represent a check on the validity of our pretentions to knowledge regarding how things work in the world, serving as *regulative principles of inquiry*: instruments for assessing intelligibility and acceptability in the conduct of our cognitive endeavors. If a characterization of the workings of nature were in substantial violation of these regulative desiderata of cognitive systematization, then it would *ipso facto* blazon forth its own inadequacy. One could not rationally rest content with such an account because – by hypothesis – it contravenes what is in fact one of the very characterizing conditions of an *adequate* account. Within the make-up of our knowledge viewed as such – considered as a distinct cognitive structure in its own right – there is no room for chance, absurdity, or the haphazard. But the role of the surd *as an aspect of reality itself* cannot be precluded. The bearing of *cognitive* systematicity is thus seen as *regulative* rather than *descriptive* in orientation, and accordingly, as lacking in substantive and ontological involvements. Nelson Goodman has given incisive formulation to the key point at issue here:

> Obviously enough the tongue, the spelling, the typography, the verbosity of a description reflect no parallel features in the world. Coherence is a characteristic of descriptions, not of the world: the significant question is not whether the world is coherent, but whether our account of it is. And what we call the simplicity of the world is merely the simplicity we are able to achieve in describing it. ("The Way the World Is," in *Problems and Projects* [Indianapolis, 1976], p. 24.)

In the days of the medieval Schoolmen and of those later rationalistic philosophers whom Kant was wont to characterize as dogmatists, simplicity was viewed as an *ontological feature of the world*. Just as it was held that "Nature abhors a vacuum" – and, more plausibly, "In nature there is an explanation for everything" – so it was contended that "Nature abhors complexity." Kant's "Copernican Revolution" shifted the responsibility for such desiderata from *physical nature* to *the human intellect*. Simplicity-tropism accordingly became not a feature of "the real world," but rather one of "the mechanisms of human thought." Kant acutely observed that what was at issue was a facet not of the teleology of *nature*, but of the teleology of *reason*, responsibility for which lay not with the theory but with the theorizers. The subsequent Darwinian Revolution may be viewed as taking the process a step further. It transmuted the teleological element. Neither nature nor man's rational faculties are now seen as an ontological locus of simplicity-preference. Rather, its rationale is now placed on a *strictly methodological* basis. Responsibility for simplicity-tropism lies not with the "hardware" of human reason, but with its "software" – i.e. with the procedural and methodological principles which we ourselves employ because we find simpler theories easier to work with and more effective.

It is not that *nature* avoids complexity, but that *we* do so – insofar as we find it possible.

The parameters of cognitive systematicity – simplicity, regularity, coherence, and the rest – generally represent principles of economy of operation. They are labor-saving devices for the avoidance of complications in the conduct of our cognitive business. They are governed by an analogue of Occam's razor – a principle of parsimony to the effect that needless complexity is to be avoided. Accordingly, cognitive systematicity remains an epistemic factor that is without ontological implications.

It may be tempting to adopt the equation "*The world itself* is systematic [or *simple* or *uniform*, etc.]" as tantamount to "*An adequate account of the world* is systematic [or *simple* or *uniform*, etc.]." For it is natural to expect certain features of *accounts* – such as "significance" – to reflect corresponding aspects of the *materials* they deal with. But this correspondence does not always obtain, and in particular the connecting linkage between cognitive and ontological systematicity must not be drawn too close. A poor intellectual workman can present information regarding even a simple and regular (etc.) configuration of objects in complex, disorganized form; and a clever workman may be able to describe a disorganized chaos in relatively simple and systematic terms. The ontological object-systematicity of what is described and the presentational knowledge-systematicity of the description are in principle quite different things – and largely independent to boot.

The implication

$$\begin{bmatrix} \text{information about} \\ X \text{ is cognitively} \\ \text{systematizable} \end{bmatrix} \longrightarrow (X \text{ is ontologically systematic})$$

thus does not represent a necessary relationship. Ontological systematicity on the part of the objects of knowledge is *not* a requisite for the cognitive systematicity of our knowledge about them. Things need not *be* systematic to admit of systematic study and discussion. The systematicity of the real is not a prerequisite for systematicity in knowledge of it. Knowledge need not share the features of its objects: to speak of a sober study of inebriation or a dispassionate analysis of passions is not a contradiction in terms. What will count as evidence for the ontological systematicity in the world is not simply *that* our account of it is systematic, but rather *how* it is systematic – i.e. what sort of systematic world-picture it envisages. It is a matter not of *structure* but of *content*. (Even a chaos can be described systematically.)

Induction, as we have seen, is the search for order, and our processes of inductive inquiry into nature are geared to reveal orderliness *if it is there*. When fishing, a net whose mesh has a certain area will catch fish of a certain size *if* any are present. Use of the net indicates a *hope*, perhaps even an *expectation* that the fish will be there, but certainly not a preassured *foreknowledge* of their presence. Nothing in the abstract logic of the situation guarantees *a priori* that we shall find order when we go looking for it in the world. (Our cognitive search for order and system may issue in a finding of disorder and chaos.) The question of whether the world is such that systematic knowledge of it is possible is an ultimately *contingent* question – one the answer to which must itself emerge from our actual endeavors at systematization.

Accordingly, one need not prejudge that the world *is* a system to set about the enterprise of striving to know it systematically. The finding of ontological systematicity (orderliness, lawfulness) in nature – to whatever extent that nature *is* systematic – is a substantive product of systematizing inquiry, rather than a needed *input* or *presupposition* for it.

3. THE REGULATIVE/METHODOLOGICAL CHARACTER OF COGNITIVE SYSTEMATICITY

The principles at issue in systematicity – simplicity, regularity, coherence, uniformity, and the rest – thus have the standing of regulative precepts of probative procedure. They implement the idea of epistemic preferability or precedence, of presumption and burden of proof, by indicating where, in the absence of specific counterindications, our epistemic commitments are to be placed in weaving the fabric of our knowledge. Such a procedural/methodological mechanism does not prejudge or preempt any ultimate substantive finding. But it does decisively guide and control the process by which the answer – whatever it may be – is attained.

A regulative presumption of the sort at issue here is basically a *principle of action* – a rule of procedure or of method – rather than an *assumption of fact*. Charles Sanders Peirce wrote:

> Underlying all such principles [of scientific methodology] there is a fundamental and primary . . . hypothesis which we must embrace at the outset, however destitute of evidentiary support it may be [at this stage]. That hypothesis is that the facts in hand admit of rationalization, and rationalization by us. That we must hope they do, for the same reason that a general who has to capture a position or see his country ruined, must go on the hypothesis that there is some way in which he can and shall capture it. We must be animated by that hope concerning the problem we have in hand . . . (*Collected Papers*, vol. VII, 7.219.)

This passage almost gets the matter straight – but not quite. To be sure, we must "act as though" the hypothesis were correct; we must, as was said, effectively deploy it as a regulative presumption that serves us as a *principle of action* in the cognitive domain. But it is not necessary (save perhaps for psychological reasons of morale) for us to *embrace* this hypothesis – we need not assume or postulate it. Initially there need be no actual credence at all, and one can proceed in an experimental spirit, by the provisional adoption of a *mere* hypothesis. (One can assume the stance of the injunction: "*Allez en avant et la foi vous viendra.*") A methodologically motivated *presumption* in favor of ontological systematicity accordingly does not involve us in any vicious or vitiating circularity.

It is a regulative or action-guiding *presumption* and not a constitutive or world-descriptive *principle* that is at issue – in the first instance at any rate.[1] We are to *proceed as though* nature in fact exhibited those modes

---

[1] In another passage, Peirce seems to me to have come much closer to getting the matter right, by holding that the principles such as those of the uniformity or systematicity of nature represent not so much a substantive *claim* as an action-guiding *insinuation*:

> Now you know how a malicious person who wishes to say something ill of another, prefers *insinuation*; that is, he speaks so vaguely that he suggests a great deal while he expressly says nothing at all. In this way he avoids being confronted by fact. It is the same with these principles of scientific inference. . . . They rather insinuate a uniformity than state it. And as insinuation always expresses the state of feeling of the person who uses it rather than anything in its object, so we may suppose these principles express rather the scientific attitude than a scientific result. (*Collected Papers*, vol. VII, sect. 7.132.)

of systematicity needed for systematizing inquiry to bear fruit. Its confirmation as in requisite degree present a matter of descriptive fact at the *substantive* level is something that must come later on, at the end rather than at the outset of inquiry.

4. ONTOLOGICAL SYSTEMATICITY AS A CAUSAL PRECONDITION OF INQUIRY

As we have seen, systematicity is a cognitive ideal and regulator whose espousal involves no ontological prejudgments or presuppositions. But one significant qualification of this otherwise accurate thesis is in order.

Ontological systematicity relates to the orderliness and to the lawfulness of nature – to its conformity to *rules* of various sorts. Now if nature were not rulish in exhibiting manifold regularities – if it were pervasively "unruly" (say because its laws changed about rapidly and randomly) – then anything approaching a scientific study of the world would clearly be impossible. The modes of rulishness at issue in the various parameters of systematicity (simplicity, regularity, coherence, uniformity, consistency, and the rest) are all related to aspects of the workings of nature that underwrite the possibility of scientific inquiry. If science is to be possible at all – if our empirical inquiry into the world is to yield any returns – then it must be the case that the world is sufficiently systematic (orderly, regular) to permit the orderly conduct of rational inquiry, and thus, *a fortiori*, the existence of intelligent beings capable of it.

If the world were not orderly (both in itself and as concerns the *modus operandi* of inquiring creatures), then there would be no uniformity in information-gathering, information-storage, etc., and consequently there would be no avenue to the acquisition of knowledge of the world – or indeed even putative knowledge of it. If the attainment – nay even the pursuit – of knowledge is to be possible for us, the world must be at any rate sufficiently orderly to permit of our cognitive functioning. This rulishness is basic to the very possibility of natural science. The aims of science – the description, explanation, prediction, and control of nature – would clearly be altogether unrealizable in a world that is sufficiently badly asystematic. A significant degree of ontological systematicity IN the world is (obviously) a causal requisite for the realization of codificational systematicity in our knowledge OF the world. Thus while the ontological systematicity of the world is not a *conceptual presupposition* for the success of systematizing inquiry, it is nevertheless – at least in some degree – a *causal precondition* for this success.

To be sure, the pivotal question at this juncture is not the ontologically oriented question: "Why *are* there laws of nature?" but the importantly different question: "Why are we able to *discover* laws of nature; that is, how is it that the laws of nature are sufficiently simple that we mere humans – limited and imperfect cognizers that we are – can discover these laws?" This question clearly poses an issue that is crucial for legitimating systematicity – with its pursuit of regularity, simplicity, and the like – as a regulative principle of inquiry. For to this end we must ensure that there is a *rational* basis for our hope that the systematizing venture – based on these parameters – has good prospects of meeting with success.

We must recognize that an impressive body of opinion among current scientists and philosophers approaches this issue with counsels of despair. Erwin Schrödinger, for one, says it is "a miracle that may well be beyond human understanding that we men can discover lawful regularities within the multifarious events of a complex world."[2] Karl Popper sees the success of science as something fortuitous, accidental, literally *miraculous*, and totally unintelligible: "However, even on the assumption (which I share) that our quest for knowledge has been very successful so far, and that we now know something of our universe, this success ·becomes miraculously improbable, and therefore inexplicable. . . ."[3] And he goes on to insist that "no theory of knowledge should attempt to explain why we are successful in our attempts to explain things."[4] Again, E. P. Wigner joins Schrödinger in the view that: "It is a miracle that in spite of the baffling complexity of the world, certain regularities in the events could be discovered," and goes on to maintain that "it is not at all natural that 'laws of nature' exist, much less that man is able to discover them."[5]

However, there is good reason to dismiss all this sort of thing as quite improper and unnecessary mystery-mongering. For man's capacity to discover the laws of nature has a perfectly natural and straightforward evolutionary explanation. There is a good rational basis to support our

[2] Erwin Schrödinger, *What is Life* (Cambridge, 1945), p. 31.
[3] Karl Popper, *Objective Knowledge* (Oxford, 1972), p. 28; cf. p. 204.
[4] *Ibid.*, p. 23.
[5] Eugene P. Wigner, "The Unreasonable Effectiveness of Mathematics in the Natural Sciences," *Communications on Pure and Applied Mathematics* (vol. 13 [1960], pp. 1–14), pp. 4–5.

hope of finding natural laws to answer our questions about the *modus operandi* of nature.

From one point of view it is not particularly surprising that men should succeed in acquiring knowledge. This is something only natural and to be expected because *if we did not succeed in this cognitive venture we wouldn't be here.* The rationale for this is fundamentally Darwinian: rational guidance is necessary for successful action; successful action is crucial for the survival of creatures constituted as we are; accordingly, our survival is indicative of cognitive competence.

This important fact was already clearly perceived by C. S. Peirce around a century ago. Peirce saw man's evolutionary adaptation as an evolutionary product which endows his mind with a kind of functional sympathy for the processes of nature:

> [M]an's mind has a natural adaptation to imagining correct theories of some kinds, and in particular to (sic.) correct theories about forces, without some glimmer of which he could not form social ties and consequently could not reproduce his kind. In short, the instincts conducive to assimilation of food, and the instincts conducive to reproduction, must have involved from the beginning certain tendencies to think truly about physics, on the one hand, and about psychics, on the other. It is somehow more than a mere figure of speech to say that nature fecundates the mind of man with ideas which, when those ideas grow up, will resemble their father, Nature. (CP, 5.591 [1903].)

For Peirce the validation of man's scientific talent lies in evolution. Under the pressure of evolutionary forces, mind of man has come to be "co-natured" with physical reality.[6] Peirce's argument is clearly on the right track. Man has evolved in nature as a creature who tries to make his way in the world by his wits. It is no more a miracle that the human mind can understand the world than that the human eye can see it.

Cognitive evolution is doubtless no different from all evolution in consisting of a long series of improbable accidents. But this does not make them any more inexplicable than any other improbable developments *in rebus naturae*.[7] (The fact that one could not have

---

[6] For a fuller exposition of Peirce's views, see the author's *Peirce's Philosophy of Science* (Notre Dame, 1978).

[7] Consider the analogy of quantum phenomena like radioactive decay of atom of a heavy element. Here the fact that one cannot predict does not mean one cannot *explain* the phenomena at issue.

predicted them does not mean that one cannot explain them with the wisdom of *ex post facto* hindsight.) There is no mystery or unintelligibility.

The key point is that there is a perfectly good explanation – to wit, an *evolutionary* explanation – of our success of discovering laws (and systematizing factual knowledge in general). And this explanation is clearly such that the past successes at issue augur good future prospects. All the indications are that the structure of this explanation affords an adequate basis of supportive warrant for the ongoing pursuit of systematicity as a regulative ideal.

To be sure, a world that admits of knowledge-acquisition need not be a *total* system, *partial* systematicity will do – merely enough to permit orderly inquiry in our cosmic neighborhood by beings constituted as we are. For example, various thinkers (from Plato in the *Timaeus* to Herbert Spencer and C. S. Peirce) have seen the ontological systematicity of nature in evolutionary terms as a developmental process that is as yet largely incomplete. Such a view would be quite compatible with a construction of ontological systematicity as a causal prerequisite of an inquiry.

This perspective makes manifest the duality of ontological systematicity as both an ontological precondition for the conduct of scientific inquiry and also a substantive product thereof, so that its regulative presumption comes to be retrovalidated by the products of the inquiry process. Cognitive systematicity emerges as a regulative ideal governing the conduct of inquiry – an ideal whose adoption is appropriate because its pursuit enables us to realize more effectively the fundamental aims and purposes of the cognitive enterprise with respect to understanding (description and explanation), prediction, and control over nature.

5. COGNITIVE SYSTEMATICITY AS AN INDICATOR OF ONTOLOGICAL SYSTEMATICITY

Suppose, for the moment, that our most carefully drawn picture of the world ultimately manifests imperfect systematicity. Should this happen, would the ground be one of epistemology or one of ontology? If our best efforts to endow our knowledge of the world with a high degree of systematic unity and coherence prove unavailing, should this be seen as due to deficiencies on *our* part as inquirers (we simply do not probe deeply enough or think with enough subtlety and comprehensiveness), or is it to be construed as meaning that *the world itself* fails to be sufficiently systematic?

The former, strictly epistemological grounding can never be ruled out finally and decisively: in theory it is always a real prospect that the responsibility for an imperfect systematicity in our picture of reality actually lies – in the final analysis – with us inquirers rather than with the object of inquiry. Nevertheless, it is certainly *possible* that the responsibility is ontologically rooted in nature itself – and it might in fact be plausible, in suitable circumstances, to suppose that this is indeed so.

While its converse fails, as we have seen, the implication

$$(X \text{ is ontologically systematic}) \longrightarrow \left[\begin{array}{l} \text{information about } X \\ \text{is in principle} \\ \text{cognitively systematizable} \end{array} \right]$$

is nevertheless a necessary one. Ontological systematicity is in fact a sufficient condition for cognitive *systematizability*. For clearly such implications as the following will hold.

If no simple *account* of a thing is in principle realizable, then it cannot itself be simple, ontologically speaking.

If no coherent *explanation* of a process is in principle realizable, then it cannot itself be coherent, ontologically speaking.

If no uniform *description* of a thing is in principle realizable, then it cannot itself be uniform, ontologically speaking.

The parameters of systematicity are accordingly such that the following basic principle holds:

If a thing *is* itself ontologically simple (uniform, coherent, etc.), then a simple (uniform, coherent, etc.) *account* of it must in principle be possible (however difficult we may find its realization in practice).

We have seen that cognitive systematicity cannot serve as *deductive* evidence for ontological systematicity. But the present relationship indicates that cognitive systematicity provides an *inductive* indication of ontological systematicity.[8] In fact, cognitive systematicity of a suitable kind affords the *best* – perhaps the *only* – empirical evidence we can ever actually obtain on behalf of ontological systematicity; the former constitutes the best available criterion or evidential indicator of the latter.

To be sure, a further objection might well be propounded at this stage:

> Might there not be a theory which, qua theory, is extremely complex, but according to which the *modus operandi* of nature itself is extremely simple?

Notwithstanding its surface plausibility, this objection rests on a mistake. Man is a part of nature. The efforts of his mind form part of the processes of nature. If our intellectual dealings are not simple (or regular or – generally – systematic), then nature itself does not allow this character either. For nature cannot be simple (etc.) if our mental processes are not, seeing that we ourselves are a *part* of nature. If cognitive systematicity (or regularity or simplicity, etc.) proves to be ultimately unattainable, then ontological systematicity (etc.) will be unrealizable as well.

Cognitive and ontological systematicity must thus be seen as symbiotically interrelated. Ontological systematicity – in some adequate degree – is fundamental in the *causal* order: it is a causal requisite for any prospect of the attainment of systematized knowledge. On the other hand, cognitive systematicity is fundamental in the *epistemological* or *conceptual* order. And such conceptual systematicity affords the prime – perhaps the sole – entryway through which evidence of ontological systematicity can be secured.

6. THE LEGITIMATION OF TAKING SYSTEMATICITY AS A REGULATIVE IDEAL OF INQUIRY

Systematicity – in the cognitive sphere – is a regulative ideal of inquiry, correlative with the procedural injunction "So organize your knowledge

---

[8] We thus take the stance – standard of the theory of plausible reasoning – that when "If X then Y" obtains, then Y will (in suitable circumstances) serve as an inductive indicator of X. Cf. the author's *Plausible Reasoning* (Amsterdam, 1976).

as to impart to it as much systematic structure as you possible can!"
But does not the prospect that its objective may well be unattainable
destroy the validity of this ideal? Surely not. The validation of this
cognitive ideal does *not* lie in the fact that its realization can be
guaranteed *a priori* from the outset. We may in fact never realize this
ideal. But this possibility should never be allowed to impede our efforts
to press the project of systematization as far as we possibly can. Here,
as elsewhere, the validity of an ideal does not call for any prior
guarantee of its ultimate realization. (What ideal is ever validated in this
way?) To be sure, a hope of its eventual realization can never in
principle be finally and totally demolished. But this feeble comfort is
hardly sufficient to establish its propriety. The long and short of it is that
while we have no *a priori* assurance of ultimate success in the quest for
systematicity, a standing presumption in favor of this key cognitive ideal
is nevertheless rationally legitimate because of its furtherance of the
inherent aims and objectives of the cognitive enterprise.

The validation of systematicity as a cognitive ideal lies in the more
practical consideration of its proven utility. A very general point at issue
here: The legitimation of anything whose status is instrumental or
methodological hinges decisively on *teleological* considerations. As
with any methodological instrumentality, the validity of an ideal
accordingly lies in its purposive efficacy – its capacity to facilitate the
realization of the aims and purposes that determine the objectives of its
correlative enterprise. We are thus led back to the issue of the legitimation of the commitment to systematization as facilitating the pursuit and
promoting the attainment of the goals of cognition: understanding,
prediction, and control over nature. The justification of systematicity as
a regulative ideal in the pursuit of our cognitive affairs must thus be seen
in essentially instrumental terms. "Design your cognitive procedures
with a view to the pursuit of systematicity!" is a regulative principle of
inquiry whose legitimation ultimately lies in its being pragmatically
retrovalidated by its capacity to guide inquiry into successful channels.

It merits reemphasis that this essentially *methodological* legitimation
of the pursuit of systematicity on the *cognitive* side involves no
substantial prejudgment of the substantive question of the systematicity
of nature on the *ontological* side. Cognitive systematicity characterizes
the procedural structure of our endeavors to *organize* our knowledge of
the world. It embodies methodological or regulative principles of
plausibility and presumption – principles in the sense of rules governing

how we are to proceed in the conduct of our cognitive affairs, and not (at any rate in the first instance) principles in the sense of theses describing how things work in the world. Acknowledgment of the importance of systematicity as a cognitive desideratum must *not* be construed as preempting the issue of the ontological systematicity of nature.

IX

Limits to Cognitive Systematization – I

Issues of Erotetic Completeness

SYNOPSIS

(1) What factors might render it impossible to systematize our factual knowledge about the world? There are three prime possibilities here: *incompletability, inconsequence*, and *inconsistency*. The present chapter will deal with the first of these only. (2) A closer look at the idea of the "state of knowledge" at a particular stage of scientific development and an examination of some conceptions regarding "completion" and "completeness" in the context of cognitive history. A critique of the geographical exploration model. (3) An examination of some aspects of the historical availability of questions in empirical inquiry. (4) The dynamics of questions gives a different and characteristic dimension to the idea of cognitive progress. (5) A survey of various interpretations of the idea of the question–answering *completeness* of a body of knowledge, leading to (6) A consideration of cognitive limits and the idea of unanswerable questions. (7) Examination of the traditional paradigm example of an "ultimate" question: *Why is there anything at all?* A critique of the contention that such questions represent *insolubilia*. (8) The completability of science is presumably not realizable in the sense of the attainment of a "complete and final state" of knowledge-ossification. And its completability in the erotetic sense of "all questions answered" is also presumably unattainable. The pursuit of completeness nevertheless remains legitimate and proper in its role as a regulative ideal.

1. NONSYSTEMATIZABILITY

This chapter will begin an examination of the key issue of what – if anything – could decisively block the attempt to endow our factual knowledge with systematic unity. Its focus is the problem: What factors might render it impossible to achieve an adequate systematization of our knowledge about the world?

Let us start with the question: How could it actually come about that a body of knowledge is *not* smoothly systematizable? In general terms, the answer is simply that one or more of the essential elements of systematicity cannot be realized. The three prime possibilities here are *incompletability, inconsequence* (disconnectedness), and *inconsistency* (incoherence). The present chapter will deal with only the first of these, and its successors with the rest.

2. KNOWLEDGE AND ITS DYNAMICS: A CRITIQUE OF THE GEOGRAPHIC
   EXPLORATION MODEL

The incompleteness of knowledge is a familiar conception, but nevertheless it deserves closer scrutiny. A body of knowledge is *incomplete* when it is defective in point of comprehensiveness, self-sufficiency, and scope. In such a case, the body will have gaps, omissions, or such-like deficiencies in the inclusiveness of its overall "coverage." The whole is then lacking in mutual support – like a broken statue with missing pieces. Some parts of it will demand the operation of elements that are simply lacking, there is a collective inadequacy to the common task.

To probe more deeply into the workings of this idea of cognitive completeness in the context of our factual knowledge of the world it is useful to introduce some formal machinery, as follows:

K'_t : the set of theses (propositions, contentions, claims) explicitly endorsed as warranted (correct, acceptable, true) according to the systematization of scientific information actually accepted (i.e., *generally* accepted) at the time t.

Thus K'_t is simply the "state of 'knowledge' (i.e. *putative* knowledge) at *t*," comprising the broad consensus of the scientific community of the day.

This family of actually endorsed theses can be amplified so as to embrace also its various inferential consequences, which may or may not be explicitly recognized and overtly admitted:

K_t'' : the set of theses that are "consequences" of K_t' (in some appropriate sense of the term). This is the totality of implicit (potential) "knowledge" (i.e. *putative* knowledge) at the time *t*.

Note that while the *actually* espoused theses of K_t' must always, in the very nature of the thing, be finite in number, this limitation is removed with the transition to K_t''.

For abbreviative convenience we shall use K to indicate indifference as between K' and K'', as long as the filling-in is done *uniformly* throughout a given thesis.

The ambiguity of $p \notin K_t$ should be noted. This could mean either (1) at *t* people simply don't yet know about *p*, their ignorance is such that the whole question of *p vs.* not-*p* has not yet occurred to them, or (2) at *t* people do indeed ask the *p vs.* not-*p* question, but are simply unable to settle it: they simply do not know whether *p* or not-*p*, or (3) *p* is actually blocked from K_t because $\sim p \in K_t$, that is, because its contradictory is in fact known: the question of *p vs.* not-*p* is a live issue, and has been resolved in favor of not-*p*.

Since it is *putative* or *purported* "knowledge" that is at issue – knowledge as it is claimed by imperfect men, and not the capital-K Knowledge set down in the book of some infallible recording angel – we shall *not* have a

Law of the Conservation of Knowledge

What is once "known" always remains "known":

$$(\forall t)(\forall t')(\forall p)([t < t' \ \& \ p \in K_t] \supset p \in K_{t'})$$

Such a "law" fails for two reasons: (1) "knowledge" can be forgotten, as in fact much of Greek astronomy was lost in the "Dark Ages"; and (2) "knowledge" can be abandoned: the scientific community may no longer accept a once accepted thesis, and indeed such a thesis may even be replaced by its contradictory (as much of Galenic medicine is actually inconsistent with modern medicine). The progress of science not only exhibits *additions* but *subtractions* as well.

Our "knowledge" is not cumulative: the body of "accepted scientific fact" can be a matter not merely of augmentation but also of outright replacement.

The ramifications of the idea of this theme of knowledge-stabilization are worth exploring at greater length.

One acute contemporary analyst of physics moots the prospect of its ultimate completion in the following terms:

> It is possible to think of fundamental physics as eventually becoming complete. There is only one universe to investigate, and physics, unlike mathematics, cannot be indefinitely spun out purely by inventions of the mind. The logical relation of physics to chemistry and the other sciences it underlies is such that physics should be the first chapter to be completed. No one can say exactly what completed should mean in that context, which may be sufficient evidence that the end is at least not imminent. But some sequence such as the following might be vaguely imagined: The nature of the elementary particles becomes known in self-evident totality, turning out by its very structure to preclude the existence of hidden features. Meanwhile, gravitation becomes well understood and its relation to the stronger forces elucidated. No mysteries remain in the hierarchy of forces, which stands revealed as the different aspects of one logically consistent pattern. In that imagined ideal state of knowledge, no conceivable experiment could give a surprising result. At least no experiment could that tested only fundamental physical laws. Some unsolved problems might remain in the domain earlier characterized as organized complexity, but these would become the responsibility of the biophysicist or the astrophysicist. Basic physics would be complete; not only that, it would be manifestly complete, rather like the present state of Euclidean geometry.[1]

Extended from physics to natural science in general, such a position views the realm of potential discovery as one of ultimately limited proportions.

A position of just this sort was maintained by the great American philosopher Charles Sanders Peirce (1839–1914). Peirce, in effect, saw the history of science as progressing through two stages: an initial or preliminary phase of groping for the general structure of the *qualitative*

[1] D. A. Bromley, et al., *Physics in Perspective: Student Edition* (Washington, D.C., 1976; National Research Council/National Academy of Sciences Publication), p. 26.

relations among scientific parameters, and a secondary phase of *quantitative* refinement – of filling in with increasing precision the exact values of parameters that figure in equations whose general configuration is determined in the initial phase. Once the first phase has been gotten over with – as Peirce believed to be the case in his own day, at any rate with regard to the physical sciences – ongoing scientific progress is just a matter of increasing detail and exactness, of determining the ever more minute decimal-place values of quantities whose approximate value is already well-established.[2]

We have here a metaphysical view of cognitive evolution according to which science will finally reach a condition of ultimate cumulativity – that science is evolving along a winding and circuitous route into a condition of eventual stability in point of thesis-retention:

Law of the Ultimate Conservation of Knowledge
$$(\exists t)(\forall t')(\forall p)([t' > t \,\&\, p \in K_t] \supset p \in K_{t'})$$

On such a view, science will ultimately reach – or at any rate asymptotically approximate – such a conservationist state in which whatever is "known" will always remain "known," so that everything then "known" always remains "known" thereafter.

A very different but related idea is that of knowledge-completion (at *t*). This envisages a circumstance where everything ever "known" is then "known":

Law of the Completion of Knowledge (at *t*)
$$(\forall t')(\forall p)([t' > t \,\&\, p \in K_{t'}] \supset p \in K_t)$$

The combination of these two may be characterized as knowledge-*ossification*. Its definitive principle may be formulated as follows:

$$(\exists t)(\forall t')(\forall p)(t' > t \supset [p \in K_t \equiv p \in K_{t'}])$$

This principle envisages the eventual arrival of a condition of cognitive stability: the evolution of science towards a totally fixed and unchanging cognitive posture. Such a theory envisages a completion of the scientific enterprise, at any rate as far as really important findings

---

[2] The background of Peirce's position will be described more fully in the next chapter. See also the author's *Peirce's Philosophy of Science* (Notre Dame, 1978).

are concerned. It sees the development of science on analogy with the course of terrestrial exploration after the Middle Ages – the ongoing exhaustion of an essentially finite domain. The plausible-seeming analogy of geographic exploration, though often invoked in this context, is nevertheless fundamentally mistaken. It views scientific progress as a whole on the basis of one particular (and by no means typical) *sort* of progress, namely the sequential filling-in of an established framework with greater and greater detail – the working out of more decimal places to lend additional refinement to a fundamentally fixed result. This view encompasses the erroneous idea that the progress of science proceeds by way of *cumulative accretion* (like the growth of a coral reef). But science – as we have already noted – progresses not just *additively* but in large measure also *subtractively*.

Theorists of scientific method of an older school were deeply committed to the view that science is cumulative, and indeed tended to regard the progressiveness of science in terms of its cumulativity.[3] But in recent decades this view has come under increasingly sharp attack – and rightly so. As Thomas Kuhn and others have persuasively argued, today's most significant discoveries always represent an *overthrow* of yesterday's: the big findings of science inevitably take a form that *contradicts* its earlier big findings and involve not just supplementation but replacement on the basis of conceptual and theoretical innovation. It will not serve to take the preservationist stance that the old views were acceptable as far as they went and merely need supplementation. The medicine of Pasteur and Lister does not add to that of Galen or of Paracelsus, but *replaces* them. The creative scientist is every bit as much of a demolition expert as a master builder. Significant scientific progress is generally a matter not of adding further facts – on the order of filling in a crossword puzzle – but of changing the framework itself. Science in the main develops not by addition but by way of substitution and replacement.[4] (Its *progress* lies not in a monotonic accretion of more

---

[3] See, for example, George Sarton, *The Study of the History of Science* (Cambridge, Mass., 1936), esp. p. 5 and *History of Science and the New Humanism* (Cambridge, Mass., 1937), esp. pp. 10–11.

[4] This shibboleth of the contemporary philosophy of science is not all that new. Already at the turn of the century, Sir Michael Foster wrote:

The path [of progress in science] may not be always a straight line; there may be swerving to this side and to that; ideas may seem to return again and again to the same point of the intellectual compass; but it will always be found that they have reached a higher level – they have moved, not in a circle, but in a spiral. Moreover, science is not fashioned as is a house, by

information, but in superior performance in point of prediction and control over nature.[5])

The doctrine of convergent cumulation must, accordingly, be abandoned.

But a very important point looms up at this stage. Even if science were in fact ultimately "completed" by way of the eventual stabilization envisaged by Peirce, this sort of "completion" may still leave the issue of *completeness* in a very unsatisfactory condition. This becomes clear once we must turn from scientific *theses or answers* to consider also scientific *problems or questions*.

3. QUESTIONS AND THEIR AVAILABILITY

Epistemic change over the course of time relates not only to what is "known" but also to what is *asked*.

Some notational machinery will help in setting out the relevant issues:

> Q_t' : the set of scientific questions or problems actually (but appropriately!) posed on the basis of the "state of knowledge" at t; that is, all those (sensible) questions currently raised with reference to the then-extant systematization of scientific information.

Thus Q_t' is the problem-field as actually formulated at t, comprising all the questions explicitly contemplated by the scientific community of the day. It represents the "state of questioning" of the day.

This family of *actually* posed questions can be broadened to embrace the entire stock of questions *in principle available* at t.

---

putting brick to brick, that which is once put remaining as it was put to the end. The growth of science is that of a living being. As in the embryo, phase follows phase, and each member or body puts on in succession different appearances, though all the while the same member, so a scientific conception of one age seems to differ from that of a following age. . . . ("The Growth of Science in the Nineteenth Century," *Annual Report of the Smithsonian Institution For 1899* [Washington, 1901], pp. 163–183 [as reprinted from Foster's 1899 presidential address to the British Association for the Advancement of Science]; see p. 175.)

[5] A detailed exposition and defense of this view of cognitive progress is given in the author's *Methodological Pragmatism* (Oxford, 1976).

Q''_t: the set of questions that can appropriately be asked on the basis of what is "known" (or "knowable") at the time t; viz., K'_t or K''_t, respectively. (We need not for present purposes resolve this choice.)

Again, we shall drop the primes and speak equivocally of Q_t when this can be done without creating problems. And we shall let a, a', etc., represent questions.

All questions have presuppositions.[6] And thus Q_t can be construed as the set of all questions that have only the theses of K_t (viz., K'_t or alternatively K''_t) as their presuppositions. Accordingly, we have it that, specifically, Q''_t is the set of all questions that can be asked on the basis of K''_t – the questions whose presuppositions are all available from K'_t:

$$Q''_t = \{ a : (\forall p)(a \ni p \supset p \in K'_t) \}$$

Here "$a \ni p$" represents: "The question a presupposes that p." (This is intended in the sense in which "Does John still beat his wife" presupposes (1) that John has a wife, and (2) that John used to beat her.[7]) Different ranges of assertion will underwrite different sets of questions precisely because they provide different sets of background presupposition that p is the case is met, but not with respect to S_2 where while S_2 includes not-p, then we can ask the rationale-demanding question "Why is it that p is the case?" with respect to S_1, where the presupposition that p is the case is met, but not with respect to S_2 where this presupposition fails.

The idea of question-propagation is important and well worth consideration. The answering of a question can serve to provide the presupposition for yet another question – one which would not have arisen had the former question not been answered. Questions have a dynamic of their own. One question gives rise to another (in a certain historic context) if its answer (in that context) is a requisite presupposition of the other.

Questions should thus be regarded as entities that exist in an *historical* context: They arise at some junctures and not at others. A

---

[6] R. G. Collingwood, *An Essay on Metaphysics* (Oxford, 1940), chp. V, "On Presupposing."

[7] Note that there can be *incompatible* questions – questions based on mutually incompatible presuppositions.

question *arises* (i.e. can meaningfully be posed) at t iff all its presuppositions are then-known. Accordingly, questions can come into being and pass away. Specifically:

a originates at t iff a arises at t and a does not arise at any time prior to t.

Consider the following putative principle:

Law of the Conservation of Questions
$(\forall a)(\forall t)(\forall t')([t < t' \& a \in Q_t] \supset a \in Q_{t'})$

Note that the failure of the Law of the Conservation of Knowledge also ensures the failure of this law. For a presupposition of a that is satisfied at t by K_t may fail to be satisfied at t' by $K_{t'}$. Not only is it possible for answers to questions to be forgotten, but the scientific community may well come to reject the presupposition of a question altogether. In the course of scientific progress questions may not only be *solved* but also *dissolved*. We no longer ask about the properties of "caloric" fluid or about the behavior of phlogiston.

The idea of questions that cannot be answered needs closer scrutiny. To begin with, it deserves note that some questions are not just *unanswerable*, but actually *unaskable* because – in the given state of knowledge – they cannot even be posed. Caesar could not have wondered whether plutonium is radioactive. It is not just that he did not know what the correct answer to the question happens to be – the very question not only *did* not, but actually *could* not have occurred to him, because he lacked the conceptual instruments with which alone this question can be posed. Cases of this sort are typical in the history of science. In the main, today's scientific problems could not even have arisen a generation or two ago: they could not have been formulated within the cognitive framework of the then-existing state of knowledge. Their presuppositions were cognitively unavailable.

Ignorance (i.e. the lack of knowledge) will accordingly be of two very different types. It prevails at a surface level when we can grasp a question but lack – under the circumstances – any means of giving an answer to it. (Think of the status of claims about mountains on the far side of the moon made in 1850.) Ignorance prevails at a more fundamental level when we could not even pose the question – and indeed could not even *understand* an answer should one be vouchsafed us by a benevolent oracle.

The thesis that there are unanswerable scientific questions must be clarified in the light of this distinction between unaskable *vs.* merely unanswerable questions. For this thesis can be understood in two very distinct senses:

(I) *Sense A*: There are potential scientific questions that will never be answered because we will forever remain in a position of *fundamental ignorance* with regard to them. We do – and always shall – lack the means of probing nature at a level of comprehensiveness and/or detail *needed even to develop the operative concepts of the question* itself. Not just the answer but the very question lies beyond our grasp.

(II) *Sense B*: There are some scientific questions that will never be answered because we will forever remain in a position of *effective ignorance* with regard to them. While these questions can – or will – indeed be asked (since the means of their formulation are or will come to hand), yet they will never be resolved – presumably for essentially practical reasons relating to the techniques required for their resolution.

This second sense envisages an essentially economic limitation. The means of probing nature at the requisite level of comprehensiveness and/or detail needed to answer the question lie beyond our grasp.

The first conception is the more troublesome, because one cannot as a matter of principle exhibit any such fundamentally inaccessible questions. But their reality is rather easily envisioned on the basis of past experience. The fact that some *current* ideas were unrealizable at *all earlier* historic stages[8] is readily generalized to the more drastic conception that some ideas may be unrealizable at *all* historic stages.

---

[8] The 19th-century English scientist George Gore offers some illustrations:

> That which is inconceivable by one man, or in one age, is not necessarily so by another man, or in another period. . . . Ideas which at one period are beyond reason, do in many cases, by the progress of knowledge, come within its domain. . . . Some discoveries which are unattainable in one age or state of knowledge become attainable in another; for instance, the laws of electro-magnetism or of electro-chemical action could not have been discovered in an age when electro-currents were unknown, nor could the principle of conservation of matter and of energy have been arrived at when science was in its infancy. (George Gore, *The Art of Scientific Discovery* [London, 1878], pp. 19–20.)

4. COGNITIVE PROGRESS AND THE DYNAMICS OF QUESTIONS

Cognitive progress is commonly thought of in terms of discovery of new facts (new theses). But the real-life situation is more complicated.

Progress on the side of questions is a crucial mode of cognitive progress, correlative with – and every bit as important as – progress on the side of information. The questions opened up for our consideration are as crucial and definitive a facet of a cognitive system as are the theses which it endorses. Information is developed in the context of questions. And the new facts (theses) we discover can bear very differently on the matter of questions. Specifically, we can discover:

(1) New (i.e. *different*) answers to old questions.
(2) New questions.
(3) The impropriety or illegitimacy of our old questions, in that they were based on erroneous presuppositions – i.e. once-purported "facts" which are no longer viewed as tenable.

With (1) we discover that the wrong answer has been given to an old question: we uncover an error in our previous question-answering endeavors. With (2) we discover that there are certain questions which have not been posed at all: we uncover an "error of omission" in the context of our former question-asking endeavors. Finally, with (3) we find that one has asked the wrong question altogether: we uncover an "error of commission" in the context of our former question-asking endeavors. Such improper questions rest on incorrect presuppositions (and are thus generally bound up with type (1) discoveries). Three rather different sorts of cognitive progress are involved here – different from one another and from the traditional view of cognitive progress in terms simply of "an accumulation of further facts."

This line of thought suggests the following:

Principle of Question Propagation (Kant's Principle)
The solution of any scientific question gives rise to yet further unsolved questions.

This phenomenon of the ever-continuing "birth" of new questions might be designated as the "Kant Proliferation Effect," after Immanuel Kant who described it in the following terms of a continually evolving cycle of questions and answers:

> Who can satisfy himself with mere empirical knowledge in all the cosmological questions of the duration and of the magnitude of the world, of freedom or of natural necessity, since *every answer given on principles of experience begets a fresh question, which likewise requires its answer* and thereby clearly shows the insufficiency of all physical modes of explanation to satisfy reason.[9]

The italicized passage indicates an aspect of the phenomenon of scientific inquiry which is empirically as well established as any in our study of nature itself: the operation of a conservation-law for scientific problems.

This principle indicates a fact of considerable importance for the theory of scientific progress. One need not claim longevity – let alone immortality – for any of the *current* problems to assure that there will be problems ten or one hundred generations hence. (As immortal individuals are not needed to assure the immortality of the race, so immortal problems are not needed to assure the immortality of problems.) It suffices for the prospect of endless scientific progress to rely on the operation of Kant's principle to the effect that old problems when solved or dissolved give birth to others – no recourse to *Welträtsel* or *insolubilia* need be made. Moreover, even a theory which holds that there indeed *are* such insolubilia need not regard them as being *identifiable* at any given stage of scientific development – we may never even get as far as their recognition because they may well prove to be inaccessible to scientific inquiry at any given *actually realizable* state. It is thus by no means necessary for a theory of endless scientific progress – one which envisages an inexhaustible pool of scientific problems – to accept the idea that there are insolubilia identifiable as such *at this stage of the game.*

The thesis of endless scientific progress is thus perfectly compatible

---

[9] Immanuel Kant, *Prolegomena to any Future Metaphysics* (1783), sect. 57. Compare the following passage from the British chemist George Gore (1826–1909):

> New knowledge is not like a cistern, soon emptied, but is a fountain of almost unlimited power and duration. . . . The area of scientific discovery enlarges rapidly as we advance; *every scientific truth now known yields many questions yet to be answered.* To some of these questions it is possible to obtain answers at the present time, others may only be decided when other parts of science are more developed. (*The Art of Scientific Discovery* [London, 1878], p. 27.)

with the view that *every* question that can be asked at *every* stage is going to be answered at some future stage: it does not commit one to the idea that there are any unanswerable questions placed altogether beyond the limits of possible resolution. It suffices that in the course of answering old questions we constantly come to pose new ones as per Kant's Principle.

5. COGNITIVE COMPLETENESS: QUESTION-ANSWERING (OR "EROTETIC") COMPLETENESS

The conception of question-and-answer gives rise to a characteristic sense of "completeness" for cognitive systems. It will be useful to adopt the notation A^*pa for the thesis "p is a correct answer to the question a." And we shall need to temporalize this conception to its relativized cousin:

$$A_t pa \text{ for } p \in K_t \, \& \, A^*pa \in K_t$$

where K_t again represents the body of (putative) knowledge accepted at t. Thus $A_t pa$ represents "p is offered as an appropriate answer to the question a within the state of knowledge prevailing at t." And here the qualification "appropriate" does not necessarily mean *true per se*, but rather *true according to the best available standards of the day*. (Recall the dictum *ultra posse nemo obligatur*.)

Now the idea of cognitive completeness can also be construed in line with the formula that "every question is answered." We may thus say that the "state of science" at the time t has achieved a condition of Q-completeness (question-answering or "erotetic" completeness) if the following condition obtains,

$$(\forall a)(a \in Q_t \supset (\exists p) A_t pa)$$

or equivalently:

$$(\forall a)(a \in Q_t \supset (\exists p) [p \in K_t \, \& \, A^*pa \in K_t]).$$

Given the equivocation implicit in Q and in K, we see that the idea of the Q-completeness of a state of knowledge (i.e. the state of knowledge obtaining at a given time) can be construed in four combinatorially available ways:

(i) *Perceived Q-Completeness*
Every then-asked question has a then-given answer:
$$(\forall a)\,(a \in Q_t' \supset (\exists p)\,[p \in K_t' \;\&\; A^*pa \in K_t'\,])$$

(ii) *Weak Q-Completeness*
Every then-asked question has a then-available answer:
$$(\forall a)\,(a \in Q_t' \supset (\exists p)\,[p \in K_t'' \;\&\; A^*pa \in K_t''\,])$$

(iii) *Strong Q-Completeness: Completeness in Principle*
Every then-askable question has a then-available answer:
$$(\forall a)\,(a \in Q_t'' \supset (\exists p)\,[p \in K_t'' \;\&\; A^*pa \in K_t''\,])$$
(*Note* that condition (iii) entails condition (ii).)

(iv) *An Unrealistic Case*
Every then-askable question has a then-given answer:
$$(\forall a)\,(a \in Q_t'' \supset (\exists p)\,[p \in K_t' \;\&\; A^*pa \in K_t'\,])$$

We thus arrive at only three distinct viable modes of the idea of Q-completeness. Each of these alternatives reflects a way in which an available answer-set K_t can be construed as being large enough to "cover" an existing questions-set Q_t.

It is important to note – specifically in relation to the first two modes of Q-completeness – that erotetic completeness does not necessarily betoken the comprehensiveness or abundance of K, but might simply reflect the paucity of the range Q' of questions we are prepared to contemplate. If we are sufficiently restricted (or unimaginative) as regards the questions we raise, the completeness of our knowledge will reflect this restrictedness rather than its own adequacy.

The idea of strong Q-completeness specifically points to the idea of an *equilibrium* between questions and answers: the questions that can be raised on the basis of a body of knowledge can be answered with recourse to this same body of knowledge.

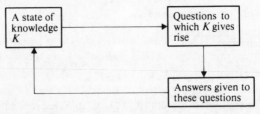

This sort of question-answering (or *erotetic*) completeness of a "state of knowledge" is a particularly attractive and useful idea. For it does not construe completeness in terms of some state-of-knowledge external, absolutistic standard of "perfect information," comparing our "knowledge" with that of some hypothetical cognitively infallible being. Rather, it develops a standard of completeness that is *internal* to our intellectual horizons: all the questions that *we* do (or can) pose are questions which *we* do (or can) answer. The issue of completeness is correlative with our "state of knowledge" on *its own* terms, and is not posed in terms of some transcendental absolute.

This perspective has important implications for the issue of the completability of science. Conceivably, if improbably, science might reach a fortuitous equilibrium between problems and solutions. It could be completed in the *effective* sense – in providing an answer to every question one *can* ask in the then-existing (albeit still imperfect) state of knowledge, yet without thereby being completed in the *fundamental* sense of answering the questions that would arise if only one could probe nature just a bit more deeply (as, alas, one cannot). The idea of erotetic completeness thus remains a relatively weak one – our corpus of scientific knowledge could be erotetically complete and yet substantially inadequate.

6. THE ISSUE OF UNANSWERABLE QUESTIONS: TWO VERY DIFFERENT SORTS OF COGNITIVE LIMITS

The preceding section explored the idea of question-answering *completeness*. The correlative idea of *incompleteness* clearly points towards the issue of *cognitive limits*, relating to the prospects of the question-resolving capacity of our knowledge in the long run. Now one significant way in which the question-resolving capacity of our knowledge might be limited is by the weak limitation asserted in the following thesis:

Weak-Limitation (The Permanence of Unsolved Questions)
There are *always*, at every stage,[10] questions to which no answer is in hand. At every stage of cognitive history there are then-unanswerable questions (which, however, may well be answerable at some later stage):

$$(\forall t)(\exists a)(a \in Q_t \, \& \sim (\exists p) A \, pa).$$

---

[10] Or perhaps alternatively: always, at every stage subsequent to a certain juncture.

This thesis maintains a permanence of cognitive limitation – that our knowledge is never at any stage completed, because unanswered questions always remain on the agenda.

Note that if Kant's Principle of Question Propagation were accepted, then this situation of the permanence of unsolved questions would be assured. For if every answer generates further new questions, then we should never reach a position where all questions are answered. It should also be observed that this position is perfectly compatible with the circumstance that *every* question arising at any given stage can be answered (or dissolved) at *some subsequent stage*. Weak limitation envisages the immortality of questions, and not the existence of immortal questions (insolubilia).

A second way in which the question-resolving capacity of our knowledge may be limited can accordingly envisage the far more drastic situation:

Strong-Limitation (The Existence of Insolubilia)
There will (as of some juncture) be then-posable questions which will *never* obtain an answer, identifiable questions whose resolution lies beyond the reach of science altogether, questions that are always on the agenda, yet never soluble:
$$(\exists a)(\exists t)(\forall t')(t' > t \supset [a \in Q_{t'} \ \& \ \sim(\exists p)A_{t'} \, pa]).$$

This thesis has it that there are immortal problems, permanently unanswerable questions, in short, genuine *insolubilia*.

Limits or restrictive boundaries upon knowledge can thus function in two very different ways. Consider the analogy of a reference library of a rather unusual sort – one with an *infinite* number of volumes. Suppose, as a first possible case, that only some finite number of its shelves are accessible. Then we have the situation of what may be characterized as a *terminating* limit on the information to be obtained: since only finitely many volumes can be attained, the body of knowledge to be derived – however vast it may be – must in the end remain finite. An inquirer will, in principle, have to come to the end of the road as regards the knowledge he can eventually secure: although still drastically incomplete, it will be incapable of any extension.

By way of contrast, consider the case in which only the last volume on every shelf of the infinite library is inaccessible. Clearly this too is a circumstance of restrictive limits. But such an *excluding* limit on the information to be obtained is something very different from the preceding *terminating* limit. For despite the undoubted existence of a very real limitation, the prospects of further substantial advances in knowledge are now always open. An inquirer can evermore extend his information in any given subject-matter direction as far as he pleases.

The point at issue was already clearly put by Kant, who was prepared to grant the actuality of excluding limits while vehemently denying that of terminating limits.

> [In] natural philosophy, human reason admits of *limits* ("excluding limits") but not of *boundaries* ("terminating limits"), namely, it admits that something indeed lies without it, at which it can never arrive, but not that it will at any point find completion in its internal progress. . . . [T]he possibility of new discoveries are infinite: and the same is the case with the discovery of new properties of nature, of new powers and laws, by continued experience and its rational combination. . . .[11]

This Kantian distinction between terminating and excluding limits is crucially relevant to our discussion. For in the context of scientific progress we must carefully distinguish two very different issues:

1. Can we always improve (more than marginally) on the body of scientific findings we already have in hand?
2. Does anything within the realm of the potentially discoverable lie entirely beyond our grasp, in being outside the range of what is possible for us to realize?

The former issues comes down to "Does science have terminating limits?" and the latter to "Does science have *any* limits, be they terminating or excluding?" And note that the problem of the prospects

---

[11] *Prolegomena to Any Future Metaphysic*, sect. 57. Compare the following passage from Charles Sanders Peirce:.

For my part, I cannot admit the proposition of Kant – that there are certain impassable bounds to human knowledge. . . . The history of science affords illustrations enough of the folly of saying that this, that, or the other can never be found out. Auguste Comte said that it was clearly impossible for man ever to learn anything of the chemical constitution of the fixed stars, but before his book had reached its readers the discovery which he had announced as impossible had been made. Legendre said of a certain proposition in the theory of numbers that, while it appeared to be true, it was most likely beyond the powers of the human mind to prove it; yet the next writer on the subject gave six independent demonstrations of the theorem. (*Collected Papers*, vol. VI, sect. 6.556).

of ongoing scientific progress relates only to item (1) – it pertains to the question of *terminating* limits, and leaves that of *excluding* limits aside.

The distinction between the two types of limits thus carries the important lesson – already drawn by Kant – that to accept the idea that scientific knowledge is limited is *not* tantamount to accepting the idea that science is finite or completable. The existence of unsolvable questions in natural science – of genuine *insolubilia* – will emphatically *not* entail the consequence that our knowledge in this sphere must ultimately terminate at some dead-end, issuing in a "completed" state of knowledge whose boundaries we can extend no further. (Think of the ever more comprehensive exploration of a limitless flatland punctuated by high peaks that one simply cannot scale.)

7. ULTIMATE QUESTIONS

The issue of the question-answering completeness of an explanatory framework for systematizing our knowledge is in fact more complex than first meets the eye. It is an important consideration here that any scientific framework for the systematization of our factual knowledge is entitled to establish certain sorts of questions as improper – as "just not arising." Thus when a certain form of motion (be it in Aristotle's circles or in Galileo's straight lines) is characterized as "natural," then we are enjoined to refrain from asking why objects move in this manner in the absence of imposed forces. Or again, considering that the half-life of a certain species of californium is 235 years, we must not ask – given modern quantum theory – just why a certain particular atom of this substance decayed after only 100 years. If an explanatory framework actually *eliminates* a certain group of questions, then we must presumably not regard its failure to answer them as counting to its discredit.

It is thus important to distinguish between:

1. *insolubilia*: questions that one can meaningfully pose, but which one cannot *then*, and indeed will not *ever* be able to answer. Such questions transgress "beyond the limits" of our explanatory powers, admitting of no resolution within any explanatory framework that we devise.
2. *"improper questions"*: questions which are unanswerable

only because there is good and sufficient reason for holding that they cannot really arise within the framework of discussion, in that its fundamental commitments violate the essential pre-suppositions of such a question. The framework effectively *disallows* the question.

Question-answering completeness should accordingly be assessed in terms not of *all* questions, but of all proper or *legitimate* questions. And an explanatory framework is entitled to play a part in the determination of such legitimacy.

But of course the matter does not quite end there. We must not be *too* liberal in allowing an explanatory framework to eradicate awkward questions with utter impunity. One must reserve the right in the final analysis to dismiss the framework itself under the charge: "There are more things in heaven and earth, Horatio. . . ."

Over and above the limit-transcending questions of types (1) and (2), they are also

3. *"ultimate questions"*: questions which clarify the fundamental commitments of an explanatory framework because they indicate or delineate rather than *violate* its limits.

Such "ultimate" questions cannot be resolved *within* the framework to which they relate: from a framework-internal point of view they are insoluble, because they demonstrate where the boundaries of the framework lie, which fact need not, of course, render them insolubilia as such. Nor are they improper questions. They *arise* on a framework-relative basis even though they cannot be *answered* within it.

It is worthwhile to consider briefly the traditional paradigm example of an ultimate question for the scientific framework of causal explanation, Leibniz's question: "Why is there anything at all?"

In dealing with this question it is crucial not to fall into "the causal trap" of attempting to provide an answer of the general form: "Because X exists, and X constrains existence." It is patent that such a response is inappropriate – "anything at all" includes X itself.

With respect to the "ultimate" question "Why is there anything at all?" the approaches that can be (and have been) envisaged may be grouped as follows:

I. The Dissolutionist Approach
II. Solutionist Approaches
    A. The *no-cause* solution
    B. The *necessitarian* solution
    C. The *teleological* solution

Let us consider each in turn.

The dissolutionist approach maintains that the very question is improper and illegitimate. It maintains that one can ask for why-exists explanations of items *within* nature, but not for nature as a whole. But why not? No really satisfactory answer is ever given here. In general we are simply shunted round in the circle which brings the impropriety of the question on the supposed impossibility of providing a proper answer to it.

All the remaining, solutionist approaches accept the validity of the question on its own terms.

The *no-cause* solution in effect says "just because." It takes the stance that there is no particular reason for existence. "That's just the way it is" – take it with no further questions asked. (Think of Carlyle's remark on being informed that some lady had learned to accept the world – "By G–d, she'd better!")

The necessitarian solution has it that things exist because that's how it's got to be. We have here a Spinozist necessitarianism which holds that things are as they are because this is *inevitable*.

The teleological solution holds that *being* rests on *value*. Things exist because "that's for the best." To be sure, this leaves the residual issue: "But why should what is fitting exist?" And there one does not want to say "What is fitting exists because there is something [God, Cosmic Mind, etc.] that brings what is fitting to realization." This simply falls back into the causal trap. We shall have to answer question simply in its own terms: "Because that's fitting." Fitness is seen as the end of the explanatory line.[12]

How can we tell which approach is "the correct one"? Clearly we cannot *demonstrate* correctness here. The best we can hope to do is to show that some one approach is on balance the most advantageously tenable in the light of the available arguments.

And from such a cost-benefit standpoint, each approach has significant drawbacks.

[12] See John Leslie, *Existence and Value* (Oxford, 1978).

1. *The Dissolution Approach*
   Just why is the question illegitimate – apart from its proving difficult for us? Is this not simply another instance of the fox and grapes phenomenon?
2. *The No-cause Solution*
   This is surely nothing but a solution of last resort. It is like the explanation "on impulse" offered to account for someone's action. It is not so much a solution as a concession of defeat – an indication that other solutions are not available.
3. *The Necessitarian Solution*
   The line taken here is simply too problematic. Given that alternatives can readily be conceived, how can one establish necessitarian inevitability?
4. *The Teleological Solution*
   Teleology already began to fall from credit in the Renaissance, and has suffered a steady succession of blows from Copernicus to Darwin.

The last of these approaches is nowadays the least fashionable and perhaps for that very reason the most interesting. The general strategy by which such a solution might conceivably be made to work runs somewhat as follows.

One looks to the fundamental equations defining the physical "laws of nature" as obtained in our best attempts to explain the *character* (that is, the *modus operandi* of nature). One then endeavors to show that these in themselves suffice to indicate the fact of existence. That is, one endeavors to exhibit that the *existence* of the world is implicit in its lawful *essence*. The strategy here is to show that the most simple, most elegant, most aesthetic solutions of the cosmic equations are those which accord to the key parameters values $\neq 0$ (i.e. values which are existence-requiring). The overall strategy is to argue that given the "essential nature" of the real as physics reveals it to be, its existence is "more fitting" than its nonexistence would be. And indeed going beyond this, it might emerge that the optimal solution of the cosmic equations (the most simple, elegant, etc.) are exactly those correlated with the parameter values being exactly as they are – that is, being such as to yield the world as we have it.

If such a general line of argumentation can be developed satisfactorily (admittedly a big IF), then the Teleological Solution could presumably become a live option.

The reader can readily work out for himself how an analogous treatment could handle such other "ultimate questions" relative to the scientific framework of causal explanation as: Why are there any laws of nature? Why are there relatively simple laws of nature (i.e. laws simple enough that naturally evolved creatures can discover them)? Why are the laws of nature such as they are (e.g. involve the universal constants taking on their actual values)?

It is unsatisfying to try to answer such questions, with Descartes, through recourse to the *mere will* (or, with Leibniz, through recourse to the *good* will) of the divine creator – not so much because God is dead as because of the rational proprieties of the situation implicit in the scholastic dictum *non in philosophia recurrere est ad deum*. Again, it is unsatisfying to try to answer these questions, with Peirce, in evolutionary terms by arguing that it is somehow natural that laws as we have them should evolve from a primal chaos. (For one thing, why a primal chaos; for another, why those particular principles of natural development?) To dismiss the question as improper and illegitimate is little more than an intellectual equivalent of kicking in vexed frustration the chair against which one has barked one's shin. Finally, it is no less unsatisfying to speak of an intrinsic *mystery* here, for this serves rather to highlight the difficulty than to remove it.[13]

We must simply recognize that such questions *cannot* be handled in the usual way – in virtue of their status as ultimate questions for the causal framework within which questions are usually resolved within the ambit of scientific explanation. We must here rest the Archimedean level of rationalization wholly outside the usual causal arena. Perhaps a teleological approach will serve; perhaps some other ingenious approach as yet ignored or obscured can be made to serve. But the crucial fact that the whole basis of reasoning not only can but *must* here be shifted wholly outside the purview of causal principles.

This perspectival approach has important implications for our analysis. It illustrates the need to avoid classing a question as "ultimate" pure and simple, but only as ultimate with respect to one particular explanatory framework. And this framework-relative ultimacy need not make the question insoluble as such. For, as we have seen, in the context of that paradigmatically ultimate question "Why is there

---

[13] Cf. Erwin Schrödinger, *What is Life* (Cambridge, 1945), p. 31. E. P. Wigner, "The Unreasonable Effectiveness of Mathematics in the Natural Sciences," *Communications on Pure and Applied Mathematics*, vol. 13 (1960), pp. 1–14. Cf. p. 122 above.

anything at all" and its various cognates, the fact that such questions are indeed ultimate for *the causal framework* (which, given its own nature, cannot come to grips with the issue) does not mean that there may not be some other framework (e.g. the teleological) which can deal with them more or less successfully.

Here again we do well to avoid the temptation to classify certain questions as in principle insoluble. For "ultimate questions" bear upon the issue of cognitive limits in a rather special sort of way – by indicating where the limits of a particular explanatory framework lie. They are "insoluble" not as such, but merely *within the framework*. If we take resort to "higher ground" by expanding or supplementing or replacing the framework, such questions may well become answerable. They have a distinctive and characteristic standing in our cognitive scheme: they are neither unanswerable insolubilia nor illegitimate "improper questions," but rather framework-indicators. They accordingly bear upon the framework-relative rather than the absolute or globe aspect of the issue of the "limits of knowledge."

8. THE INCOMPLETABILITY OF "OUR KNOWLEDGE"

Let us briefly review the bearing of these deliberations upon our starting-point issue of the possible nonsystematizability of scientific knowledge on the grounds of its incompletability. We have seen that two quite different things are at issue with completeness. One is the attainment of a "completed and final state" of factual knowledge by way of an eventual knowledge-ossification of the sort envisaged in section 2. Given the realistic prospects of continuing scientific progress *ad indefinitum*, this sort of completability is itself an implausible prospect. And even completability in the weaker, erotetic sense of reaching a condition in which all questions are answered is also an unrealistic prospect, given the processes of question-propagation.

The completion of our factual knowledge is accordingly not a circumstance we can reasonably hope to realize. Facing this prospect of incompleteness, the crucial consideration is that completeness is not an all-or-nothing issue but a matter of degree. The fact that we cannot expect fully to attain the ideal at issue provides no argument against the regulative injunction to "strive to make your knowledge of the world as complete as you find it possible to do." Such an upshot of these deliberations is accordingly wholly consonant with the role envisaged for this parameter of systematization throughout these deliberations. It remains a perfectly legitimate and proper *regulative ideal* for factual inquiry.

All the same, the incompleteness – indeed presumptive incompletability – of "our (purported) knowledge" has profound impliciations for its status. For one of the clearest lessons of the history of science is that where scientific knowledge is concerned, further information does not just supplement but generally *corrects* our prior knowledge. Accordingly, we have little alternative but to take the humbling view that the incompleteness of our information entails its incorrectness as well – incompleteness must be presumed to carry incorrectness in its wake. This aspect of the matter endows incompleteness with an import far graver than meets the eye on first view.

X

Limits to Cognitive Systematization – II

Issues of Explanatory Completeness

SYNOPSIS

(1) There are two very different senses of "explanatory completeness": *comprehensiveness* or all-inclusiveness on the one hand, and *finality* or completion on the other. (2) Comprehensiveness is of necessity only partially attainable on the subsumptive-inference construction of explanation. But if explanation is thought of in terms of systematic coordination – as is the case on the coherentist approach – then comprehensiveness is in principle attainable and its pursuit represents a legitimate desideratum. (3) Finality, on the other hand, is not attainable *as a matter of principle* and its pursuit is a vain and Quixotic quest. (4) The completeness of science in another sense – that of self-sufficiency – is guaranteed by its autonomy: no explanatory issues within the domain of its problems and concerns fit appropriately into the range of some variant enterprise.

1. TWO SENSES OF "EXPLANATORY COMPLETENESS": COMPREHENSIVENESS AND FINALITY

Two importantly different things can lie in view when "explanatory completeness" is spoken of. On the one hand there is *comprehensiveness*, the circumstance which obtains when every explanatory problem has been solved and every explainable issue has actually been explained (or, at any rate, has a potentially available explanation in terms of the machinery that has been forged). No explanatory questions remain unanswered. On the other hand, completeness in the sense of *finality* or *completion* means that a condition of finality has been reached: that the *definitive* explanation is in hand (or "available") for every explanatory problem that in fact has a solution – the *ultimate* explanation which admits of no further correction or amendment. No explanatory answer can be improved upon: the end of the line has been reached. With comprehensiveness-completeness we can answer – perhaps wrongly – every (answerable) question that we can ask; with finality-completeness we have answered *definitively*, beyond further improvement, every question that we can answer.

The matter of the explanatory completeness of our endeavors at scientific systematization will accordingly stand on a very different footing depending on which of these two senses of completeness is taken to be at issue.

2. IS COMPREHENSIVENESS ATTAINABLE?

It is generally agreed – more generally, it would seem, than is the case with most other issues in the epistemology of science – that scientific explanations are *subsumptive* inferences that place the items to be explained within a rationale-providing context of covering laws. (The subsumptive argument at issue can, of course, be probabilistic rather than deductive.) Thus if asked to explain why *this* object is *now* falling with a velocity of 8g we would frame our reply with reference to Galileo's law of falling bodies, viz.,

> Whenever an object has been released from altitude for free fall in *vacuo* for a period of t seconds, it will move towards the earth's surface with a velocity of $\frac{1}{2}gt^2$.

And we would, accordingly, note that this object was released 4 seconds ago for free fall *in vacuo*. What such an explanation clearly achieves is the rationalization (indeed in this case the *deductive* rationalization) of its *explanandum*, the item to be explained, with reference to the appropriate *laws* and certain *background facts* (or "boundary value conditions").

This line of approach leads to a theory of explanation that might be characterized as *subsumptive inferentialism*, considering that it sees explanation to proceed by a deductive or probabilistic inference that effects a subsumptive reference to the laws of the relevant domain.

But consider now the question of the *comprehensiveness* of its explanatory range. Can science actually explain everything? It might seem at first sight that the answer here would have to be a negative one, as indicated by the upshot of an argument as old as Aristotle's *Posterior Analytics*.[1] In brief summary this argument goes as follows: To give an explanation of one fact as explanandum invariably involves the use of others in the explanans. An infinite regress will thus result. This regress can be terminated only if there are certain "ultimate" facts – facts not themselves explained at all, although they are available for use in the explanation of other facts. Such "ultimate" facts will play the role of basic premises in science much as the axioms are basic in a system of geometry. And these ultimate facts will represent the limits of scientific explanation, for although science uses them in giving explanations, they will themselves lie outside the range of scientific explicability.

This regress argument to an eventual bedrock of "ultimate" facts indicates one of the serious defects of the subsumptive approach.

But this entire approach to explanation stands in contrast to a very different one, namely, with *nonsubsumptive* explanation on basis of "best-fit" considerations in the spirit of the coherentist approach. The best fit ("coordination") at issue may involve *inferential connectedness* but it may also be a matter of analogy, uniformity, simplicity and the other parameters of cognitive systematization. Thus we have here a wholly different approach to explanation; one that takes systematization itself as the key, relying not on subsumptive inference, but on systematic coordination. Here the issue is not *subordination to*, but *coordination with*: it is not a matter of *inference* from other theses at all, but one of *coordination* through mutual attunement with them. On such an approach, if we explain *A* with reference to *B* and *C*, we do so not by inferring *A* from *B* and *C*, but by showing that *A* is more smoothly co-systematizable with *B* and *C* than is the case with its alternatives *A'*, *A''*, etc.

This distinction between inferentially subsumptive and systematically coordinative explanations has an important bearing on the attainability of explanatory comprehensiveness.

[1] See Bk. I, sect. 3.

As a matter of principle, comprehensiveness is just not going to be attainable in purely a subsumptive setting. The subsumption of this under that involves us in an explanatory regress that will soon have to come to a halt. We can only go on so long to place the obligation on the back of the elephant on the back of the tortoise; ultimately, we are driven back to the first principles that are never themselves *explained*, but only *rationalized* in terms of "producing the right consequences." In this subsumptive context, explanatory completeness in the sense of comprehensiveness is *not* attainable as a matter of theoretical principle, and must accordingly be abandoned as a goal.

But the situation is very different in the context of the systematically coordinative approach to explanation in terms of best-fit considerations. Here there is no difficulty with the idea that *everything* can be explained. No vitiating regress is involved in explaining A with reference to B and C and then turning round to explain B with reference to A and C. It now makes perfectly good sense to adopt explanatory completeness as a regulative ideal. The pursuit of explanatory completeness in the sense of the comprehensive systematization of our explanatory understanding is an important facet of adopting systematicity as a regulative ideal of inquiry.

To be sure, this ideal of comprehensiveness-completeness involves an element of hopefulness. And this hope is just precisely that – a hope. It is certainly not the case at this present historical juncture that every physical or biological fact can be satisfactorily explained through the discipline as it now stands. And it is perfectly possible this circumstance will always continue. It is even conceivable that it should so continue even in a finally-completed physics or biology – one which human effort has pushed as far as it is capable of doing.

Of course, the idea of a perfect science is always at the back of our thinking – a state of science which is capable, in principle, of furnishing an adequate explanatory rationalization for *every* fact of its subject-matter domain. But it is certainly an open question now – and perhaps will always remain irresolvably so – whether such a perfect condition can ever be realized by us in any sort of fundamental scheme of rational systematization. Nothing guarantees us that even after everything humanly realizable has been said and done it cannot eventuate that certain particular facts will not still resist an adequate explanatory rationalization. But there is no denying that outright failure in the coordinative mode of explanatory comprehensiveness would be a serious flaw. For when a thesis cannot be explanatorily coordinated it remains disconnected, and this failure to be integrated into the "fabric of our knowledge" has serious consequences. For this could mean that we do not really understand the thesis at issue, and that our system of knowledge itself would be marked as inadequate (incomplete) through the existence of such a "surd" that it cannot accommodate.[2]

We must conclude that explanatory completeness in the sense of comprehensiveness is not only realizable when construed along coordinative and coherentist lines, but represents an appropriate desideratum correlative with a legitimate regulative principle.

3. IS COMPLETION (i.e. FINALITY-COMPLETENESS) ATTAINABLE? THE DYNAMICAL ASPECT OF OUR KNOWLEDGE

We come now to the issue of explanatory completeness in the sense of *completion*. Is this a plausible desideratum? Can we ever reach a condition in which it is reasonable to expect that no further *corrections* (indeed not even significant *improvements*) to our explanations are ever going to be needed?

This is clearly an unrealistic prospect. There can never be a complete explanation of anything for reasons akin to those why there can never be a complete description of anything. In describing a man we can go on *ad indefinitum* to give greater detail about more and more aspects – the exact shape of his fingernails, lips, and so on. In explaining we can go more fully into the reasons why of the reasons why. Improvements are always possible. And best-fit explanations are similarly open-ended. Although one explanation can certainly be more complete than another, no explanation can ever be totally "complete as such." We can never push the process of explanation "through to the bitter end," and must always keep our completeness-claims in comparative rather than the categorical mode.

Moreover, this is simply the *static* aspect of incompleteness. Its *dynamic* aspect within the framework of cognitive *change* is no less significant.

The preceding considerations relate to the limits of explanations that can be rationalized on a *fixed and given* conceptual basis. But in real life

---

[2] As we shall see, such incompleteness threatens not only the *completeness* of our "body of knowledge" but may endanger its consistency as well.

a conceptual basis is never "fixed and given." Our conceptions of things do not present an easy object of scrutiny – they are a *moving* rather than a *fixed* target for analysis. We form our conception of the sun in terms of reference very different from those of Aristotle, and that of a heart in terms of reference very different from those of Galen.

Consider how many facts about his own sword were unknown to Caesar. He did not know that it contained carbon or that it conducted electricity. The very concepts at issue ("carbon," "electricity-conduction") were outside Caesar's cognitive range. There are key facts (or presumptive facts) even about the most familiar things – trees and animals, bricks and mortar – that were unknown 100 years ago. And this is so not just because of an ignorance of detail (as with a missing word in a crossword puzzle). Rather, the ignorance at issue arises because the very *concepts* at issue had not been formulated. It's not just that Caesar didn't *know* what the half-life of californium is, but that he couldn't have *understood* this fact if someone had told it to him.

The language of emergence can perhaps be deployed profitably to describe this situation. What is at issue is not an *emergence of the features of things*, but an emergence in our *knowledge* about them. The blood circulated in the human body well before Harvey; uranium-containing substances were radioactive before Becquerel. The emergence at issue here relates to our cognitive mechanisms of conceptualization, not to the objects of our conceptualization in and of themselves.

We do – and must – recognize that we may well be wrong about the nature of a thing not only in regard to its descriptive make-up, but in more fundamental regards as well. Things may be misconceived in very basic ways (for example, a pre-Copernican "sunrise," or again a "case of cancer," should it turn out that future physicians take a very different view of what goes on where we see the occurrence of a particular "disease entity").

And any adequate metaphysico-epistemological world-view must recognize that this is always so. It must recognize that the ongoing progress of science is a process of *conceptual* innovation that always leaves certain issues wholly outside the cognitive range of the inquirers of any particular period.

This means that there will always be explanatorily significant facts (or plausible candidate-facts) about a thing that we do not *know* because we cannot even *conceive* of them. For to grasp such a fact means taking a perspective of consideration that we simply do not have, since the state of knowledge (or purported knowledge) is not yet advanced to a point at which its formulation is possible.

The properties of a thing are literally open-ended: We can always discover more of them. Even if we view the world as inherently finitistic, and espouse a Principle of Limited Variety which has it that the world can be portrayed descriptively with the materials of a finite taxonomic scheme, there can be no *a priori* guarantee that with the progress of science we will not go on *ad indefinitum* to change our mind about the membership of this finite register of descriptive materials.

And thus our notion of nature is – and must be – such that the possibility of learning more about any thing will always have to be kept in mind as an open, theoretically feasible prospect. This "inexhaustibility" of the potential knowledge of things is implicit in the very conception of a "real thing" as it figures in our conceptual scheme.

It is of course *possible* that natural science will come to a stop, and do so not in the trivial sense of a cessation of intelligent life, but in Peirce's more interesting sense of eventually reaching a condition after which even indefinitely ongoing inquiry will not – and indeed, given the inherent limitations of man-nature interaction *cannot* – produce any significant change. Such a position is *in theory* possible. But we can never *know* – be it in practice or in principle – that it is actual. We can never know that science has attained such an ω-condition of final completion – from our point of view, the possibility of further change lying "just around the corner" can never be ruled out finally and decisively.

To be sure, some writers think that one can guarantee more or less *a priori* that science must (in principle) ultimately terminate in the acceptance of one single final theoretical structure. There must, they believe, be a single "real truth" of things which inquiry is bound in the long run to reach or approximate.[3] For – so they argue – if this were not so, then there would be no real nature of things and no actual reality to serve as object of inquiry. But this view seems somewhat optimistic in its presupposition that reality cannot have a nature that is

---

[3] This idea is central in the thought of Charles Sanders Peirce. For more recent variations see William Kneale, "Scientific Revolutions Forever?," *British Journal for the Philosophy of Science*, vol. 19 (1967), pp. 27–42; and Robert F. Almeder, "Science and Idealism," *Philosophy of Science*, vol. 40 (1973), pp. 242–254.

impervious to the intellectual assaults which inquiry of the sort at issue in *"our* science" is able to mount against it.

A further, economic, line of consideration is important here. Man's material resources are limited. And these limits inexorably circumscribe our cognitive access to the real world. There are interations with nature of such a scale (as measured in such parameters as energy, pressure, temperature, particle-velocities, etc.) whose realization would require the deployment of resources of so vast a scope that we can never realize them. And if there are interactions to which we have no access, then there are (presumably) phenomena which we cannot discern. It would be unreasonable to expect nature to confine the distribution of phenomena of potential cognitive significance to those ranges that lie within the horizons of our vision.

Where there are inaccessible phenomena, there must be cognitive incompleteness. To this extent, at any rate, the empiricists were surely right. Only the most hidebound of rationalists could uphold the capacity of sheer intellect to compensate for the lack of data. Where there are unobserved phenomena we must reckon with the prospect that our theoretical systematizations may well be (nay, presumably are) incomplete.

Moreover, if certain phenomena are not just undetected but in the very nature of the case inaccessible (even if only for the merely economic reasons mooted above), then our theoretical knowledge of nature is (presumably) incompletable. It would, accordingly, appear that certain fundamental features inherent in the very structure of man's inquiry into the ways of the world conspire to indicate the finality-incompleteness of the knowledge we can attain in this sphere.[4]

We are thus led back to the thesis of the great Idealist philosophers (Spinoza, Hegel, Bradley, Royce) that human knowledge inevitably falls short of "perfect science" (the Idea, the Absolute), and must accordingly be *presumed* deficient both in its completeness and its correctness.

The crucial point thus emerges that the pursuit of finality-completeness (unlike that of comprehensiveness-completeness) is not a valid regulative ideal but represents a vain and Quixotic quest. Even if a state of finality-completeness were attained we could never know it.

---

[4] This rather compressed discussion is developed more fully in the author's book on *Scientific Progress* (Oxford, 1977).

And this unaccessibility *as a matter of principle* destroys the prospect of finality-completeness serving as an appropriate cognitive ideal.

4. THE COMPREHENSIVENESS OF SCIENCE AND ITS AUTONOMY

We arrive finally at the question of the explanatory range of science. Is science so limited that certain factual issues simply fall outside its scope?

What sorts of things are candidates for scientific explanation; what is the potential range of the explanatory problems of scientific inquiry? The answer to this question is simply: "Any and all facts about the world whatsoever." Nothing is in principle placed outside the purview of science. The conceivable subjects of scientific explanation therefore exhibit an enormous, indeed an endless variety. All the properties and states of things, any and all occurrences and events, the behaviour and doings of people, in short, every facet of "what goes on in the world," can be regarded as appropriate objects of scientific explanation.

But although science does not exclude any facts from its purview, there is perhaps some range of fact that is located outside the effective range of scientific explanation. Certain facts within the field of view of science may yet lie outside the reach of its grasp. Perhaps there are *a priori* theoretical grounds for having to exclude certain facets of nature from the effective scope of science as lying beyond its operative limits.

It is not for any reason of principle that the thesis that "Science can explain everything" must be rejected; it is because modern science itself, in the context of irreducibly stochastic processes, brings to light certain "unanswerable" questions. Quantum phenomena of radioactive decay afford an example of the explanatory restrictedness of science: there is, and cannot be an explanation of why a certain atom of plutonium disintegrated after $3\frac{1}{2}$ hours. In the light of such considerations, the dictum in view must be revised to "Science can explain everything explicable." We arrive at the (somewhat more modest) thesis that all facts can be explained scientifically that can be explained at all in ways acceptable to a rational mind.

Whatever be its lack of completeness, science is self-sufficient. And this is how the matter *must* stand, given the crucial fact that *science is autonomous*. Corrections to science must come from science. Science is necessarily "complete" in regard to its self-sufficiency. Shortcomings in scientific work can emerge only from further scientific work. The mistaken results of science can only be improved or corrected by further results of science – tea leaf reading, numerology, the Delphic oracle, etc., cannot at this time of day be put forward as plausible candidates. Scientific claims must – whenever corrected at all – be corrected by further scientific claims. A "science" viewed as subject to *external* standards of correctness is simply not deserving of this name.[5]

[5] Issues relating to the autonomy of science are explored more fully in the author's *Methodological Pragmatism* (Oxford, 1977).

XI

Limits to Cognitive Systematization – III

Issues of Consistency

SYNOPSIS

(1) *Inconsequence* (disconnectedness), and *inconsistency* (incoherence) as factors which might render it impossible to systematize our knowledge about the world. (2) The prospect of inconsistency must not be dismissed out of hand. It is a force to be reckoned with, because incompleteness and inconsequence may so conspire together as to issue in inconsistency. (3) Inconsistency might also issue from attempts to (over)compensate for explanatory indecisiveness. (4) And there is no reason of principle why inconsistency cannot be tolerated – up to a point. Even consistency, like the other parameters of systematicity, is a mere *desideratum*, and not an indispensable requisite – a matter of absolute necessity. (5) To be sure, inconsistency is in theory always avoidable; but the over-all price of such avoidance might be too steep. Paradoxically, the very pursuit of adequate systematization may itself press inconsistency upon us. (6) Conclusion: Only with the wisdom of hindsight can one finally tell if systematized knowledge of the world can be attained. Cognitive systematicity is at bottom a regulative ideal the extent of whose actual realizability cannot be prejudged in advance on the basis of general principles.

1. NONSYSTEMATIZABILITY

As was observed above (p. 130), there are three prime factors that may render it impossible to systematize a body of knowledge: incompletability, disconnectedness, and inconsistency. The preceding two chapters have focused upon the first of these by dealing with incompletability under the aspect of both erotetic and explanatory completeness. The present chapter will examine the remaining two issues of connectedness and, above all, consistency.

(1) *Inconsequence (or Disconnectedness)*

A body of knowledge is *inconsequent* when it is disconnected – when it is deficient in point of wholeness, architectonic unity, cohesiveness, or functional interrelatedness. In such a case, this body will consist of disjoint compartments which fail to link up because they represent regions of assertion that are disconnected from one another. (Egyptology and, say, nuclear physics might perhaps be a plausible example.) When this sort of disjointness obtains, the ideal of a systematic cohesiveness under the aegis of unifying principles cannot be realized.

Now it is clear that such inconsequence cannot possibly characterize *the body of our factual knowledge as a whole.* Any two sectors here can always be joined by a series of mediating connections of common relevancy. (To return to the preceding example, the sun's functioning enters centrally into Egyptology with regard to agricultural practices, to religious celebrations, etc., and nuclear physics accounts for solar phenomena.) All areas of natural science address themselves to one common nature, and consequently deal *with different facets of the same thing.* The ultimate connectability of all departments of our factual knowledge is guaranteed by its common focus on a single unifying objective, "the real world" – its *mundocentrism* (as it might be called). This fact of a common bearing upon a single object under its various aspects – all of them linked by a vast network of causal interrelationships – assures the connectability of all of the diverse component specialities of the overall corpus of empirical inquiry. In this synoptic, all-comprehending context, all branches of knowledge are linked together, so that "total science" must necessarily – as a matter of general principle – be capable of a connected treatment.

It should, however, be noted that while there will always be mediating connections of common *relevancy* between any two sectors of science-as-a-whole through the operation of connecting causal principles, there could well fail to be connections in *meaning* between the subject-materials of two branches of science. Take neurophysiology and phenomenological psychology, for example. The former might well tell us through what processes and under what conditions certain phenomena occur (e.g. experimental color vision or psychological feeling-tones). But the physics and chemistry at issue here, though they can causally *explain* the experiential qualities at issue, cannot serve to *describe* them. Their mutual relevance is of a causal rather than substantive nature.[1]

Moreover, the connectedness of our factual knowledge that is in theory guaranteed by its generic orientation towards one common world which constitutes one overriding causal matrix in which all natural occurrences are bound together – its *mundocentrism* (as we have called it) – might merely be a purely formal unity, lacking any sufficient substantive basis of functional connectedness. The universal relevance consequent upon mundocentrism is something purely theoretical. We might well come to have powerful evidence that nature is in various respects *inconsequent* (compartmentalized, disconnected) in its *modus operandi*. Again, the inconsequence of our overall knowledge of nature can result from its incompleteness. For it might well be – given the inevitable gaps in our actually attainable knowledge – that the pervasive interconnectedness which "must be there" represents a goal we are in practice blocked from ever realizing. Here again we encounter a facet of systematization that has, in the final analysis, the status of a regulative ideal, rather than reflecting an issue of descriptive fact.

(2) *Inconsistency (or Incoherence)*

A body of knowledge is *inconsistent* when it lacks consonance, internal

---

[1] To be sure, this is irrelevant from the angle of scientific explanation: Explanatory connections can be merely causal in orientation and need not correspond to meaning-connections. (If this case were otherwise scientific inquiry could proceed by studying the language of science instead of nature.)

regularity, and self-concordance. Such a body embraces incompatible constituents – components which cannot be conjoined without generating internal conflict or contradiction in the resulting whole. With *inconsequence* we have components that stand apart in being substantively DISjoint; whereas with *inconsistency* we have components which, albeit connected, must be kept apart because their CONjunction creates problems since they are mutually incompatible.

For any but a convinced Marxist, the thesis of the consistency of nature may seem to be a trivial truism. But the idea that man's endeavors to systematize his knowledge of nature might end in inconsistency is a real prospect that cannot be dismissed out of hand. For this could eventuate as the result of a combination of two perfectly possible circumstances: that our knowledge of nature may in the end prove inconsequent, and that then, in this situation, incompleteness may issue in inconsistency. Let us examine this prospect more closely.

2. INCOMPLETENESS PLUS INCONSEQUENCE CAN ISSUE IN INCONSISTENCY

Consider how the "natural" endeavor to achieve the best possible systematization of our knowledge might realistically come to issue in inconsistency. Take the example of a theoretical regimentation of limited data as in the curve-fitting situation of Figure 1. Projecting a

Figure 1

CURVE-FITTING IN RESTRICTED PURVIEW CASES

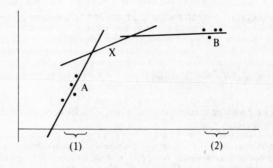

"best-fit" curve basis of data obtained in region (1) alone we might well arrive at the line A. Again, on the basis of region (2) data we might well arrive at the line B. Moreover – so let us assume – no practicable, physically accessible way is open to us for securing data outside of (1) and (2). Now if our "science" were to contain two separate branches, one of which deals with the data of region (1) alone, and the other with those of (2), then an inconsistency would at once result. The prospect of a transitional phase X would not arise to yield a unified picture. The one branch of science would hold the overall situation to be A-like, while the other would hold it to be B-like.

Consider another example, that of filling a gap in two different but intersecting or interrelated contexts, as seen in Figure 2. The data of the P-series (column) context yields 5 as best estimate for Z; the Q-series (row) context yields 4. Again, if our science contains two different branches, one with P alone in its purview as a data-base, and the other with Q alone, we would arrive at mutually incompatible claims. We are up against the old difficulty of discordant views based on the systematic projection of somehow incomplete views of things.[2]

The examples also illustrate the important point that it is not the given "facts" of the case in and by themselves, *but the very drive to achieve their smooth systematization* that produces the inconsistency at issue in such circumstances. In each case we have several *partial*

---

[2] An amusing but vividly clear picture of the problem is given in John G. Saxe's poem "The Blind Men and the Elephant" which tells the story of the wise men of Indostan who investigated the elephant:

. . . six men of Indostan,
To learning much inclined,
Who went to see the elephant,
(Though all of them were blind).

One sage stumbled against the elephant's "broad and sturdy side" and declared the beast to be "very like a wall." Another, who has felt its tusk, pronounced the elephant to be rather like a spear. The third, who held the elephant's squirming trunk in his hands, compared it to a snake; while the fourth, who put his arms around the elephant's foreleg, was sure that the animal resembles a tree. A flapping ear convinced another that the elephant has the form of a fan; while the last blind man was convinced that it has the form of a rope, since he took hold of the tail.

And so these men of Indostan,
Disputed loud and long;
Each in his own opinion
Exceeding stiff and strong:
Though each was partly in the right,
And all were in the wrong.

Figure 2

GAP-FILLING IN DISTINCT BUT INTERSECTING CONTEXTS

```
              (P)
               1
               2
               3
               4
(Q) 1 2 3 Z 5 6 7 8 9 10
               4
               3
               2
               1
```

perspectives on an over-all set of facts – incomplete and to all appearances mutually inconsequent. And the isolated (as it were) *systematization* of each context then leads to an extrapolation-result which is incompatible with an analogous result of the other.[3]

It should be observed, however, that the assumption of distinct branches of knowledge is crucially important in both these examples. In the absence of such compartmentalization, the discords at issue would not arise, since they stem from the overextension of what is actually an incomplete purview. But the examples do show that – and how – inconsequence can cooperate with incompleteness to issue in inconsistency.

In this context, we must not fail to remark that compartmentalization is, after all, a basic aspect of the division of labor achieved by dividing science into branches – a part of the very reason for being of scientific specialization. The presence of fragmentation of this sort is presumably an ineliminable feature of the structure of the scientific enterprise as we humans are able to pursue it. And in these circumstances it is not only possible, but even likely that the resulting theories arrived at by extrapolation from an incomplete basis may prove incompatible with one another. To be sure, if our knowledge were more synoptic then (no doubt) we would presumably be able to shape a more complex but unified and self-consistent picture, as in the Figure 1 diagram itself. (Thus if one line of inquiry addresses itself to the issues of

---

[3] Just here lies the profound lesson of the story of the blind men and the elephant. The inconsistencies at issue do not result from "the data" available to the men – what they feel and experience. It is their systematizing extension of these data that produces the conflict.

physiological psychology, another to those of behavioral psychology, inconsistencies of perspective might well develop which a suitably unified psychological theory – were one available – should be able to transcend.) The mere quantitative growth of a scientific field in terms of its literature and its findings may, however, so operate as to preclude such unification. In the actual state of scientific development, even our most valiant efforts may fail to yield this happy condition.

Indeed, a situation of this sort seems currently to be developing in natural science, as Eugene P. Wigner (Nobel laureate in physics for 1960) has detailed in the following terms:

> We now have, in physics, two theories of great power and interest: the theory of quantum phenomena and the theory of relativity. These two theories have their roots in mutually exclusive groups of phenomena. Relativity theory applies to macroscopic bodies, such as stars. The event of coincidence, that is in ultimate analysis of collision, is the primitive event in the theory of relativity and defines a point in space-time, or at least would define a point if the colliding particles were infinitely small. Quantum theory has its roots in the microsocpic world and, from its point of view, the event of coincidence, or of collision, even if it takes place between particles of no spatial extent, is not primitive and not at all sharply isolated in space-time. The two theories operate with different mathematical concepts – the four dimensional Riemann space and the infinite dimensional Hilbert space, respectively. So far, the two theories could not be united, that is, no mathematical formulation exists to which both of these theories are approximations. All physicists believe that a union of the two theories is inherently possible and that we shall find it. Nevertheless, it is possible also to imagine that no union of the two theories can be found.[4]

There is, to be sure, no actual *paradox* here: it is, of course, perfectly conceivable both that "a union of the two theories is inherently possible" and that yet "no union of the two theories can [ever] be found [by us]." This combination of circumstances could arise – for example – when the information needed to forge a workable unifying theory lies

---

[4] Eugene P. Wigner, "The Unreasonable Effectiveness of Mathematics in the Natural Sciences," *Communications on Pure and Applied Mathematics*, vol. 13 (1960), pp. 1–14 (see pp. 11–12). Wigner has suggested in private conversation that a more radical disunity is at issue. The space-time metric of general relativity requires mathematically *punctiform* occurrence configurations, whereas the quantum theory excludes the prospect of such point-events. The requirements of the two domains are to all appearances incompatible with one another.

beyond the reach of our resources (e.g. because it requires interactions with nature on a scale we men cannot afford to mount in a world of limited resources). It is thus a perfectly real prospect that science might in fact evolve (in a seemingly settled way) into a Wigner-condition of internal inconsistency. One certainly cannot rule out this prospect on any grounds of general principle.[5]

Accordingly, it is important (and perhaps shocking) to recognize that incompleteness may well exact its price not simply in *ignorance* – that is, in blanks in our knowledge – but in actual *inconsistency*. As long as our purported knowledge of the world remains – as it always must – both fragmented and incomplete, we must reckon with a potential infeasibility of imparting to it that systematic unity and coherence which has been a regulative ideal for science since the days of the *epistēmē* of the Greek philosophers. The inevitability of incompleteness and of compartmentalization assures that inconsistency can conceivably prove a real prospect – and indeed one that need not prove to be a merely transient feature of "the presently imperfect state" of the current state of our knowledge, but might well be ultimately ineradicable, affecting every realizable state thereof.

To be sure, we are never absolutely *forced* to accept this sort of inconsistency as irrevocably final and as demanding an ultimate and inescapable sacrifice of the regulative principle at issue. For, as the very nature of the preceding example indicates, the inconsistency at issue can be viewed as "the result of mere incompleteness." A recognition of the actual incompleteness (and possible incompletability) of our knowledge might thus be seen as an ever-available protection against finding our knowledge of the world to be unsystematic. And so, one might try to argue as follows here:

> Nothing can finally constrain us to the view that our knowledge of the world is not systematizable. For as long as this knowledge is incomplete – an ever-present possibility – the prospect of finding the missing pieces that restore systematicity can never be ruled out.

Thus even if the prospect mooted by Wigner were realized – even if

---

[5] The situation is reminiscent of the late 19th-century split between physicists (especially William Thompson, later Lord Kelvin) on the one hand the geologists and biologists (especially T. H. Huxley on the other) over the issue of the age of the earth. See the discussion in Stephen G. Brush, "Science and Culture in the Nineteenth Century," *The Graduate Journal*, vol. 7 (1969), pp. 479–565.

nature as best we grasp it is inconsistent to all scientific intents and purposes – still, this would not finally and irrevocably refute the principle of the coherence of nature. We could always tell ourselves in a hopeful tone – "If only we now a bit more, if only we could push inquiry around the next corner, then we could eliminate the inconsistency which now confronts us; if only our information were enhanced and our science more synoptic, the difficulty would presumably be overcome." One can take the stance that if only science were to enter into a sufficiently complete state (a condition whose realization may conceivably lie beyond our feeble powers), that then the anomaly characteristic of the Wigner-condition would be removed. We are not unavoidably constrained to give up our regulative commitment to consistency.

But the availability of this line of approach does not really settle the problem. For the following objection is now in order:

Yes, this recourse to a hopeful view of what would happen in the light of more complete information could indeed be taken. But is it *rational*? Is it more than "an act of pure faith" – of what is, in the final analysis, a matter of quixotically holding aloft the standard after the troops have been routed from the field? Perhaps our difficulties might indeed be removed "by overcoming these limitations." But is this always a realistic prospect? May not circumstances arise in which an enlargement of our information is simply not realistically feasible in the practically attainable circumstances? Could there not prove to be decisive horizons to our inquiry into nature resulting from limitations upon our access to data and their theoretical exploitation?

This objection is, in the final analysis, decisive. In theory, we *can* always save the ideal of consistency, but the crucial fact remains that beyond a certain point it would – in practice – become *unreasonable*, nay Quixotic, to do so.

3. OVER-COMPREHENSIVENESS: INCONSISTENCY THROUGH (OVER)COMPENSATING FOR EXPLANATORY INDECISIVENESS

Yet another possible route to inconsistency arises from the theoretical indeterminacy inherent in what one might call the *explanatory indecisiveness* that can characterize particular states of knowledge.

Suppose our explanatory resources are such as to put us into a position that is wholly indecisive with respect to the alternative (mutually incompatible) explanations $A_1, A_2, \ldots, A_n$, preserving this indecisiveness even "with everything taken into account" – with all theory-internal considerations duly accommodated. Then one might simply (over)compensate for this explanatory indecisiveness by adopting the difficult but not necessarily indefensible stance that *all* of the incompatible possibilities are conjointly realized.

Let us consider a way of making this problematic prospect less implausible – an illustration which figures in the physical literature under the name of the Everett-Wheeler theory in quantum mechanics.

The focal point of this theory is the issue of measurement in quantum mechanics specifically the well-known "problem of the reduction of the wave packet." With such quantum-theoretic measurements as the nucleonic decay-timespan of a very heavy radioactive element, the result of a measurement is formally speaking a superposition of vectors, each representing the quantity being measured as having one of its possible values; that is, each being a distinct, observational result of measurement. The obvious difficulty is how this superposition of distinct outcomes can be reconciled with the fact that in practice only one value is to be observed. How is it that in experimental trials at quantum measurement only one unique single outcome can be encountered observationally when the theory itself provides no means for collapsing the state vector into a single one of its values? How can the process of actual observational measurement force an inherently pluralistic situation into producting a unique result?

The orthodox quantum-theoretical line of response to this question is to say that only one outcome is real, and that the other alternatives are *unactualized possibilities*, merely possible but utterly nonactual alternatives. The fundamental problem of this approach is put by the question: How can an experimental trial of physical measurement single out as uniquely real and actual one specific situation whose status in all departments of physical theory is altogether similar to that of others? Given that physics is inherently nondiscriminatory as between these alternatives, how is the measuring process able to constrain nature to select one single alternative as the uniquely real observed value? How can a mere measurement force reality to make up its mind, so to speak?

The Everett-Wheeler hypothesis cuts the Gordian knot of this problem with the daring thesis that *all* of the possible alternative outcomes are in fact actual. We come here to its notorious hypothesis of the "self-multiplication of the universe." Intuitively, its physical picture is that of a universe continually splitting into a multiplicity of distinct but equally real sub-worlds, each embodying a unique but definite result of the quantum measurement. The cosmos is the internally complex counterpart of a linear superposition of vectors, each of which represents observable reality as having assumed one of its value outcomes. The seeming uniqueness of our actual quantum observation is a simply *perspectival* aspect of the relationship between the observer and what is observed: being placed within the subworld where a given result obtains, the other no less real outcomes are simply observationally inaccessible to the observer. The reason why all observers agree on a given result inheres in the merely parochial fact that they hail from the same subworld, and accordingly lack all prospect of causal interaction with the rest. We have simply lost to another subworld those observers whose view of reality conflicts with our own.

The Everett-Wheeler theory thus illustrates a more general line of thought. In cases where the totality of information at our disposal indicates the impossibility of a preferential choice within a certain group of alternatives $A_1, A_2, \ldots, A_n$, we have the prospect of "taking the bull by the horns" by holding that *all these alternatives are concurrently realized* – their mutual incompatibility and discord notwithstanding. (To be sure, we would not be tempted to take this drastic course simply when the information at our disposal did not decide between the alternatives A_i, but only if the overall character of the existing state of our knowledge indicates that the decision between these alternatives is unresolvable in principle.[6]) In this way, explanatory indecisiveness provides another avenue of approach which may also issue – in suitable cases – in an acceptance of inconsistency.[7]

4. CAN INCONSISTENCY EVER BE TOLERATED?

The preservation of consistency is, to be sure, one of the prime tasks of the systematizing enterprise. And here we must look to "the other side

[6] In this case the source of inconsistency is thus not rooted in the negative fact of the incompleteness of our information (as in § 1 above), but rather lies in its positive bearing.

[7] This section draws upon the discussion of the Everett-Wheeler hypothesis in Chapter V of the author's *The Primacy of Practice* (Oxford, 1973). For a good semipopular account of the theory see B. S. De Witt, "Quantum Mechanics and Reality," *Physics Today* (Sept., 1970), pp. 30–35.

of the coin" of the story of the blind men and the elephant. For often it is "experience" that insinuates inconsistencies and "theory" that restores harmony rather than destroying it. Think of the old sceptics' example of sight telling us the stick is bent while touch informs us it is straight. Each eye presents a somewhat different picture of the world: the brain alone enables us to "see" it consistently. To assert the consistency of nature is to express one's faith that the mind will be able ultimately to impress consistency upon the results of our inquiry. But this confidence may in the final analysis prove to be misplaced.

It would be a mistake to think that inconsistency necessarily poses an altogether intolerable threat to the intelligibility of a cognitive enterprise. For one thing, it will be reasonable for someone to accept each statement in an inconsistent set when it is reasonable (even if presumably incorrect) for him to think this set of statements to be consistent. (As we know from the work of Kurt Gödel, there is no way in which the consistency of a set S of – sufficiently complicated – propositions can ever be determined by routine, automatic means.)

Moreover, it may even be reasonable in certain circumstances for a person to accept a set S of statements of whose inconsistency he is certain, for example when the following conditions obtain:

1. There is powerful reason for accepting each and every member of the propositional set S.
2. The set S is inconsistent (and is recognized as such).
3. Although consistency can always in theory be restored regarding S by *deleting* certain of its elements, this can (as ever) be done in various ways, and *given the limitations of information-access and processing under which we actually labor in practice* there simply is no feasible way of justifying any one of these consistency-restoring resolutions *vis-à-vis* its alternatives.

In circumstances of this sort it would be quite reasonable to retain one's commitments to S – at any rate provisionally, until further notice. For in such a case, the desideratum of consistency-elimination conflicts with other cognitive desiderata (viz., adhesion to the probative standards that endorse the S-elements) in such a way that the latter could well outweigh the former in the specific circumstances of particular cases.[8]

[8] The discussion of this section is indebted to Keith Lehrer, "Reason and Consistency" in *idem* (ed.), *Analysis and Metaphysics* (Dordrecht, 1975), pp. 57–74.

But is inconsistency something we can ever tolerate in the framework of rational inquiry? Can a system ever admit contradictions without yielding up all its claims to consideration? Indeed, is inconsistency like all the other, seemingly more flexible parameters of systematicity, also to be viewed as itself matter of degree?

It seems plausible to say that a system is either consistent or not – "a little bit inconsistent" seems as odd as that proverbial paradox, "a little bit pregnant." But this is misguided. The thesis that any inconsistency – no matter how minor and peripheral it may seem to be – inevitably metastasizes to spread pervasively throughout the entire system in which it figures only holds with respect to one special and highly particularized body of logical machinery.

There is no decisive *logical* (i.e. purely theoretical) impediment to the contemplation of systems purporting to characterize an inherently inconsistent nature. A steadily growing sector of recent logical theorizing has so evolved as to indicate that the automatic diffusion of contradiction is not true in general, but only in the setting of the particular framework of the logical machinery now generally characterized as "classical." Over this past generation, logicians are increasingly chary of the view that inconsistency is necessarily disastrous because inconsistent premises yield any and every conclusion whatsoever. They have come to recognize that one may distinguish between pervasive inconsistency (of the disastrous, "anything goes" form) and merely local anomalies, isolable incompatibilities whose logical perplexity is confined to within a small, localized region of a wider system.

This local-anomaly theory indicates that consistency too is a matter of degree. Like the other parameters of systematicity (coherence, simplicity, and the rest), consistency is not a matter of yes-or-no but one of more-or-less. It too emerges as *a degree-admitting desideratum rather than an absolute requirement*. Like the other facets of systematicity, consistency may defensibly be sacrificed on a limited basis in return for sufficient gains within the overall framework of systematic desiderata. Thus toleration of inconsistency is not a holus-bolus abandonment of the systematic ideal.[9]

One important aspect of the abandonment of consistency as an absolute requisite deserves stress. If we are prepared to tolerate

---

[9] The considerations at issue here are crucial for the present line of reasoning, but they are somewhat technical in character. For a fuller development of the theory of inconsistency at issue here see N. Rescher and R. Brandom, *The Logic of Inconsistency* (Oxford, 1979).

inconsistency in systematizing our factual knowledge of the ways of the world, then we would do well to abandon also the stance of a classical Euclidean deductivism as an ideal of systematization in this domain, and go over to something like a network approach of degree of enmeshment. (Compare Chapter III above.) The work of Kurt Gödel has revealed the breakdown of classical deductivism in the systematization of the *formal* sciences. The present considerations indicate the prospect of a breakdown of classical deductivism in that of the factual sciences as well. As Routley and Meyer have rightly noted:

[A] logical or mathematical theory can always be saved – at varying costs – by making sufficient changes or revisions in scientific theories, since logical principles rarely confront empirical data in isolation and generally only do so rather indirectly in continuation with other theoretical assumptions. But though a non-empirical principle, such as the consistency [of the world] hypothesis, never directly encounters the hard empirical data and can always be saved in one way or another, with greater or lesser art, by changes elsewhere, the costs may be too high, and it might be better to give up the principle. A convincing microphysical theory based on a dialectical [i.e. inconsistency-tolerating] logic might provide such a reason. The decline of classical deductivism invites a greater tolerance of inconsistency.[10]

5. INCONSISTENCY ITSELF ROOTS IN THE URGE TO SYSTEMATICITY

But if one is really intent on avoiding it, is inconsistency not always in fact avoidable? Of course it is! It results from accepting too much – the whole of some group of incompatible theses. Inconsistency can thus always be avoided by the simple step of refusing to accept those theses that generate it. Scepticism, the abstention from acceptance, therefore affords a sure-fire guarantee against inconsistency.

But this prospect is not the end of the matter. As William James emphasized, the aim of the cognitive enterprise is not just to avoid error but to engross truth. To secure truths we must *accept* something: Nothing ventured, nothing gained! And to accept something rationally, we must have rules or standards of acceptance. But if these rules or

---

[10] Richard Routley and Robert K. Meyer, "Dialectical Logic, Classical Logic, and the Consistency of the World" (Melbourne, 1975; unpublished typescript), p. 27.

standards indicate the acceptability of mutually discordant theses (as they indeed can), then there is something unsatisfying – something too pristine, purist, and pernickety – about rejecting them *en bloc* simply and solely on this account. To be sure, no sensible person would court inconsistency for its own sake. But this is not the issue. The point is that one can reasonably be in a position of tolerating inconsistencies when driven to it by the operation of (otherwise defensible) acceptance-principles. As emerged in previous discussion (pp. 166–168), it is a crucial fact that it is the very drive towards *completeness* – itself a key parameter of systematic adequacy – that can and does so operate as to enjoin the toleration of inconsistency upon us.

As we saw in the opening chapters, the systems concept itself reflects the systematic fusion of various parameters of systematization. In the very attempt to realize the systematic ideal (as far as possible under the recalcitrant circumstances of actual situations) we might be forced into some partial sacrifice of one or another of the parameters that serve as constituent components of the systematic ideal. And this potential sacrifice of one parameter in the interests of others may affect even consistency itself.

The key point is that the acceptance of an inconsistency-embracing world-picture is governed by the same basic cognitive ground-rules as the acceptance of *any* such picture – to wit, a cost-benefit calculation with the usual parameters of inductive inquiry: evidential strength, systematic convenience, simplicity, uniformity of treatment, etc. A complex constellation of systematic considerations is at issue, producing a situation in which there can be reciprocal give and take in the mutual adjustment of component elements, a give and take from which even consistency itself is not altogether exempt.

This recognition that the various parameters of systematicity are matters of degree which must themselves stand in a reciprocal balance and coordination with one another has far-reaching consequences. Perhaps the most important of these is that the very question from which we commenced in our present deliberations rests on a mistaken footing. For we began with the question: Might certain factors render it impossible to systematize our knowledge about the world? We can now see that this question oversimplifies the problem. The issue is realistically to be formulated as a matter of degree rather than being posed in on-or-off terms; it is not "systematizable-or-not?," but "how-smoothly-systematizable?" The prospect that realistically confronts us in our attempts to systematize our knowledge of nature is not that of no system at all, but rather that of obtaining only an ungainly system; not that of asystematicity, but that of deficient systematicity.

6. CONCLUSION

We have seen that systematicity is both a matter of degree, and a matter of respect. With the ideal of systematicity, as with other desiderata, one must presume it infeasible to realize the objective in a total and absolute way. Even the consistency of nature – that cynosure of traditional philosphy – is an ideal which may, in certain circumstances, have to be abandoned or at any rate compromised. We may conceivably have to settle for half a loaf, or even less.

For example, our knowledge of the law-structure of the world might be *incompletable* – ontologically so, quite apart from any cognitive limitations on our part. For – as C. S. Peirce maintained a century ago – nature might well be ever-evolving; it might be the stage of a continually changing and open-ended structuring of things and laws. (And this change might well not just transpire in a predictable pattern, but in ways that fundamentally encompass the fresh emergence of fundamental novelty at every step, moving ever onwards to the production of situations of novel kinds that have never existed before.) Such a never-ending series of changes in the *modus operandi* of nature might accordingly render our knowledge of it in principle incompletable on strictly ontological grounds, and thus necessarily preclude its synoptic systematizability.

No guarantee is available on the basis of general principles that it cannot ultimately eventuate that man's scientifically attained world-picture is very imperfectly systematic.

To be sure, this is a *mere* possibility. One cannot say on grounds of general principles whether or not it will be realized. We must wait and see. Only with the wisdom of a yet unavailable hindsight will it be possible to say that we have been able to attain knowledge of the world within the framework of a comprehensively systematic development. As has been stressed time and again, systematicity is at bottom a regulative ideal the extent of whose actual realization cannot be prejudged. In its pursuit we must simply forge ahead and do the best we can. No assurances of ultimate success can be issued in advance on the basis of general principles. The legitimacy of the systematic ideal does not lie in an *a priori* demonstration of its inevitable efficacy, but in its proven conduciveness to a fuller realization of the aims and objectives of the cognitive enterprise.

And here we must realize that the "fuller realization" at issue will doubtless never be a *perfect* one. We have to face up to the facts:

1. The (essentially historicist) circumstance that we must inevitably operate within those cognitive systems (conceptual and propositional) that are available to us in terms of the state of knowledge of the day.
2. The profound lesson of the history of science that this state of knowledge will ultimately be found imperfect with the wisdom of hindsight of a future perspective.

Realism requires us to recognize that as concerns our scientific understanding of the world our most secure knowledge is presumably no more than presently acceptable error. But this recognition of the fallibilism of our cognitive endeavors must be construed rather as an incentive to do the best we can than an open invitation to scepticism. In human inquiry, the cognitive ideal is correlative with the striving for optimal systematization. And this is an ideal which, like other ideals, is worthy of pursuit, despite the fact that we must realistically recognize that its full attainment lies beyond our grasp.

XII

Cognitive Metasystematics: the Morphology of Knowledge Systems

SYNOPSIS

(1) Cognitive systems can themselves be related systematically, a prospect which gives rise to the enterprise of *cognitive metasystematics*. (2) The classificatory taxonomics of our knowledge systems appears as a focal aspect of this enterprise. (3) The distinction between *classifying* sciences and *evaluating* them is examined. Despite the long tradition of linking these two activities they can – and should – be separated. (4) The hierarchial ordering of successive system-inclusions represents a particularly prominent mode of cognitive taxonomy. (5) Taxonomic proliferation is a characteristic facet of scientific progress. (6) Despite its prominence here, hierarchial ordering is insufficient for the needs of the taxonomy of science. The over-all taxonomic structure of natural science is not that of a hierarchy but that of a chain-mail network interlinkage. (7) The history of science exhibits not only taxonomic *proliferation* but taxonomic *complexification* as well. The historical trend of growing complexity: linear order to hierarchy to network. (8) What explains taxonomic complexification? The answer lies in our ongoing discovery of the complexity of nature itself, rather than in homocentric considerations relating to the *practice* of scientific research. (9) The issue of morphological eschatology: Must the morphological evolution of science come to a stop? There seems to be no cogent reason for insisting that it must. (10) This fact, however, does not mean that the unity of science is endangered.

1. THE IDEA OF COGNITIVE METASYSTEMATICS

Throughout its applications, the concept of a system indicates a whole composed of elements that are joined together by linkages operating under the unifying aegis of a connecting principle. This conception of wholes composed of parts – which may themselves be wholes – gives rise to the idea of a system that is itself composed of systems. Such a system comprises modular systems duly intermeshed with one another – it is a *hypersystem* composed of *subsystems*, to use the standard terminology. Such systematic synthesis of parts-conjoined-into-a-unified-whole is clearly capable of iteration, leading to a hierarchy of successive levels of a micro/macro sequence: systems, systems of systems, and so on – systems of the 0th-order, the 1st-order, etc. This iterative process means that there will be systems at different levels of aggregation – that systemic synthesis can occur at varying strata, so as to yield systems-composites in successive stages of comprehensiveness.

Consider, for example, the following series:

- atoms, molecules, molecular configurations, material macroobjects, celestial bodies (suns, planets, meteors), solar systems, galaxies, galactic systems.
- bio-molecules, cells, tissues, organs, organisms
- worker, work team, work section, department, factory, division, firm
- letters, words, sentences, paragraphs, discussions (articles, chapters), books, libraries, library-systems
- problems, problem-areas, subspecialties, specialties, disciplines, branches of knowledge

As these illustrations show, systemic synthesis can occur iteratively on both the physical and the cognitive side, giving rise to analogous nestings in either case.

These considerations open up the prospect of a new and characteristic enterprise which might be designated as *cognitive metasystematics*. This enterprise roots in the reflexive character of knowledge. As one can endeavor to know about knowledge and theorize about theorizing, so one can endeavor to systematize our cognitive systems – and for the same reason, viz. the enlargement and enhancing of the information at our disposal. It is appropriate – and potentially illuminating – to study the structure of our knowledge-systems in the attempt to systematize these systems in their turn. For if our knowledge itself is to be adequately systematic, then our knowledge about this knowledge must also be put upon a systematic basis. The over-all project of cognitive systematization must accordingly include a consideration of the systematic order that obtains within the proliferation of cognitive systems themselves.

2. THE TAXONOMY OF KNOWLEDGE

The definitive task of cognitive metasystematics is the introduction of systematic order into the setting of our knowledge-systems. And this enterprise has a long and distinguished history. Since the days of Plato's stress on *dihairēsis* (taxonomic division) there has been general agreement that the principal instrument by which we introduce systematic order into our knowledge is *classification*.

Classification is, of course, a tool of cognitive systematization in general – quite apart from any specific concern with cognitive METAsystematics. For such systematization seeks to provide an account of the operation of the ordering principles that reveal the rational relationships and factual interconnections among systematic constituents, a task for which the mechanism of classification is ideally suited. The whole of a taxonomic *scheme* results when classificatory distinctions are themselves placed into a framework of systematic interconnection. The taxonomy of knowledge, with its systematically structured interplay of classificatory ordering principles, is thus a prime task of cognitive metasystematics.

To be sure, there are both natural or substantive and artificial classifications in the cognitive domain. The natural ones are those demanded by the theoretical exigencies of the subject-matter itself. (When we distinguish between organic and physical chemistry, for example, or between vertebrate and invertebrate zoology, we draw lines of division along boundaries which mark the key segmentations of the factual anatomy of the subject-matter in hand, differentiating in our discussion where we perceive differences *in rerum natura*.)[1] William Whewell long ago cogently put the key point as follows:

[1] First, the taking in of scattered particulars under one Idea, so that everyone understands what is being talked about. . . . Second, the separation of the Idea into parts, by dividing it at

> The Classification of the Sciences must result from a con-
> sideration of their nature and contents. . . . The Classification
> thus obtained, depends . . . upon a . . . natural and fundamental
> element; – namely, the *Ideas* which each science involves. The
> ideas regulate and connect the facts, and are the foundations of the
> reasoning in each science. . . . (*Novum Organon*, ch. IX, sect. 2).

With a "natural" taxonomy, an ordering appears that arises from the
objective properties of the materials at issue, and reflects the organic
exfoliation of the subject in line with the discoverable features of its
content. (The Hegelian dictum that "The order of sciences is the order
of things" becomes applicable.)[2] The issue of the classificatory taxonomy of the sciences is to proceed on the basis of content-connections
as established by explanatory considerations. (This stress on the
explanatory aspect of the matter renders our concern for the metasystematics of the sciences continuous with that of the systematization
of our scientific knowledge itself.)

Artificial taxonomies, on the other hand, are those introduced for
strictly *practical* reasons whose rationale lies wholly on the side of the
systematizers – reasons of convenience, of efficiency of operation (in
learning or teaching or application, etc.), or accessibility, and the like.
The classificatory distinction between algebra and geometry is of the
former sort, that between elementary and higher mathematics is of the
latter. An encyclopedic arrangement of information by letters of
alphabet is the very paradigm of an artificial arrangement of
knowledge.[3]

The practical approaches to the taxonomy of science include
preeminently the following:

1. the *bibliographic* (attempting to order the literature of the
   subject)

---

the joints, as nature directs, not breaking any limb in half as a bad carver might. (Plato,
Phaedrus, 265D.)

[2] Cf. Ernest Cushing Richardson, *Classification: Theoretical and Practical*, 3rd edn. (New
York, 1930), pp. 9–11.

[3] Sensitivity to this issue lead the editors of the more recent edition of the *Encyclopaedia
Britannica* to endeavor to superimpose (in the *Micropaedia*) a more organic mode of
organization upon the strictly alphabetical organization of information in the main body of the
encyclopedia itself (the *Macropaedia*). The dualistic approach is a somewhat uneasy (but
understandable) compromise between convenient artificiality and complex naturalness.

2. the *expository* (for the sake of recording information in handbooks, encyclopedias, etc.)
3. the *pedagogical* (the subdividing of subject matter for the sake of instruction and learning)
4. the *methodological* (arrangement by methods of data-acquisition in data-processing a data exploitation)
5. the *manpower-utilizing* (for the sake of inventorying skills and capabilities)
6. the *historical* (for describing the evolutionary course of development by which the continuing growth of one branch of learning gives rise to others)

It might, perhaps, go without saying that our present concern with cognitive classification must focus solely on the former (substantive) aspect of the matter, and that artificial classifications – however significant in their own way – are beside the point of present purposes.

When one turns from the student's *textbook* to the expert's *treatise*, the artificial and merely practical approaches to classification are usually left behind. An advanced treatise generally ignores artificialities; at this level, the demands of practical desirability are put aside in the interests of realizing a schema of classification warranted as theoretically adequate by *substantive* considerations alone.

Some theoreticians (e.g. Immanuel Kant) have held that while the *content* of our empirical knowledge is something *a posteriori* and experiential, the issue of its rational *form*, its taxonomic structure, is at bottom *a priori* and strictly theoretical. The prominence of distinctions like that between *statics* and *dynamics* in physics may on first thought lend credence to such a view. But the aura of aprioricity always vanishes on closer inspection. (As the discovery of the relativity of simultaneity in special relatively brings home reference to the temporal element in the static/dynamic distinction and leads to substantial enmeshment in factual/substantive issues.) The rational structure of our factual knowledge emerges from its content, and its systematic architectonics is as empirical an issue as that of the constituent theses: in the domain of cognitive systematics, *form is built into content, and conversely*.

The development of principles of cognitive classification is itself a major product of cognitive progress. The organic connections that obtain among parts of empirical knowledge are a key aspect of the subject-matter of that knowledge. With the advance of science (e.g. physics) we not only acquire more information about how things happen in the world, we learn how to organize our information more systematically. Cognitive progress is progress not only with respect to the *volume* of information, but with respect to its *structure* – its mode of organization – as well. Indeed the indications of scientific progress are certainly no less striking on the side of form – organization, systematic structure – than on that of substantive content.

It is interesting to consider an issue that agitated the medieval schoolmen, that posed by the question: Would an omniscient and omnipotent being – a divinity – need to *order* his knowledge? Would he, for example, divide it into fields and branches and specialties, etc.?

Some argued that a deity has no need to impose any form of structure on his knowledge: for such a being knowledge would be a *totum simul* where everything is co-present, lying on an even plane of synoptic awareness, so to speak. There would be no need – and indeed no point – for distinguishing between the axiomatic and the theorematic, the general and the special. Were an intellect freed from the limitations of a finite capacity – with its concerns for learning, teaching, recollection, reconstruction, etc. – the requirement for any division of labor would be removed, and the need for organizing knowledge vanishes with it.

But here they are wrong. For the indicated grounds remove only those particular classificatory distinctions that we have characterized as artificial, and *not* those that are natural and inhere in the intrinsic anatomy of the substantive content itself. It is a crucial feature of certain geometric theses that they can serve as axioms in a particular deductive systematization of Euclidean geometry, and of others that they will invariably be theorematic in any efficient axiomatization. *The knowledge of interrelationships on the structural side of natural taxonomy in cognitive systematization is a key aspect of factual knowledge itself.* For the very reason of his omniscience, an omniscient being could not possibly do without it.

3. THE LINEAR RANK-ORDERING OF THE SCIENCES

Closely related to the problem of *classifying* the sciences is the ancient enterprise of *ranking* them. In fact, these two issues were linked together as far back (at least) as Plato's teaching that mathematics, as the science of the eternal and regular, is inherently superior to medicine, and that astronomy, as a science of the imperishable objects of the heavens, is inherently superior to biology, as a science of the perishable constituents of the sublunary sphere.[4] The various medieval discussions of the ranking of the sciences (*de ortu scientarium*), which we shall consider more closely below, represent a continuation of this enterprise.[5]

Nor has this venture become less popular in modern times. Comte's ranking views mathematics (i.e. arithmetic, geometry, and "pure" mechanics), astronomy, physics, chemistry, biology, sociology as a series of increasing complexity and specialization where, as one expositor puts it, each successive member "depends upon the facts of all the members preceding it, and cannot be fully understood without them."[6] Until Herbert Spencer's critique of Auguste Comte in the middle of the last century, it was the generally favored view that the sciences admitted of some such strictly serial rank ordering in a *linear* arrangement.[7] And even today one can still occasionally find contemporary writers who think within the framework of this same tradition, viewing a science "the more fully developed" to the extent to which it uses mathematical techniques – and accordingly relegating psychology, say, or sociology to the outer reaches of inferiority.

It is not difficult to see that this project is futile. In each area of inquiry one does the best one can to solve the problems of the field by whatever methods prove themselves adequate to the purposes at hand. It is both pointless and misleading to say that physics is something inherently superior to biology as a cognitive discipline because its objects are more numerous or more pervasive or more stable. The value of objects does not rub off on the studies thereof: the numismatics of gold coins is no more noble than that of copper ones. Rank-ordering on a scale of superiority has no place in the taxonomy of cognitive disciplines.

The fact is that *ranking* and *classifying* branches of knowledge are very different projects. The latter is eminently useful; the former an outdated facet of the Greek tradition which (quite wrongly) viewed

---

[4] But compare *Parts of Animals* I, v., 644b23–45a8, where Aristotle contrasts the two sciences and allows biology to come off a pretty good second best.

[5] See Joseph Mariétan on *Problème de la classification des sciences d'Aristote à St.-Thomas* (St. Maurice and Paris, 1901).

[6] See the article on Comte in the *Encyclopaedia Britannica*, 11th ed., vol. VI, p. 819.

[7] See Spencer's *Essays on the Genesis of Science and the Classification of the Sciences*, 3rd edn. (London, 1871).

evaluation as an inseparable aspect of ordering. Despite the long-lived temptation of conjoining these enterprises – a temptation in which many of the great names of the history of thought find a prominent place – they can *and should* be separated. And once this separation is made, we free ourselves from the vain project of ranking sciences in a linear order of relative superiority or "development" or whatever.

4. THE HIERARCHICAL VIEW OF COGNITIVE TAXONOMY AND ITS DIFFICULTIES

But how – more realistically – do interrelationships among cognitive systems manifest themselves? What is the nature of the structure to which their mutual relationships in an explanatory ordering will give rise?

Unquestionably the form of interrelationship encountered most frequently in the historical discussions of the subject is that of a *hierarchy*, taking the form of an inverted tree. Virtually all writers on the subject after the mid-1800's – by which time the classical paradigm of a linear rank-order had finally fallen into disfavor – favored a hierarchical of the taxonomy of the sciences.

System-inclusion of this sort amounts to *speciation* and its iteration produces a taxonomic nesting, as per the sequence: fields, branches, specialties, subspecialties, problem-areas. Such sequences always make patterns of order of the standard hierarchic form:

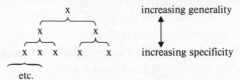

With successive additions a strict hierarchy is maintained through the basic relationship of *system-inclusion*, the containment of something within a systematic whole as a constituent element thereof. Such system-inclusion generally proceeds by way of the substantive supplementation of a further specification of subject-matter focus. The additions at issue in such a superaddition of further thematic elements proceed preeminently through introducing further subject-matter restrictions. An example of this is that of the transitions:

biology → human biology
medicine → tropical medicine

We have to do here with a narrowing of focus that produces a subdivision of the subject-matter.

It is clear that if the classical idea of a *linear* rank-ordering is coupled (as, historically, it standardly was) with the idea of system-inclusion, then serious difficulties will soon develop. Trouble is encountered even by something as simple-minded as the well known antique ordering of cognitive disciplines: *hylology* (sciences of material things: physics, chemistry, etc.), *biology* (sciences of living things: zoology, ecology, etc.), *noology* (sciences of thinking things: psychology, anthropology, etc.), *theology* (science of divine things). For this involves the sequential additions of an ordering of successive inclusions (matter, life, thought) only until the last item, where the material element utterly disappears, so that a linear ordering must be abandoned at this stage. The proper order here must thus be nonlinearly hierarchical:

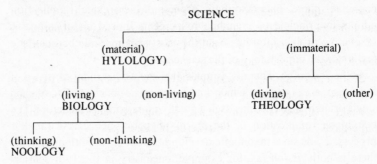

In technical terms we are forced to the transition from a strict rank-order to a merely *partial* ordering.[8] Such a listing is clearly not a linear ranking under the guidance of some single undirectional principle. With the rising prominence of taxonomic speciation in science, the idea of hierarchy thus came into its own.

---

[8] To be sure, the difference between a linear and a hierarchical ordering is ultimately not as severe as seems on first view, since a decimalization can always transpose a hierarchical "table of organization" into a sequential order (as per the Dewey Decimal System of library classification). Compare p. 63 above.

5. TAXONOMIC PROLIFERATION IN COGNITIVE MORPHOLOGY

A sequence of system-inclusions always leads to an hierarchically nested ordering of cognitive systems. The successive members of these hierarchies are arranged with respect to generality through the introduction of delimiting assumptions that produce a more and more specialized focus, so that the successive members may be described as sectors or branches of one another. Such hierarchical classification schemes – generically inherent in the process of system-division – accordingly have a particular importance in cognitive systematization. They are pervasive throughout what one might call "the descending order" in the taxonomy of knowledge, an ordering that reflects the successive resolution of cognitive systems into their subsystems at every level in the course of increasing specialization. And in theory, at any rate, one can always envisage the introduction of further intermediate groupings between any taxonomic unit and the particular cognitive problems that represent the *infima species* at issue in the cognitive sphere. This taxonomic process of hierarchical ramification admits in principle of unending refinement. Indeed historically this taxonomic proliferation has been the most striking and characteristic feature of the morphology of the sciences.

In the days of St. Thomas Aquinas, the whole of learning consisted of five or six areas each of which had five or six subfields.[9] Today each single branch of science has itself a greatly more complex structure. The taxonomic ramification of the morphology of science is a familiar process. To be sure, taxonomic development occurs in both directions: there is both *fission* (as, for example, chemistry in the 19th century came to divide into organic and inorganic chemistry) and also *fusion* (as Newton's gravitational theory provided a conjoining framework for the theory of terrestrial fall in ballistics, etc. with the theory of planetary motion, or as Maxwell's field theory fused the theory of light and that of electromagnetism).

Moreover – and very importantly – there is also *absorption*, which is the inverse of "reduction" in the sense in which chemistry has been effectively reduced to physics in the course of the 20th century.[10] This

[9] See Joseph Mariétan on *Problème de la classification des sciences d'Aristote à St. Thomas* (St. Maurice and Paris, 1901).

[10] On "reduction" in this technical sense see Ernest Nagel, *The Structure of Science* (New York, 1961). (This work does not deal with the structure of *science*, but with that of *scientific reasoning*.)

morphological process is a very important aspect of scientific progress, a fact neatly illustrated in the following passage:

> Science tends to generalize, and generalization means sim-
> plification. My own science, biology, is today not only very
> much richer than it was in my student days, but is simpler, too.
> Then it was horribly complex, being fragmented into a great
> number of isolated principles. Today, these are all fused into one
> single complex with the atomic model at its center. Cosmology,
> quantum theory, DNA and genetics, are all, more or less, parts of
> the same story – a vast wonderful simplication.[11]

But it is misleading to speak of "simplification" here. The topmost branches of the inverted tree of scientific taxonomy are pruned only at the price of proliferating the lower ones: the amalgamation of high-level branches effects a theoretical economy that is in practice always bought at the price of overall complexification. For fusion and absorption – the processes which lessen the number of taxonomic elements at issue – tend to occur only at the higher levels of the taxonomic hierarchy where the impetus towards an increasing generality (or abstraction) that unites previously disparate taxa is particularly pronounced. (And anyway, such higher-level fusion generally does not lead to lower level absorptions.) At the lower levels of specialties and problem-areas there is, however, an overwhelming predominance on the side of fission. Hence there is a substantial tendency to quantitative growth here.

This process has produced a massive proliferation of the taxa of science that is among the most characteristic features of scientific progress. For throughout modern times the morphology of science has grown at an exponential rate, expanding in the manner of a bacterial culture growing under ideal conditions. At all of the lower taxonomic levels – problem-areas, subspecialties, specialties, branches, etc. – the subdivisions of science have been increasing in a geometric progression, doubling with inexorable regularity during every repetition of a fixed-size period.

Herbert Spencer maintained long ago that evolution is characterized by von Baer's law of development "from the homogeneous to the heterogeneous," and manifests an ever-increasing "definiteness of detail

---

[11] Albert Szent-Györgyi, "Teaching and the Expanding Knowledge," *Science*, vol. 146 (1964), pp. 1278–1279.

and complexity of structure." This may or may not be correct for *biological* evolution, but it certainly does seem to hold for *cognitive* evolution, where *changes in the taxonomical structure of a science* continually appear as an integral part of the progress of science itself. As the French physicist Pierre Auger has written:

At the time of Auguste Comte, the sciences could be classified in six or seven main categories known as disciplines, ranging from mathematics to sociology. Since then, during the nineteenth century and at the beginning of the twentieth, there has been what might be described as an intra-disciplinary dismemberment, each of the main categories splitting up into increasingly specialized fields, each of which rapidly assumed comparable importance to that of the actual disciplines from which it sprang. Chemistry, for example, in the days of Lavoisier formed a reasonably homogeneous entity, but chemists were soon obliged to choose between inorganic and organic chemistry; within the latter, a distinction arose during the second half of the nineteenth century between the chemistry of aromatic compounds and that of aliphatic compunds, the latter shortly being further subdivided into the study of saturated compounds and that of unsaturated compounds. Finally, at the present time, a chemist can devote a most useful research career entirely to a single chemical family. The same process can be discerned in physics and in biology.

But this very over-specialization has provoked an inverse or rather a complementary process, that of interdisciplinary synthesis; thus, from physics and chemistry there has grown up a new discipline of physical chemistry, which is influenced by both these sciences. This process has given rise to a whole series of new sciences with double or even triple names – astrophysics, biochemistry, mathematical chemistry, physico-chemical biology, etc. Thus, the diverging lines of the subjects of scientific research are connected by cross-links which restore unity to the whole.[12]

Consider the example of taxonomic structure of physics. We may assume a three-layer taxonomy: the field as a whole, the principal branches thereof, and the sub-branches of the branches (= specialties). The taxonomic situation towards the beginning of this century is given in Table 1.

[12] Pierre Auger, *Current Trends in Scientific Research* (Paris, 1961; UNESCO Publications), pp. 15–16.

Table 1

THE TAXONOMY OF PHYSICS
IN THE 11th EDITION OF THE *ENCYCLOPAEDIA BRITANNICA*
(1911)

Astronomy
  – Astrophysics
  – Celestial Mechanics

Acoustics

Optics
  – Theoretical Optics
  – Spectroscopy

Mechanics

Heat
  – Calorimetry
  – Theory of Radiation
  – Thermodynamics
  – Thermometry

Electricity and Magnetism
  – Electrochemistry
  – Electrokinetics
  – Electrometallurgy
  – Electrostatics
  – Thermoelectricity
  – Diamagnetism
  – Electromagnetism

Pneumatics

Energetics

Instrumentation

Note: Adapted from the Classified List of Articles at the end of Vol. **XXIX** (Index volume) of the 11th edition of the *Encyclopaedia Britannica*.

It is interesting to contrast this picture of the taxonomic situation in physics with the picture of the situation in subsequent decades as given in Table 2.

Table 2

PHYSICAL SPECIALTIES IN THE "NATIONAL REGISTER OF SCIENTIFIC AND TECHNICAL PERSONNEL" FOR 1954 AND 1970

(1954)	(1970)
Astronomy (16 specialties)	Astronomy
Acoustics (7 specialties)	– Solar-Planetary Relationships (9 specialties)
Optics (8 specialties)	– Planetology (6 specialties)
Mechanics and Heat (13 specialties)	– 11 Further Astrophysical Specialties
Electromagnetism (6 specialties)	Acoustics (9 specialties)
Solid State (8 specialties)	Optics (10 specialties)
Atomic and Molecular Physics (5 specialties)	Mechanics (10 specialties)
Nuclear Physics (9 specialties)	Thermal Physics (9 specialties)
Theoretical Physics: Quantum Physics (4 specialties)	Electromagnetism (8 specialties)
(= Elementary Particles and Fields)	Solids (25 specialties)
Theoretical Physics: Classical (3 specialties)	Fluids (9 specialties)
Electronics (7 specialties)	Atmospheric Structure and Dynamics (16 specialties)
Instrumentation and Miscellaneous (4 specialties)	Atoms and Molecules (10 specialties)
	Nuclei (3 specialties)
	Elementary Particles and Fields (6 specialties)
	Physical Chemistry (25 specialties)
	Biophysics (6 specialties)
	Solid Earth Geophysics (10 specialties)
	Instrumentation (28 specialties)

Data from *American Science Manpower: 1954–1956* (Washington, 1961; National Science Foundation Publications) and "Specialties List for use with 1970 National Register of Scientific and Technical Personnel" (Washington, 1970; National Science Foundation Publications).

These tables tell a significant story. In the 11th (1911) edition of the *Encyclopaedia Britannica*, physics makes its appearance as a discipline composed of 9 constituent branches (e.g. "Astronomy" or "Electricity and Magnetism") which are themselves partitioned into some 20 further specialties (e.g. "Thermoelectricity" or "Celestial Mechanics"). The 15th (1974) version of the *Britannica* divides physics into 12 branches whose subfields are – seemingly – too numerous for explicit survey. (However, the 14th [1960's] edition carried a special article entitled "Physics, Articles on" which surveyed more than 130 special topics in the field.) In 1954, when the National Science Foundation launched its inventory of physical specialties with the National Register of Scientific and Technical Personnel, it divided physics into 12 areas with 90 specialties. By 1970 these figures had increased to 16 and 210, respectively.

Substantially the same picture emerges in every field of natural science. The springing up of new disciplines, branches, and specialties is manifest throughout. And as though to negate this tendency and maintain unity, one finds the evolution of interdisciplinary syntheses – physical chemistry, astrophysics, biochemistry, etc. The historical situation has been such as to indicate that the very attempt to counteract fragmentation produces new fragments. Historically, scientific speciation has proceeded exponentially – at a relatively constant per-period percentage growth-rate – doing so with increasing rapidity as one moves downward on the taxonomic scale.[13]

6. NONHIERARCHICAL MODES OF ARCHITECTONIC

As long as this process of taxonomic ramification goes on – no matter how far we press such descent from any given unit to its successive subdivisions – we shall always remain in a hierarchial order if we begin with one. (This fact, of course, lends a special prominence and importance to the principle of hierarchial organization.) And so the question inevitably arises: Can *all* of natural science be developed within the framework of a single hierarchy? In pursuing this question, let us begin with a general, abstract consideration of the ways in which

---

[13] The historical situation is pictured in considerable detail in Derek J. Price, *Science Since Babylon* (New Haven, 1961).

the basic relationship of system-inclusion can generate structural relationships within families of related systems.

The basic mode of system-relatedness by inclusion itself yields the simple pattern of outright *containment*:

But this mode of relatedness immediately leads to a further, derivative pattern of system-relatedness – in particular (and most fundamentally) the following:

(i) *Association*

The *association* of systems results from their inclusion as subunits within a common generic superunit as per the pattern:

An illustration of this form of relatedness is afforded by the fact that optics and thermodynamics are both comprised within physics.

(ii) *Overlap*

The *overlap* of systems consists in the inclusion of a common subunit as per the pattern:

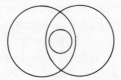

An illustration of this form of relatedness is that of physics and chemistry which nowadays share a common-core system of quantum theory, a common element which they supplement in rather different ways so as to give rise to distinct systems based on different subject-matter foci.

The introduction of this second mode of level-coordinating relationship gives rise to much more complex *patterns of affiliation* (cognitive orderings) than the merely hierarchial. As long as no overlaps are present, a hierarchical structure can always be developed. Thus, for example,

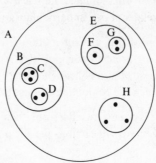

results in

But when the affiliation scheme includes overlaps, the prospect of achieving a hierarchical ordering is removed. Thus, for example, consider

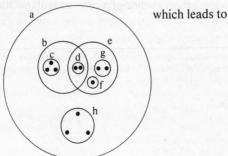   which leads to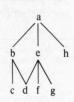

The result is no longer a strictly hierarchical arrangement seeing that such a "hierarchy with overlaps" is not really a *hierarchy* at all.

But this analysis also shows that in giving up the neat-partition view of specifically hierarchical arrangement, we do not abandon the more general notion of "integrative levels" – successive strata of order on the scale of complexity and of organizational sophistication.[14]

Thus while in the *downwards descent* of the successive division of one initial unit into the sequence of its successive subunits (field into specialties into problem areas, etc.) we will always maintain a hierarchial order, in the *upwards ascent* of the associative relationship of various units in a conjoining fusion, one may – and indeed will – encounter such a nonhierarchial order.

The introduction of this variant mode of relatedness provides for cognitive systems of greater morphological complexity than can be captured within the structure of a single hierarchial tree. The structural architectonic to which the conjoining of these two modes of relatedness gives rise can take on a form which is not that of a hierarchy at all, but rather that of chain-mail-work interlinkage reminiscent of medieval armor.[15]

The future's functional equivalent of a Dewey-Decimal-like classification of the sciences will thus not have a hierarchical basis. Its rationale will be map-like, with branches of learning positioned on a two-dimensional or pluri-dimensional manifold whose relative distances reflect the volume of the commerce between them. (Perhaps coordinates will be used, perhaps some other coding to indicate position relative to a fixed reference base.)

The upshot with respect to our initial question as to the adequacy of a hierarchial model for the taxonomy of science in general is thus negative. The overall structure of natural science is *not* that of a hierarchy. To be sure, in the *descending* order of successive subdivision in taxonomic fission we always remain within a hierarchial pattern. But in the *ascending* order of associative relatedness we will obtain the complexity of a chain-mail network interlinkage.

[14] This important instrumentality of systems theory goes back at least to Joseph Needham's 1937 Herbert Spencer Lecture, "Integrative Levels: A Revaluation of the Idea of Progress" reprinted in his book *Time: the Refreshing River* (London, 1943).

[15] It seems plausible to conjecture that a detached study of the interrelations of scientific disciplines (based on citation indexing) will reveal a two-dimensional pattern of relative "proximity" and "distance" among loci of *intellectual* productivity akin to the established patterns of geographical relatedness among loci of *economic* productivity. Regarding the economic side of this analogy see K. S. O. Beavon, *Central Place Theory* (London, 1977).

7. SCIENTIFIC DEVELOPMENT AND TAXONOMIC COMPLEXIFICATION

The history of thought regarding the taxonomy of knowledge deserves brief scrutiny.

The turn-of-the-century revolution of physics had the effect of riveting the attention of philosophers of science upon scientific *theories*. The *formulation*, *testing*, *confirmation* or *invalidation*, and *change* (modification or replacement) of scientific theses and hypotheses has accordingly been the leading themes of the philosophy of science during the present century. However, throughout this concern with the theses and theories of science, the question of its taxonomic *structure* has been ignored. Contemporary philosophers of science have been so concerned with issues of ontogenesis that they have abandoned the issue of phylogenesis.

In the 19th century, a different situation prevailed. Then, all of the great figures of the philosophy of science of this era – Comte, Whewell, Mill, Spencer, Peirce – made substantial examinations of the systematic structure of science as a whole, including the inventory and arrangement of its component branches and subdivisions.[16] The rapid expansion of interest in this subject in the 19th century (in the wake of the growth of historical interests) is a phenomenon as striking in its modern neglect when the extent to which science presents an ever-changing and ever-growing target of study became clear. No major 19th-century philosopher of science failed to give extensive consideration to the problem of classifying the sciences, no major 20th-century philosopher of science has touched it.[17]

It is understandable why this subject of the disciplinary taxonomy and morphology of science should have fallen into neglect. To some extent, the nominalistic tendencies of recent philosophy have militated against devising synoptic schemes. The growing stress in philosophy on matters of microscopic detail and the aversion to large-scale syntheses

[16] The better older surveys of the historical situation are: Julius Pelzholdt, *Bibliotheca Bibliographica* (Leipzig, 1866), Charles W. Shields, *Philosophia Ultimata*, vol. II = "The History of the Sciences and the Logic of the Sciences or the Science of the Sciences" (New York, 1889); Robert Flint, *Philosophy as Scientia Scientiarum and History of the Classification of the Sciences* (New York, 1904); and E. C. Richardson, *Classification: Theoretical and Practical* (New York, 1930; 3rd edn.).

[17] For an interesting recent analysis see R. G. A. Dolby, "Classification of the Sciences: The Nineteenth-Century Tradition" [unpublished study issued for its author by the University of Kent at Canterbury ca. 1975].

are also a hindrance. Most importantly, the process of growth and change within the sciences themselves has so proceeded as to countervail against any attempt to provide the orderly fixity of a taxonomic framework.

With the development of science, the morphology of our cognitive systems also grow more complex. Even a brief glance at the history of learning suffices to reveal that man's view of the structure of knowledge has become vastly more intricate. Not only is there proliferation within existing units, as we have just seen, but there is also the origination of new units making for increasingly complex affiliation patterns of overlap and association. The history of science exhibits not only taxonomic *proliferation* but taxonomic *complexification* as well.

From Greek antiquity until the Latin middle ages, the standard view was that the branches of knowledge could be arranged in the linear sequence of a rank ordering that begins with the "trivial" subjects of the foundational disciplines (i.e. those of the Scholastic *trivium*: grammar, logic, and mathematics [i.e. arithmetic and geometry]) and moves onwards through natural, theoretical, and moral philosophy (i.e. science, metaphysics, and ethics) to culminate in theology, the queen of the sciences. Medieval philosophers were pretty generally agreed on such an essentially linear presuppositional ordering of the established branches of knowledge, roughly following the sequence of treatises in the established canon of the Aristotelian corpus. Treatises on the ranking of the sciences (*De ortu scientiarum*) produced in both the Arabic and the Latin side of medieval philosophy concurred in this linear and sequential picture of cognitive taxonomy, an approach which – as we saw above – can be found as late as the positivism of Auguste Comte in the 19th century. (He took the view that the natural order of the theoretical sciences stood in a *pari passu* alignment with the historical order of their emergence.)

Three factors conspired to overthrow this doctrine. One was the demise of the linearly sequential, prior/posterior oriented medieval Aristotelian world picture. The second was the rapid development of the sciences themselves in the post-Galilean era. The third was the Darwinian theory of evolution with its picture of the tree-like exfoliation of increasingly ramified relationships. This changed orientation gave rise in the course of the last century to the view of science as itself a tree-like hierarchy developed along evolutionary lines. The quintessential model of this view of the structure of knowledge is no longer a sequence of treatises as per the Aristotelian corpus, but the *Dewey Decimal System*, which organizes knowledge through the successive exfoliation of a nested hierarchy ramifying ever onwards into more and more detailed subcategorizations.

In the 20th-century even this more complicated, hierarchial view of the taxonomy of science has had to be abandoned – under the pressure of necessity – in favor of still more complex and convoluted forms of interrelationship. The subject-unifications achieved through the reductive triumphs of modern science are substantive simplifications bought at the price of taxonomic complication. They have destroyed the prospect of a simple morphology of science, one based on a linear or even an hierarchical classification of the sciences. With the ongoing development of more complex patterns of overlaps and associations, the morphological structure of science has come to take on the form of a chain-mail network. To give an adequate picture of the taxonomic structure of science nowadays calls for the drawing of a complex map, rather than the sketching of an orderly tree. This sequential complication of cognitive classification and taxonomy is among the most characteristic – and important – aspects of the progress of knowledge.

8. THE PROBLEM OF EXPLANATION

The preceding considerations point inexorably towards the key question: What can be said regarding the *root causes* of taxonomic complexification of science?

Various possible explanations are in theory available here:

(A) The explanation might lie simply on the side of the essentially intellectual limitations of the *practitioners* of science. The ongoing exponential growth of the scientific literature is a phenomenon that is well known (especially in the wake of the publications of Derek Price). Science has become less and less manageable in teaching and learning. If one supposes that adequate intellectual control of a branch of knowledge requires mastery of some fixed fraction of its literature, then increasing specialization – and speciation – is an immediate consequence.

(B) The explanation might lie on side of the *practice* of scientific research. One does the easy work first, the more complex later on. As Max Planck wrote:

> With every advance in science the difficulty of the task is increased; ever larger demands are made of the achievements of researchers, and the need for a suitable division of labor becomes constantly more pressing. (*Vorträge und Erinnerungen*, 5th ed. [Stuttgart, 1949], p. 376.)

As the work gets harder, a given volume of effort can discharge less and less of it. Increasing specialization is now indicated because of growing difficulty of task.

(C) The explanation might lie in the *sociological* factors. As more people crowd into a given area of scientific work it could be necessary to divide it more finely to prevent overcrowding in one specific compartment of practice, leading to its division into smaller-scale subunits defined by various "craft guilds," as it were. ·

(D) The explanation might lie in the *structure of nature* itself. For nature itself may well be structured through a stratification of complexity levels. And then there would be continually increasing difficulties in digging ever deeper through the strata,.resulting in ever narrowing concentration of effort. (The physicists D. Bohm and J. P. Vigier have offered some suggestions along these lines.[18])

These explanations are certainly not the only promising possibilities. (Nor are they mutually exclusive.) But surely (D) comes the closest towards getting the matter right. If it were not the case that ongoing inquiry were encountering increasing complexity in nature itself, we would simply have more workers criss-crossing the same terrain without any enhanced complexity in the mappings they produce. The fact that scientific progress generally takes place in *virgin territory* – at higher temperatures, pressures, particle-velocities, than have previously been explored – indicates that it is the world itself that confronts us with an increasingly more demanding phenomenology that makes increasing taxonomic demands. It is this "objective" side of the issue, rather than

[18] See the discussion in Chapter III of the author's *Scientific Progress* (Oxford, 1978).

the exigencies of our ways of inquiry, that ultimately accounts for taxonomic complexification. The basic mechanism at work here takes the sequential form: greater *variety* of phenomena → greater complexity of explanatory theories → greater complexity in the structure of knowledge. As we probe nature more deeply in our "exploration" of its phenomena, it is only natural and to be expected that our knowledge of it should grow increasingly complex. (The man who has never left the confines of his native town is likely to have a misleadingly simple picture of the world.) The fundamental metasystematic lesson of the history of cognitive systematization is surely that complexity is the price of progress. The more we know and learn about the world, the wider the range of phenomena to which our theories must accommodate themselves, and so the more complex a structure our knowledge itself assumes.

9. MORPHOLOGICAL ESCHATOLOGY

Will this process of morphological complication not ultimately reach an inevitable stop? We must face up to the question of the inherent finitude of the morphological complexity of knowledge.

There is surely no reason of theoretical principle for espousing a doctrine of morphological finitude. No considerations intrinsic to the cognitive enterprise entail that our knowledge of nature should ever stop growing — at every level of intrinsic significance. Even if nature itself is finitely complex, it is yet possible that — like a typewriter with a finite keyboard — it could trace out ever new sequences of concrete occurrences that manifest increasingly complex laws of operation.

This steadily unfolding complexity means that the fusion and (far more commonly) fission of scientific fields into subfields (etc.) is an ever-available prospect. The ongoing development of ever more complex patterns of overlap and association is a genuinely open possibility. The chain-mail structure would accordingly come to take on an increasingly elaborate form, thanks to the need to accommodate an ever-enlarging domain of phenomena as our capacity to interact with nature becomes larger and larger in the course of historical development. To be sure, as science moves into ever more difficult areas and faces ever deeper and more difficult problems, the rate of scientific discovery and innovation on the side of new findings will come to slow down. And with this deceleration of the pace of morphological change will also decelerate. But a slowing is not a stoppage.

Whatever the philosophy of science teaches us about the nature of the enterprise, and the history of science about its past evolution, conspires to indicate that there is no decisive reason why science need ever converge to a fixed condition of morphological ossification as long as the activity of scientific inquiry itself continues.

10. THE UNITY OF SCIENCE

But does its ongoing complexification not threaten the unity and coherence of science itself?

Philosophers have long emphasized the theme of the *unity* of science, correlative with the classic ideal of science as a cohesive and integral whole. In taking this issue to hand, we may begin by noting that the "unity of science" is a many-headed beast. At least three things can be in question here:

1. *Methodological* unity: the contention that exactly the same methods of inquiry and of validation are at issue in all of the sciences. (Think of the *Methodenstreit* of the natural sciences *vs.* the cultural [i.e. the human and social] sciences – the *Naturwissenschaften vs.* the *Geisteswissenschaften.*)
2. *Explanatory* unity: the claim that everything may be subsumed under one certain selfsame family of explanatory principles. (Think of ancient atomism and the physicalism of the logical positivists.)
3. *Semantic* unity: the doctrine that everything can be expressed in a common vocabulary. (Think of the historic idea of a universal medium for scientific discourse, which enables expression in – or translatability into – a common language used uniformly throughout all the branches of science.)

There are interrelationships among these modes of unity (e.g. E-unity entails both S-unity and M-unity). But in general, rather different considerations are at issue with these different modes of unity. In any case, it must be stressed that our present concern with unity in systematization is with explanatory-unity: the unity and uniformity of explanatory or justificatory principles.

Doubts as to the attainability of such unity have recently been raised in various quarters. (Already the prospectus of the St. Louis Universal Exposition of 1904 spoke of its aim "to discuss and set forth the unification and mutual relations of the sciences, and thus overcome the level of relation and harmony in the scattered specialistic sciences of our day.") And one European savant now speaks of "the currently widespread belief that the unity of the sciences has been lost" (*die verbreitete Ansicht von der verlorenen Einheit der Wissenschaften*).[19] It is necessary to reexamine this thesis of the systematic unity of science in the light of the ongoing structural complexification of the enterprise.

This worry regarding the unity of science is surely a mistaken concern. With the ever-continuing complexification of science we are not being driven to abandoning this old systematic ideal of the unity of science, but we are being constrained to interpret the nature of this unity as being more complex and – so to speak – internally diversified – than had been thought. What is in danger of being lost is not the *unity* of science, but its *simplicity*. It is not the *existence* but the *nature* of "the unity of science" that we are compelled to rethink in the wake of the growing complication of the enterprise of scientific systematization.[20]

[19] Karl Ulmer in idem (ed.), *Die Wissenschaften und die Wahrheit* (Stuttgart, 1966), p. 24.

[20] Some of the themes of this chapter are dealt with at greater length in the author's *Scientific Progress* (Oxford, 1977).

Name Index

Subject Index